Elizabeth Ann Lyon Roe

Recollections of frontier life

Elizabeth Ann Lyon Roe

Recollections of frontier life

ISBN/EAN: 9783337143145

Printed in Europe, USA, Canada, Australia, Japan

Cover: Foto ©Andreas Hilbeck / pixelio.de

More available books at **www.hansebooks.com**

To the Early Settlers of the Rock River Valley, and my loving and devoted Children, this work is respectfully and kindly dedicated.

THE AUTHOR.

PREFACE.

The following pages were written for the perusal of the author's family, with no expectation of giving them to the public in book form. But for some time past I have felt it my duty to put it into book form, hoping that it may prove gratifying to my old friends to call to mind some of the scenes of trial, privation and inconvenience we suffered; but above all, the hopes, the pleasures and the comforts we enjoyed in our new homes. Many of these venerable heads are covered with the dust of the valley, and the few of us who are left can truly say, "Blessed are the dead who die in the Lord, for they rest from their labors; and their works do follow them."

In these pages many recollections of frontier life in different localities are sketched. The climate, the soil, society, schools and churches, in many places in Kentucky, Illinois and Nebraska are described, and I hope it will interest all persons who are looking for facts instead of fiction. It is written in old style, without any attempt at literary merit. Its details may be regarded as the truth in every sense, and hoping that it may be useful in leading some precious souls to the Truth as it is in the Redeemer of the world and the Fountain that is open to all, I offer it to your kind perusal, trusting you will not criticise too closely its many defects.

E. A. ROE.

CONTENTS.

Illustrations.—Portraits of Dr. John Roe and Mrs. E. A. Roe.

	PAGE.
Preface	5
Chapter I.—My Childhood	7
Chap. II.—The Garden and the Gardener	13
Chap. III.—Earliest Recollections of Methodism and its Influence on Me	20
Chap. IV.—Religious Resolutions and How they Were Prosecuted	34
Chap. V.—Recollections of Early Married Life	49
Chap. VI.—Doctor's Adventure on the Farm	108
Chap. VII.—Removal to Rock River—Progress of Methodism	112
Chap. VIII.—Recollections of Methodism in Chicago	148
Chap. IX.—Recollections of Payne's Point	154
Chap. X.—Recollections of Rockford and our new Home on the Prairie	159
Chap. XI.—Visit to Nebraska	171
Death of Dr. John Roe	244
Funeral Sermon	267
Dr. John Roe	285
Birthday Testimony	289

RECOLLECTIONS OF FRONTIER LIFE.

CHAPTER I.

MY CHILDHOOD.

The first that I recollect of self I was a rude, playful girl, fair complexion, black hair, with rosy cheeks and hazel eyes; so much for personal appearance. Perhaps the reader may remember I was the daughter of Col. Mathew and Beaulah Lyon. I was born on the 11th of June, 1805, in the beautiful village of Eddyville, situated on the Cumberland River, Livingston County (afterward Colwell), but now known as Lyon County, Kentucky. In this place I awoke to life, which at that time seemed to have a thousand charms for me; I was loved and caressed by everyone, and almost idolized by my parents.

Nature in her rich profusion spread romance and beauty all around the village. There were the bold mountain-like bluffs which approached the village, and yet stood back in awe, as if the divine hand that made them said, "Thus far thou may'st come, but no further." They sloped off with modest beauty and formed a lovely valley, or bottom, even to the water's edge; this in its natural state, formed a canebrake growing from one inch to six feet in height.

When I can first recollect (through the perseverance and enterprise of a Yankee Colony that settled there in 1799) it was dotted all over with neat dwellings and good gardens, producing every variety of vegetables and flowers that the mind could well conceive, yielding not only plenty but an abundance to the diligent hand. While these bluffs were covered with a variety of timber, wild fruit and flowers. The timber consisted of elm, ash, hickory, walnut and sugar-maple, from which the early settlers made a great quantity of sugar and molasses,—a great luxury I assure you, at that time. The fruit consisted of grapes, blackberries, crab-apples, paupaus, dewberries, and many others. There was a great variety of wild flowers, from the gorgeous white and purple flower of the dogwood and the pink flush of the red-bud tree, to the tiny violet, arrayed in its modest robe of blue and white. (How beautiful is this tiny flower in its simplicity and humility, sending forth its rich perfume through the air, while growing so humbly at our feet.) Here I was allowed to ramble at pleasure through these scenes of romance and beauty, constantly attended by my brother, who was two years older than myself, and sometimes a number of boys and girls would join us in our rambles over the bluffs and through the lovely valley. We have often spent half a day at a time in one of these rambles.

One day, when returning from a stroll, our baskets laden with flowers, our party concluded to stop and make a playhouse in the back yard under some large shade trees. At this proposition all hearts swelled with delight. We had all had a nice ramble, and we would all have a good time building a play-house. The boys hurried about, hunting and collecting pieces of boards which had been used on former occasions. They then put up the house as best they could, suiting the taste of us girls very much. They would call out occasionally, "Well, girls, how will this do?" "How will that look? It is the best we can do now; but when we grow to be men I think we will beat it, as we shall be provided better with tools and lumber; besides, we shall have nails and all those sort of thing which will enable us to build in the right way." The girls would respond, "You have done well; the house is splendid; you are first-rate house-builders."

We girls were busy with our little hands picking up all the bits of broken ware in the shape of old flower-pots, tea pots, etc., to put our flowers in, so that we could decorate our shelves. We soon got our house in order. Then came an important thing for me to do. It was for me to go and get mother's consent to take my nice tea-ware which my father had presented to me only a few days before. As soon as this was mentioned my heart throbbed with delight and I exclaimed, "I'll go, girls; ma will let me have them, and some cake, fruit and cheese, and then we can have tea just like old folks!" I bounded away to the house, and found my mother in the sitting room. She cast her expressive blue eyes upon me, and with her usual kindness, asked, "What are you in such haste for? I hope nothing unpleasant has occurred."

"Oh, no; dear mother," I replied, "I have come to ask your leave to use my nice tea dishes that pa gave me the other day; and then, ma, I want some cake, some cheese and sauce, so that we can have tea in our play-house, the boys have built us one; do come and see it ma!" "Oh, no, dear," my mother replied, "the boys might run away if they should see me coming; here are your things, go, now, and enjoy yourselves, be careful of your tea ware, and bring them back safe." With this counsel from my mother, I started away greatly delighted. The boys and girls met me, saying, "Oh, we knew your ma would let you have them, she is so kind." The table was made of a board on four forks; a cloth was spread, and the dishes neatly arranged, and our cake, cheese and fruit were placed on the largest plates, the tea-kettle was boiled, our tea drawn, and then we were all ready to be seated. As we were sitting down, one of the party hit one of the forks which supported the table, and down went our dishes, tea, cake and cheese, all at one sweep. Some of us caught the ends of the cloth preventing the dishes from falling to the ground, so that the dishes were not broken, and of course no great damage was done.

It being too late by this time for us to go through the ceremony again, we dispersed with the hope of having a tea out of the nice teaware some other time. As my brother and I approached my mother with our dishes all in a muss, she said, "Ah, my dear children, I feared you would not enjoy all that you anticipated. This life is full of disappointments, and you must try and prepare yourselves for them; I hope and pray that you may have patience, resignation and grace to bear them."

Time with its swift wings has borne me along, but has not erased from my mind many scenes, some pleasant, and some of a more serious nature. One that I will relate now is of the earthquakes that were felt so severely in Kentucky in the years of 1812-13. We had read and heard of earthquakes, but had little idea that we should know by experience what it meant to feel the earth quake and totter and roll under our feet, but it was so.

One day, in the beginning of the winter of 1812, after spending the day in play, I retired for the night, first saying the prayer my mother had taught me—

"Now I lay me down to sleep.
I pray Thee, Lord, my soul to keep;
And if I die before I wake,
I pray Thee, Lord, my soul to take."

Then tucking me snugly in my little trundle-bed, my kind kind mother, who was ever watching over me like a guardian angel, bent over me and said, "Now, dear, go to sleep." After commenting on the uncertainty of life and the certainty of death, she turned away and left me to reflect upon what she had said to me. While reflecting, I fell asleep, comforting myself that God would hear my prayers. I realized nothing more until about midnight, when I was aroused with very strange feelings. I was rolling to and fro in my bed, not knowing the cause of the motion. Just then my mother came to my bed and caught me up in her arms, saying, "My dear Lizzie, this is an earthquake, and I fear the earth will open and take us in! This shows the power of Him who made the heavens and the earth. It is the God I teach you to pray to." Just then my father approached us and addressed my mother with: "'Madam Lyon,' I think we had better go out of the house. It reels and shakes so I fear it will tumble down. A number of those in the chamber have been thrown from their beds and have made their way into the yard." When we got out we found all the family there, both black and white, young and old, in their night clothes. Some were holding on to the trees; others were hanging to them. Those who could not keep their feet were rolling to and fro on the ground like logs. All was consternation. Some of them could not understand the cause of this commotion, and thought that the Judgment Day had come. Richard, the black preacher, remarked, "If dis yere be de Judgment Day, I shall soon see my bressed Lord an' Mas'r!" Others exclaimed, "Oh, Lord! be merciful to me, a sinner." My father reasoned with us all on the subject and told us what he thought was the cause. "But I know not what will be the result," said he. "I have read of the earth opening, and persons and even houses falling in. That may happen to us now, but I hope not." Even my father, with all his philosophy and firmness, was frightened. By degrees the quaking and shaking of the earth became less severe, and soon the crashing sound died away into a rumbling like distant thunder. And, oh! how thankful we all were to find all alive, without the least injury.

But this was not the happy result everywhere. At a number of places on the Mississippi the earth had opened, and many persons were engulfed. Friends of these unfortunate persons hastened to rescue them by digging them out, but after succeeding to get them out they were found to be mangled and dead, so that they were only taken from the earth to be replaced again. Some were never found, to receive burial; houses were shaken to atoms, and some were thrown into the river. The houses in our village were not seriously injured, chimneys were thrown down, only, and other occurences of similar nature happened here and there. But this put people in such a state of alarm that all were reading, talking and reasoning on the subject of Earthquakes. It was thought that the sink-holes in the river near us prevented us from feeling a heavier shock in Colwell County, as there could be seen something like smoke rising frome these holes after the earthquake took place, which was never seen before. Slight trembling of the earth was felt once in two or three weeks for a year afterward, but never so severely as at first.

CHAPTER II.

THE GARDEN, AND THE GARDENER.

The gardener was, at the time I write of, a man about forty years of age, an Englishman by birth, and in the beginning of the Revolutionary War had fought under the British flag. He was on board a man-of-war, they landed on an island for the purpose of getting some wood. He with others was sent out, and, for some reason, stopped longer than the rest, and the man-of-war sailed without him. The reason why he was left, we leave the reader to conjecture. He never could endure the idea of being called a deserter. He remained on the island for a number of days, and was picked up by an American vessel; afterterwards enlisted and fought under the banner of liberty, and fought like a good soldier for the rights of an American citizen, and through the mercy of God was permitted to enjoy those privileges for many years. For reasons unknown he never married. After the war had closed he was providentially directed to my father for emyloyment. He was a nailer by trade; all the nails used in America at that time were made of wrought iron. They were manufactured thus, first the iron was made into a rod by putting it through a slitting machine made for this purpose. My father having one of these machines in effective operation, he could give the old "General Whitehouse" (a fictitious name which the workmen on the place called him on account of his superior work, and the name was borne by the old gentleman to his death) steady employment. He, "Uncle General," as the children called him, became an inmate of my father's family for many years in Vermont, and when my father emigrated to Kentucky he accompanied him, and made one of that colony comprising the citizens of the Yankee village. For a number of years he supplied the community with the best of wrought nails with peculiar nice heads and sharp points; but the old gentleman became satisfied that the new mode of making nails was about to supersede his business, and soon gave it up. He now directed his attention to another kind of employment. He had been trained in his youth to gardening, and thinking he might still be useful in this line of business, my father employed him to improve and to cultivate his already large and beautiful garden. To facilitate this, and to gratify the old General, my father had a neat little home built at the foot of the garden; furnished it with many comforts and conveniences for him. He was supplied with money, and a conveyance to travel over the country and purchase flowers, fruit and shrubbery wherever he could find them, and whatever kinds of plants that would be useful and ornamental; and he was a workman to be prized, I assure you. Everything was done in order and in due season; he was in the garden early and late; there was not a weed to be seen, and every bed was made of earth molded as fine and soft as earth could be made; all seeds were gathered in due time, dried with care, put into a neat bag, marked, and placed in a dry place ready for use in the spring.

"Uncle General" was very kind to us children, and when in a pleasant humor liked the appellation which the children had given him. But if, on the contrary, he was not in a pleasant mood, he would cry out, "Oh! you rogues, I will give you 'Uncle General,' if you don't keep your distance." And we knew it was time for us to scamper off. But, oh! what hours of pleasure I have spent, rambling through that garden with my brother, and sometimes with other playmates, and "Uncle General" at our side. We never dared to enter the garden without his permission. He would lead us to the rose alley and let us pluck roses from this and that bush until we had got one of each kind; then we would proceed to the pink alley, thence to gather the violets, chamomile, sweet lavender, flowering moss, and so on, till we would have a basket full of flowers for ourselves and friends. Then we would go to one of the arbors, covered with jessamine, woodbine and grape vines, as suited our taste or convenience. These arbors were scattered all through the garden, and after we had arranged our boquets, rested and regaled ourselves with the sweet odor of the flowers, "Uncle General" would allow us to race after the butterfly or humming-bird, and while we enjoyed ourselves in the chase, we would always find him near us.

Often, while leaning with much dignity over his hoe, he would teach us some useful lesson from objects around us. On one occasion he called our attention thus: "Dear children; see yonder, how graceful that humming-bird poises above that flower, and how skillfully it extracts the sweets from its very heart, with peculiar, tiny bill. There, it has left that flower to go to another. Now, you cannot see any difference in the appearance of the flower it has extracted the sweets from, the work of its tiny bill has been effected so skillfully; but by to-morrow, perhaps, the flower will show signs of decay, and day after day it will be more visible, until it finally withers and dies. But, see here, children; here is a well-formed capsule, filled with numerous seeds. They will ripen as the flower decays, and when they fall to the ground will vegetate and bring forth another beautiful flower in the other's place to fill the air with its rich perfume. Now, dear children, here is a good lesson to be learned from this, if we would but profit by it. Time, with her sharp sickle, like the humming-bird, is striking all these frail systems of ours, and daily we feel more or less its power, and ere we are aware of it the fatal stroke is given, and we, like the flower, will droop and die. But still there is hope in the death of the righteous. While the body dies and is committed to the earth, there to lie and mold until God who formed all things shall reanimate this sleeping dust and recall those immortal spirits that they may be reunited in the majesty and glory of the Resurrection. Oh! solemn thought, we shall all be there to share in the judgment of the just and the unjust."

Thus he often labored to make good impressions on our young minds in regard to the shortness of life and the certainty of death. In this way our interviews would close with a promise if we would be good children we should enjoy these privileges again soon. Then he would see us to the gate, then he would close it, and no one dared open it without his permission. Away we ran with our load of flowers, feeling that our hearts were profitably affected by this interview. Uncle General in a few years became very feeble with rheumatism, but as long as possible he would be in the garden. When he was unable to do his work a a man was employed to take his place. but often the "General" would grow impatient with William's work and would say, "Let me come and do that, I can do it better." And time and again I have seen him work when he was scarcely able to stand, and have plead with him to let William do the work, "he can do it very well;" sometimes I would prevail upon him, and other times I would not. For a number of years before the death of my parents, he became so infirm that he could not join the family at the table, so I generally had the pleasure of carrying to him his food, in his own little house. Here he was very comfortable and happy; his furniture consisted of a table, a large trunk in which he kept his tools, another smaller one for his clothes; my mother always saw that his linen was done up in order for him, he was remarkably neat in everything; his neat cot bed was always in perfect order, which he preferred to make up himself; the old fashioned shovel and tongs stood in the corner on the newly painted brick hearth, in a very precise manner, a large arm chair well cushioned, and a foot stool, a small shelf placed over a low window with a few volumes of old fashioned books and the Bible, summed up his library; all these comprised his household comforts. Many hours have I spent in that little house, reading to him the word of life, as he called the contents of the precious Bible. Again I would read from some other book, an interesting story. Sometimes he would tell war stories to myself, brother, and our associates, who would go there often to hear them.

In this way things moved on for a number of years without much change, except that he grew so feeble, that he ceased to labor entirely, he in the meantime lost his hearing, so that if one wished to convey anything to him, they were obliged to write on a slate which he kept hanging on the back of his chair. In this manner I have conversed with him, and he would invariably remark, "Is it possible that this is the little rosy cheeked girl that used to prance about the garden, and cull the flowers and pick the fruit with such glee?" One day, at the close of such an interview, I replied, "Yes; Uncle General, it is the same, with but the changes that time has wrought; how well do I remember the many useful lessons you taught me and my brother, and to-day I deeply realize the lessons you taught us from the pink and humming-bird, and Time has come already, with his sharp sickle, and thrust his last blow on my dearly beloved brother, and must I say it? he is no more." "Alas! alas;" he said, "is it so? Can it be possible that your brother who was the very picture of health; the pride of the village, dead? he that was to be the stay and comfort of his parents' declining years, ah; yes he was like that flower just unfolding its fragrance to the earth. And he must be called from earth;—just twenty-one years old—biding fair for so useful a life; can it be possible! Why could not the enemy have chosen me for its victim, and spared him. And the tears ran down his time worn cheeks until every furrow was drenched. In silence we wept for some time; he at length broke the silence by saying, " Well my dear child, Time, like an ever-rolling stream, bears all her sons away. It will soon be my time, I'm ready and willing, I await my change, and hope, through the atonement made by my blessed Lord, to share in the resurrection of the just." Not many months passed before a procession passed the house bearing my mother's corpse; he requested the colored man who attended him to bring him his chair, as he could not walk, that he might gaze upon my mother's face once more. His request was granted; the procession halted, that he might be raised up to the bier. When he saw my mother's face, so still and cold, what an expression of feeling there was upon his features, —I cannot describe the scene. At last he lifted his eyes all bathed in tears toward heaven, and murmured, "Dear Lord, am I to out-live all this family? I desire to be called to rest, but patiently will I await Thy call, my Master, to come up higher." Only a few weeks elapsed, and time made the last stroke on his frail body. The messenger called him to rest, and we hope he entered into that rest that he so much desired.

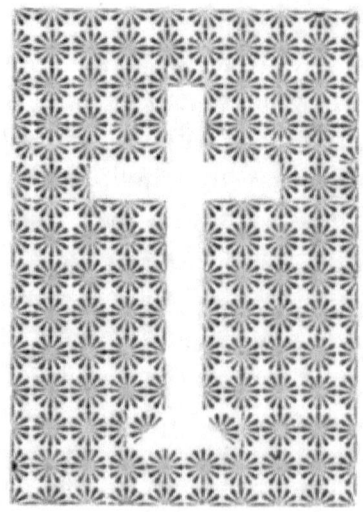

CHAPTER III.

EARLIEST RECOLLECTIONS OF METHODISM AND ITS INFLUENCE ON ME.

HAVING given the reader some ideas of my earlier associates, I will now tell you something of the religious influences which surrounded me, and the influences which were calculated to lead me into vain amusements and pleasures of a fashionable life. My father was a man who the world called, at that age, a kind-hearted, generous, noble minded deist. He believed in an all-wise Creator and preserver of the universe, was a worldly minded, business man, all absorbed in promoting the interest and improvement of the new country—Kentucky, where he had lately settled a large colony. He thought the preaching of the gospel had a tendency to improve the moral condition of society, and therefore contributed liberally to the support of the ministry,—treating them all with kind respect, no matter to what denomination they belonged. Ministers were always invited to his home, and treated hospitably, and seldom went away without a nice present; but when they ventured to bring the great truths of the gospel to bear upon his mind he would say, "My dear sir, I have no time to think of this matter now; but you go on your way, the cause you work for is a good one, and I will help you all I can." He always attended services on the Sabbath, and desired his work-hands to go; at some seasons of the year his workmen and their families would make quite a large audience. Yet he knew nothing of the saving influence of the gospel until in his last illness. Although he died away from home, from what we learned of the state of his mind, we have hopes in his death.

My mother was a daughter of Governer Thomas Chittendon, the first governor of the State of Vermont. He was re-elected until he served in that office fifteen years. He was a very pious man, and raised his children very strictly. My mother was therefore the subject of early religious impressions, but as she entered upon lights and shades of life she lost in a measure these good impressions, and became a gay fashionable woman, and enjoyed life to its fullest extent if ever any woman did. She was first in society; first in dress, and, being a handsome woman, was very much admired, both for her style of dress and neatness of housekeeping. Her intelligence, together with an amiable disposition, won for her the love and confidence of all who made her acquaintance.

Thus she glided along life's stream, till she was nearly forty-seven years of age. At that late period the Lord in mercy powerfully awakened her, she saw her danger,—sought at once, and found the Lord in the pardon of her sins. Uniting with the Methodist E. P. church, she ever afterwards lived a constant, humble christian, serving the Lord in spirit and in truth, always ready for any good work or words. I being her youngest child (then nine years old) she seemed particularly interested in me, yet she earnestly prayed for those with whom she had associated in the ball-room, at the card-table, and in all the other amusements of fashionable life. Oh, how often did she exhort them to lay aside such vain pleasures, and to seek real pleasure in the religion of Jesus. They would say, "Dear mother, you used to enjoy such amusements." "Ah, my dear children," she would say, "I feel this reproof, and I'm very sorry I ever set you the example, for those same amusements always left a sting—there was an aching spot in my heart they could not touch, and now I see the folly of it; therefore, my dear children, be persuaded to abandon them, and place your affections on a more worthy object; don't waste the prime of your life in these vain enjoyments as I have done, but seek the Lord—why will you delay? will you be lost, dear children?" Often has she thus plead with them, but with little success, as they still continued in the same course.

As I grew older, they tried to lead me and my youngest brother in the habit of doing the same by saying, "There is no use of children trying to be religious; wait until you get as old as mother, then it will do to be sober, leave off dressing fashionably, going to balls, being gay, and enjoying life. To be any body, you must act like the world, dress like the world, and make a good appearance. If you wish to be respected, this you must do, so come, you must go with us this time anyhow." These brothers and sisters were older than us, my parents having lost two children between us and the older ones, leaving a difference of twelve years. We, being so much younger, were taught to love and obey them, while they in return loved and caressed us; thus it was a difficult matter for us to think they did wrong; they exerted a great influence over us either for good or evil.

This younger brother and I were always together in all amusements; he led me to school, to church, and when we had a ramble in the woods or a race in the garden, he was always by my side. Oh, how it pained my young heart when I learned he must leave me and go away to college. He had made such rapid progress in his studies at the school that he was ready for college,—the first and only one, at that time, in the state. It was situated near Russelville; I think I remember the Principal's name, Mr. Barry. Yes, he must leave, and we were to be separated for the first time. This was the first heartfelt sorrow I remember having felt. How well I recollect how noble and manly he looked dressed in his traveling suit for the journey. He leaned over me, his face covered with tears, and kissed me saying, "Dear sister, don't weep so, brother is only going to school, to gain knowledge that he might be useful," and then imprinting another kiss upon my cheek, he was gone.

My mother, knowing the influence which my older brothers and sisters had over me, strove to counteract it by her pious examples and religious instructions. She was always at my bedside to teach me how to pray and commit myself to the care of Him who doeth all things well. I had such confidence in her piety that if there were a severe storm and I was near her I thought I was safe. I believed the Lord would take care of her and hoped he would me, for her sake. At the age of five years she dedicated me to the Lord through the ordinance of baptism administered by the Rev. Dr. P. Cartwright. How solemn I felt when he laid his hand upon my head and said, "God bless the child," and I believe the Holy Spirit sealed those impressions on my heart at that time which have never been erased. Brother Cartwright was then a young man in the field, preaching with zeal for the salvation of precious souls, and whatever he did was sealed with the spirit of God. I saw him baptise scores of children during the great revival in Kentucky, and there was a holy unction of the spirit of God resting on the minister, the subjects and the congregation. Oh, how I wish our ministers of the present day would use that ordinance in the congregation now as they did then. I believe it would be a blessing to the children, the parents, the church, and to the world generally. Brother Cartwright's preaching, with the kind instructions he gave me while visiting at my father's, made lasting impressions upon my mind. He received my mother into the church. Father often remarked to her, "You must take care of that Boy Preacher, for he is too smart and too good to want for anything we have." She generally attended to that. His preaching was the means of bringing many souls into the ark of safety. While at Eddyville he formed a class, and put Brother Rider in as leader, who was a holy, humble christian; there was father and mother White, who lived at Eddygrove, who came down and joined us, and oh! what power attended those meetings. I have seen Mother White lying on the floor, crying, "Glory! glory!" for hours. Others happy in the Lord, some crying for mercy, and new-born souls rejoicing in a sin pardoning God. At those meetings I felt the spirit striving within me, yet so young I scarcely comprehended it.

This class prospered for many years, and great good was done. But eventually Brother Rider moved away, while Father and Mother White died (and no doubt went to heaven), with the others moving away and dying, left the wicked who waxed strong; the class was broken up, and there was no more preaching for years. My mother joined a class in what was called father Reed's neighborhood, some five miles from our village. There I used to go with my mother to meeting, and the same power was manifested there, as there always is when Christians live humbly and devoted to God. The spirit of God strove within my heart under the preaching and in the class-room with her, and there I would promise (if the Lord would help me) to try and be a Christian; but when I would return home I was thrown into such a different atmosphere and the influence of those friends who were all absorbed in the world, fashion and amusements, being so young and fond of company, that ere I was aware of it would find my good resolutions shaken. I would be persuaded to go to some elegant ball, or join some giddy amusement which would drown all my good impressions; and if I ever hesitated, they would say, "I do believe mother will make a Methodist of you if you don't quit going out to old Mr. Reed's; we will not let you go out there any more." I could not bear to see dear mother go so far alone to meeting, and go she would whether any one went with her or not, and I would go with her, whether they liked it or not. I was confident she was right. Often have I heard her praying in her closet, beseeching God, saying, "Dear Lord, may I not have one sheaf to rejoice over." Then I felt that she had reference to me,— it would be borne home to my heart. I would weep as I would reason with myself,—how can I be a christian under these circumstances—such opponents to contend with; yet I feel that my mother is right, I know if she should die she would go to heaven; but should my other friends die they would die without hope, and so would I, too, for I have no hope beyond the grave. And again I would resolve to be a christian, and would try to pray. My mother watched me closely when she saw I was laboring under these good resolutions; she would exhort me to trust in the Saviour, and try to explain to me the power of saving faith, telling me it was by grace through faith we are saved. She would give me good books to read, such as the life of "Hester Ann Rogers," "Baxter's Call to the Unconverted," also "Fletcher's Appeal." These good books strengthened my good impressions, and at times I thought I was altogether persuaded to be a christian.

I recollect once when I was laboring under these convictions, there was a grand ball to be given. On the announcement of it I resolved in my own mind that I would not go, and almost promised my mother I would not go. But when the invitations came, my brothers and sisters prevailed upon me to go, by saying that as my young brother was at home on a visit and was going that I must go, too; and holding out other inducements that they would arrange my dress, and it should be the most elegant which would be worn; if I would but consent to go, I should have no trouble with it; that my brother would be very proud of me,—this they thought would touch the right cord, knowing as they did that I dearly loved my brother, and would do anything to please him. Reasoning that there was no harm in dancing, and that some religious people danced,—no ministers preached against it but the Methodist, "And I wish," they said, "they had never came here, then we could take some comfort in our balls. So come now, promise to go, there is no harm in it, will you?" At last I told them if mother would give her consent I would go. They were inconsistent enough to go and ask her. She told them she was greatly surprised that they should ask *her* consent for she had *never* given her consent for me to go, and felt much less like giving it now than ever, and if I went it would be much against her will; that I was old enough now to act upon my own responsibility. My brother said he had never been to balls much, and as he was home on a visit, thought he would go. They all said I must go.

No one, but He who knows the thoughts of every heart,

knew how I **felt**. I dearly loved **my** bothers and sisters; I loved my **mother**, and I **did not** wish to grieve her, and dreaded the guilt I would incur by going, and yet I had not the moral courage to resist their entreaties, and so concluded to go, but thought in **my** own mind I would not dance, and thus please them **all**, and **in** this manner I could get along without incurring much guilt. But when mother learned that **I** had consented to go, she looked sad and seemed depressed in spirits. I wished a thousand times I had not consented to go, **but** the tempter said, "It is **too** late now to repent, you have promised to go, and **if** you do not, you will incur a great **deal** of displeasure. You need not dance, but go, and behave **with so** much dignity that it will do you no harm." **Thus the tempter** reasoned with **my** poor young **heart**. I did **not** realize that he could so lead me when he once **got** me **on** his own ground. The **evening came; I was arrayed in style;** a number of young persons were there **to** accompany us. **As my** brother approached me I saw an expression of pride on **his** countenance as he **looked** upon the sister he loved so much. Just then mother entered the room with a look **of** grief resting upon her face. I shall never forget that look, when she said, "My dear children, **if** you will go to this ball I have one request to make, which I hope you will grant, and that is, that you will return by ten o'clock." "Oh yes, yes mother," replied my brother, "we will." I said "yes," too, as frankly as he did, and little thought but what I should do so without **a** doubt.

Brother had never paid **so** much attention to dancing as I had, and consequently did not care so much for its giddy **maze.** I had practiced it a great deal for one of my age, **and was** extremely fond of it, and wondered that I dared **to** venture under the sound of the violin, as its music had **such an** enchanting power over me. But I wish the reader to understand that I was venturing in my own strength; I knew nothing of the power of faith—in prayer—strength derived from a sweet confiding trust in a sin-pardoning God.

I had no sooner entered the dancing hall, under the sound of the violin, than my heart bounded to the music, the same as I had so often danced after before, and there joined the same circle of loved ones that I associated with in this bewitching amusement. The good resolutions my young heart had made were overpowered, but I did muster courage enough to refuse a number of warm solicitations to lead in the dance, but at last I yielded and was led onto the floor at the head of a cotillion. If I should attempt to describe my feelings my pen would fail me; but let me say it was then I felt I was a sinner; yes, I do believe the spirit of God at that moment reproached me with my sin and made me see more clearly the sureness of the judgment to come. I felt that I was sinning against God and my better judgment; I knew I was doing what would grieve one of the best of mothers; oh! how plain I could see her face with that expression of grief on her mild features before me as I glided over the floor. The wise man has said, "The way of the transgressor is hard." I felt at times like crying out, "God be merciful unto me a sinner." But I overcame those feelings, and so by degrees they wore off, and I became more cheerful the remaining part of the evening. All seemed to pass pleasantly with those around me, yet I suffered from the inward workings of a guilty conscience.

At ten o'clock my dear brother came to me saying, "Sister, it is time we were starting for home, mother will be looking for us; don't you remember what she requested of us?" "Yes, yes," said I, "and if it is ten o'clock I'll go." A number of ladies and gentlemen overhearing our conversation remarked, "Oh, no, 'tis not ten yet, and we hope you will not go at this early hour, will you?" I replied that I "must certainly go at ten." At that they surrounded us and plead with us not to go, saying as they each consulted their watches, "'Tis only nine o'clock." They looked at my brother for an answer, but he withdrew, saying to me, "Sister, I shall go soon, and you had better go with me." I said, "I will in half an hour." Then they said, "You must stay till twelve, sure." At that, brother left me, and I saw no more of him that night. When he started I had no idea he would go home without me; so when it was admitted to be ten o'clock I begged my older brother to go and find him. He sought him, but he had gone home feeling very unhappy because I did not go with him. This made me feel still worse, and the rest of my company would not go till two o'clock. I strove to throw this trouble aside and remain, but becoming so unhappy, I went to one of my brothers and told him that home I must and would go, I could not stay there any longer. At that we started, seven or eight following us. Those who had persuaded me to remain said, "You have broken up the ball at last; I knew you would if you and your company left, as the rest would follow."

When we arrived home, to our surprise, we found the doors locked. I assure you, dear reader, I felt awful, and yet felt it served me right, but did not see how I could endure this mortification. I thought my heart would break. I knew God and my mother were angry with me past forgiveness, or the doors would not have been locked. The company were about starting for a hotel, when Mr. S. (a young man who boarded with us) said, "If you will permit me to take off a slat so that I can open the shutter, I can then raise the window and go in and unbolt the door for the rest of you." "Very well," said I, "that will do," although I thought it looked bad to be forcing ourselves into the house in this way, yet we had to get in, and concluded this the only way to effect an entrance. We had knocked at every door in the house but received no response whatever. He succeeded in opening the door for us. After entering we partook of the refreshments on the sideboard, after which each one sought their own apartment. I went to my room, but not to sleep. I went to mother's room, but on looking around the apartment for her could see no sign of her. The bed had not been touched to all appearances, and I came to the conclusion that mother was away from home attending the sick, as she was often called. Having fully settled this in my mind, and feeling better, as I hoped she would never know how late it was when I returned from the ball, I proceeded at once to the clothes room to put my bonnet away. Not taking a light with me, I stumbled on—my mother—who was on her knees praying. I was sure it was her as soon as I touched her. On hearing her voice in prayer I recovered from my shock, and dragged my trembling limbs back to my room, and I thought I should never get to it. As soon as I had reached it I threw myself upon the bed, and in my agony cried out, "Lord, have mercy on me," then gave way to a flood of tears, and those tears relieved me of my intense pain. Then I tried to pray, feeling there was no mercy for me sinning as I had against God, grieving the Holy Spirit, trifling with my soul, heeding not the good resolutions I had made, and grieving my poor mother,—oh! these thoughts, how terrible they were. You may imagine that it was little rest I had the remainder of that night; but after I had thought the scenes all over, I firmly resolved never to be seen in a ball-room again; that I would go to mother in the morning and acknowledge my faults, and ask her forgiveness, and tell her of all my sorrow. This

I would do, and I resolved that, let others do what they would, I should seek the Lord in the pardon of my sins, for I felt I would be lost and undone if I did not seek and gain pardon and grace to carry out these resolutions. This was the first time I trusted in the Lord's strength, which I had before resolved in my own strength out of my perfect weakness.

After I had made these resolutions in the grace of God, I had faith given me to believe that God would help me. But how to approach my mother with my confession was the next thing to trouble me, to plan my duty was easy, but to do it was the difficulty. I had disregarded her feelings in her religious views, civility, and social life; had entered the house without her leave (as I supposed), and how could I approach her? (My mother intended to let us in herself, but not hearing us, supposed a little colored girl had opened the door instead). However, I went to my mother in the morning, and approached her with, " Mother, dearest mother, can you forgive me? I feel that I have done wrong, and am very, very sorry, and I have seriously resolved never to go to another ball." I thought I should sink at the mild, sad look she gave me, for I had expected sternness, and felt that I deserved a severe rebuke, but instead of all this she clasped me in her arms, while warm tears of forgiveness fell upon my face, and, imprinting a kiss upon my cheek, she said, " Yes, my child, I freely forgive you, and I hope the Lord will forgive you, too. I know you have sinned against His grace, and against your own religious convictions. Now I hope and pray that you will never do so again; I know you will not if you follow the dictates of the spirit, then you will be led to the fountain which washes away all sin. Again she kissed me saying, " My dear child, give your heart entirely to God, and then he will help you to overcome all temptations."

Christians, nothing but the love of God shed abroad in my heart could have given such joy and peace. It created a strong hope that the Lord would forgive me. I felt very thankful to mother for her forgiveness and sympathy for me, and more thankful to the Lord who had given me a praying mother. Mothers, pray for your erring children I entreat, and pray in faith, as a prayer in faith availeth much. My mother's prayer was answered when she saw that I was earnestly and devotedly seeking the ways of the Lord.

How carefully she watched over me; often she would come and take a vain novel from my hand which had been given me to read, given me by some of my friends, saying there was no harm in them, that I could read them without affecting my religion any, and would be more interesting to me than "Baxter's Call to the Unconverted," and "Fletcher's Appeal," which were intended for old people to read, and that those romances were calculated to improve and cultivate my mind. Oh! how wrong, and it grieves me to see how much novel reading is engaging the minds of the young people of the present time, not improving the mind in godliness, but stamping upon the mind infidelity. May the Lord have mercy and save the world, and especially the church from these influences, when the world is so full of good and profitable reading matter. You may go in the parlor or library of any fashionable house, and there you will see the center table loaded with these trifling, frivolous books, graced with a few volumes of religious works merely for good taste and looks of the thing, yet the poisoning seed of infidelity was at the foundation. For this reason parents should be very careful what kind of books they choose for their children to read. Children, I fear many of you will have cause to say, "Were it not for the reading I had at home I should have been a Christian, instead of an unbeliever, with my heart as hard as a rock, and so indifferent about the salvation of my never dying soul."

CHAPTER IV.

RELIGIOUS RESOLUTIONS AND HOW THEY WERE PROSECUTED.

From the time my mother forgave me for going to the ball, I resolved, by the grace of God, to be a Christian, and these resolutions were made in the strength of grace. I felt that I was a great sinner, but believed there was a Saviour, and hoped he would reveal himself to me in pardoning my sins. I discarded all novel reading, and read the Bible, with other good books. I found great comfort in reading "Baxter's Call to the Unconverted," and "Fletcher's Appeal;" every word seemed to suit my case. I wish those good books could be found now, on every center-table or in every book-case. In every Christian family, at least, there should be found those books, containing the pure doctrines of the Gospel by our Lord and Saviour, Jesus Christ, portrayed in every line of holy men's writings. How it glows in every sentence. I prayed much in secret; I waited on the Lord by the means of grace, whenever I had the opportunity. There were no regular services held in our village for years after the class dispersed that Brother Cartwright had organized. He traveled through the upper part of the State, except in the summer, when Brother Wilcox (a Methodist elder, half-brother to Brother Cartwright, who resided within fifteen miles of us,) came once a month and preached us a sermon. He was a very devoted Christian, and his sermons were a great blessing to me; he was gratified to learn that I was an earnest seeker of religion, and always made it a point to stop at my father's house when he visited our village. He kindly labored with me, teaching me the doctrine of faith, its great power, simplicity and importance, and I was no longer ashamed to tell to the world now, that I was a penitent sinner, and seeking the grace of God. But I was afraid to make a profession of religion, while I was not yet sure of possessing its saving power. Mother and I still attended "Father Reed's" class-meetings, and they were a great blessing to me; I never came away without feeling strengthened by going to the house of God's people, but had not yet faith to claim the blessing of justification, and say that the Lord has saved me, or saves me now; yet I was in hopes that He would save me, and this hope kept me from despairing.

While thus laboring in this state of feeling I strove to give up all the amusements of the world, and discard dressing finely,—which I had loved dearly—and had bowed at the shrine of fashion as much as any one possibly could. My pride and vanity had been gratified in every respect. My brothers were engaged in a dry goods establishment, and never failed when purchasing their stock to select for me the newest and most stylish articles of dress. Our family dressed in the richest of apparel, and moved in the most fashionable circles, and when my brothers saw me dressing so plainly they became very uneasy, and remarked, "Those Methodists will certainly drive that child crazy. If she is so determined to be a Christian, why not be led to a church where they allow dressing in style, and look and act something like the world; but no, it seems nothing will suit but those terrible Methodists. Expect they will soon have her shouting." One tried to prevent me from attending the meetings by saying that, "if he ever heard me shouting, he would disown me; and if you go any more I will give you a horse-whipping. Don't let me catch you among them again." They had seen me at Father Reed's prayer-meeting. So my friends went on for some time in this manner. They would watch mother and me so closely that we would hire the servants to slip out the horses that we rode, and then we would go by some by-road unbeknown to them. They tried to dissuade me by coaxing till they had nearly ruined my soul, and now they were trying what violent threats could do. But I was firm, and notwithstanding all their coaxing, hiring and threatening, they failed to accomplish their purpose. Now they held a council, and concluded they would send for a very fashionable cousin of ours, who lived in Tennessee, to come and spend a few months with us. She had always had a great influence over me; thinking she could no doubt turn me from Methodism, she was sent for at once, and responded promptly. I was delighted to see her, for I loved her dearly. She was a beautiful, intelligent, amiable girl, and always loved me tenderly; when she came she embraced me very warmly, telling me how happy she was to see me. But in the meantime she remarked, with a look of disapprobation overshadowing her face, "I have been feeling very uneasy about your turning Methodist. Now cousin," she commenced, "those people are turning the world up side down, they are wild, and are driving folks crazy wherever they go, and that is everywhere.

They dare go any place; they came into Clarksville, one of the most fashionable places in the country, and commenced preaching their wild Methodist doctrines, and the people are all going crazy under their influence. Their converts tear off their ribbons, ruffles, and jewelry, and shout and pray so that it is enough to set one crazy to hear them. I go to hear them preach sometimes, for I think their ministers are very intelligent and gentlemanly in their deportment, and explain the scriptures very plainly, but when they begin to shout and pray I retire as soon as possible. I don't wish to be influenced by them to throw off my jewelry, fashionable dressing, and give up every fashionable amusement. I don't think it necessary to deny oneself of everything to become a Christian, and they wont allow even fashionable novels to be read; they say they are full of infidelity which is calculated to lead the mind from God and the interests of the soul, that they induce the young to become vain and trifling in thought, and wanting in manners. They advise us to read the Bible and some other good religious books, which would help to make us Christians. I don't see why the Methodists need to be so rigid on these little matters, when other churches are not." "Cousin," I replied, "I will tell you my experience and my views on the subject. I believe the spirt of the Lord and language of inspiration teach me that it is wrong to dress extravagantly, for the blessed Word says, "Conform not to the world, but be ye transformed by the renewing of your mind, that ye may prove what is good and acceptable in the sight of God," and I think if the money used for extravagant dressing was distributed among the needy, it would greatly aid in feeding and clothing the hungry and naked, and would it not do us more good than to spend it in fashionable dressing which only pleases our vanity and selfish pride. I think every one can dress plainly and neatly without spending so much time, as it takes the greater part of our time to prepare and put on this stylish apparel. I find I have more time to read the Bible and other good books since I began to dress more plainly. Now, as to the preaching of these Methodist ministers. They do certainly preach the pure doctrines of the Bible, and it is brought home to every heart by the spirit of God, and I do sincerely believe if I follow the dictates of the blessed Spirit, I shall some day be a Christian in deed and in truth."

"Oh, well, dear cousin," she replied, "I see you are well established in this Methodist belief of yours, and that you have decided to be one; so we will drop the subject for the present."

This cousin remained with us some time, laboring to draw my mind from these impressions, still admitting that it was right to be a Christian, but it was not necessary to be so strict about dress, class-meetings, love-feasts and prayer-meetings, and I am sorry to say she partially gained an influence over my mind on the subject of dress. This pleased my friends; my brother told my cousin to spare no pains nor means in accomplishing their object; that if there was any new style of jewelry or clothing to be had, I was to have it, and she succeeded well, too, in influencing me to wear them again. She said if I did not feel a wicked pride in wearing them, that there was no harm or sin in doing so. I tried to think so, and often thought when I saw my friends of different religious denominations, dressed in such fashionable attire, why could not I? but my conscience was not at ease. My dear mother watched me closely during these proceedings. I did not neglect secret prayer entirely, nor reading the Bible, but did not take such delight in it as I had done before; I was aware that I had nearly back-slidden. My gay companions began to remark, one to another, "I told you she would come back again to our gay circle; we did miss her dancing so much.".

There was a great camp-meeting to be held by the Methodists and Cumberland Presbyterians, about twelve miles from our place. They had held these revival camp-meetings together, at this beautiful place, for a number of years, and hundreds of souls had been converted on that sacred spot. I have seen, as a general thing, five thousand persons in attendance, and have witnessed more than two hundred persons prostrate, crying for mercy, with as many more giving praise to God for the pardoning of their sins.

The time for this revival was close at hand; my mother always attended, if her health would permit, and took me with her. Father would not allow her to remain on the grounds through the night, and procured us a boarding place with a widow lady by the name of Walker, (Virginian by birth,) who lived about a mile and a half from the camp ground; she generally went to the grounds at nine o'clock in the morning and remained till nine in the evening, taking a nice dinner, in a basket, which was served under the beautiful forest trees. It was understood that mother and I were going. My cousin and other friends, insisted that I should not go, saying that it was not a fit or suitable place for a young lady. They dreaded the influence of this meeting on my mind, but mother insisted that I should go, and they concluded it would not do to oppose her, so it was determined that if I went, my cousin should accompany us, thinking that she might keep me from joining the prayer-meetings. It was necessary to make great preparations; all the aristocracy were to go, and it would be a great place to show off, and to make a grand appearance. So cousin set herself about arranging our dress, a new hat, a few articles of rich jewelry, with some new style of goods made up, to add to my wardrobe; no expense or trouble was spared to make me appear fine, and we appeared on the camp ground much to the satisfaction of this proud cousin.

My father was a candidate for congress this same year. He was a political as well as a business man, and spent about twelve years in congress. At that time camp-meetings afforded a good opportunity for electioneering, by bowing politely to this one and that one, shaking hands warmly, and occasionally talking of the great business matters which were to occupy the next congress, during the intermissions; for this purpose my father went with us."

When we arrived at the camp, Cousin said to me, " Now, I hope you will not disgrace yourself and your friends by going into those prayer-meetings; keep on the outside among the 'genteel people,' then you will not come under the influence of this fanaticism. We can hear the minister just as well here as if we were nearer the altar, where there is so much praying and groaning going on." For the first day I adhered to her counsel; but let me tell you, my dear reader, when I heard the groan of the heart-stricken penitent, the fervent prayer of the righteous, the shout of the new-born soul, it went to my heart like electricity. I felt I had sinned, and come short of the glory of God, and if I continued in that course my soul would be lost and forever. I left the camp-meeting that evening as miserable as I could possibly be. Mrs. Walker's house was crowded with the aristocracy. I spent a sad night resolving I would take off my jewelry (for this cousin had me adorned with one or two hundred dollars' worth of jewelry), then I would put on a plain garb and join the prayer-circle and confess my sins, and see if the Lord would not have mercy upon me, and pardon me. But my heart failed me in the morning; I dared not appear at the breakfast table without my jewels, as I knew that I would incur great displeasure, and receive a reproof from my father and cousin; so I appeared as usual. Breakfast over, and we were soon on the camp-ground. There had been a short sermon, and now they were engaged in a prayer-meeting. The ground was covered with the slain of the Lord, and among them who were slain were a Mr. McAvoy, a wealthy farmer who resided in that vicinity, and his wife. "Oh!" said Mrs. Walker, "who would ever have thought Mr. McAvoy would come to this. He has persecuted these Methodists so; he has said everything against them he could think of. I begin to think there is more in this than mere enthusiasm, or it would never affect them so greatly —never throw them into agony so entirely unendurable. Do go and see them; they say they cannot live long in this state of mind. He says he will go crazy or die if he does not get to the camp-ground to ask the ministers and people to pray for him." Mrs. McAvoy had been religiously inclined for some time, but her husband would not allow her to go to the meetings. But now, to see them in such agony! Who can account for it? It was,—it must have been from the Lord.

We started toward the altar, where they were; we heard a shout among them; Mrs W. remarked that she "hoped they felt better." Just then we met a lady as happy as she could be. "Oh!" she exclaimed, "Mr. and Mrs McAvoy have got religion; the Lord has blessed them, and their sorrow and mourning has been turned to joy; they love everybody now—the poor as well as the rich; bless and praise the Lord for religion." We approached a little nearer: it seemed everybody around them were rejoicing; not only the angels in heaven rejoiced, but the children of God upon the earth rejoiced over those converted souls that were justified by a Saviour's blood, through a living faith. But my poor heart was dark and gloomy. I wanted to get right down there and ask the people to pray for me, but I dared not. How heavy my jewelry felt; I thought it heavier than the convict's chain, and gladly would I have shaken them off. Just then the horn sounded for the public service, and oh! what a congregation assembled; not less than six thousand persons, and nearly all seated. Mr. Barnet ascended the pulpit, read a chapter, sang a hymn, selected his text; it was these words: "Rejoice, oh, young man in the days of thy youth, and let thy heart cheer thee. But remember for all this, God will bring you to judgment." "Uncle William Barnet," as the members of his congregation called him, but was called by *outsiders*, "the patent bellows," because he was a powerful minister, often preaching from one to three hours at a time. On this occasion the Lord's Supper was observed, and he preached three hours. He made a very commanding appearance in the pulpit, being a large, portly man. He lingered on the first lines of his text, "Rejoice, oh, young man in the days of thy youth, and let thy heart cheer thee," and handled it in a masterly manner. He held up to view all the vain pursuits of pleasure-seeking minds, to those young persons present, and said "rejoice, oh! young man or young woman." He held up the devices and habits of the profanely wicked, in such a manner as to bring home powerful convictions to the heart, that all was not right, although he said, "rejoice in the days of thy youth," and then he brought home the latter clause of his text.

He then made the usual divine appeal, which was powerfully attended by being borne home to the heart of every sinner. He gave an invitation for all who wished the prayers of God's people to come to the altar. The invitation was accepted by many, who crowded around the altar for prayers, seeking pardon of God for their sins. Many fell prostrate to the ground, who could not get to the altar, crying aloud to the Lord for mercy. Then I resolved to give expression to my feelings, and make known my desires by going to the altar, and with some difficulty, I made my way there, kneeling down, begging the Lord to have mercy on me, feeling that I could bear any reproach or persecution that might be heaped upon me in consequence of this act, even horse-whipping, which I had been threatened with.

My mother rejoiced at this decisive move of mine, and managed to keep near me. A younger cousin went with me, and we had not been there long, when the cousin that acted as watch over my moves, followed us, endeavoring to get us away from the altar, saying to my mother, "Aunt, do let me get them away from there, for they will certainly be smothered to death." She was almost frantic, and caught hold of me, attempted to drag me out; but mother told her to give herself no uneasiness about us, that she thought we would not smother, and that she thought she could attend to us, in case danger threatened, but had no idea that any such misfortune would occur, and that she would attend to us, and therefore to give herself no further uneasiness about it.

My cousin retired after my mother said that, but she came back soon after, and said, " Your father says you must come out immediately; he says the horses are ready and we must go now to Mrs. Walker's." Mother then told us "we had better come out and go with father, if we could consistently with our feelings." We made our way through the weeping and praying crowd. I felt I had done my duty for once, and that my heavenly Father approved of the course I had taken. I felt a degree of peace in believing and trusting him,—his grace would sustain me under any treatment that awaited me. I expected the frowns of my father and friends, and feared the whipping my eldest brother had threatened me with, but oh, how sweet those words were applied to my mind, " when thy friends all forsake thee, then will I take thee up." As we left the campground we could hear the cries of the penitent for mercy, and the shouts of new born souls. Even the outskirts of the congregation were as solemn as death. The whole camp ground seemed sacred on account of the presence of the Lord.

We were taken to Mrs. Walker's. Father left us there, and then went to a political meeting in that neighborhood. There was a house full of aristocrats, who gazed at me with inquisitive looks. I thought if I could retire from the parlor I would be glad. I felt as though I wanted to get to some retired spot and pour out my heart to Him who hears the prayer of the truly penitent. I longed to be stripped of my gay clothing and jewelry. They felt like weights clinging to me, and that they had been the means the enemy of my soul and my friends had used to divert my mind from God and my best interests, I was convinced.

I soon had an opportunity to pass into the dressing

room. My cousin followed me, and said, "Now, Cousin, you have acted a very silly part to-day, but your friends will overlook it and forgive you, as you are young. Come, wash up and comb your hair, change your apparel, and come out and be cheerful and social among your friends; it will all be overlooked. Let me assist you, do. Look here, here is that beautiful and costly pin hanging loosely, I wonder it did not get lost during that hubbub. Oh, dear me, I wish we had never come to this meeting." By this time I was weeping bitterly. "Come," she said, "wipe away these tears and wash, and comb your hair, and come into the parlor; you will soon get over these feelings if you go into the right company." I said, "Cousin, do leave me alone, if you please. I will try and come out as soon as I improve my appearance a little." She left me, and I prayed most fervently for the Lord to direct me in the pathway of duty, regardless of the smiles or frowns of anyone, and I believe He did. I took off all the jewelry which hung upon me and tied it up in my handkerchief, except one plain pin, which I thought I might use. I took off my rich, costly robe, bought especially for this occasion, and put on a plain, dark gingham dress, and pinned a handkerchief around my neck with that plain pin. I went to the mirror to arrange it a little. Upon glancing in the mirror I felt convicted. I do believe the impression was made by the spirit of God; I felt it, and almost spoke out loud, "This has been your stumbling block, if there is sin in wearing a great deal there is sin in wearing a little, 'Touch not, handle not the unclean thing.' 'Be not conformed to the world, but be ye transformed by the renewing of your mind.'" I thought if these badges of heathenism had shut the life of God out of my soul, they shall not do it any longer; I will cast them from me. So I put that with the rest. I did then, and do now, believe that the spirit of God led me to do as I did, and I never have worn any jewelry since. To me it was a sin, and I do believe it will hinder a growth of the spirit. I pray the Lord to save the church from this sin. I then combed my hair down plain; it was fashionable then to wear curled hair, and mine had been curled at a great expense of time and trouble. In this plain dress I went into the parlor, and tried to be cheerful. My cousin pounced upon me, while all the company looked astonished. But my mother, and dear Mother Johnson, a pious old lady who was there, they looked upon me with a smile of approbation. My mother whispered to Mrs. Johnson, "I hope the victory is gained; dress has been a a great detriment to her. I hope, as she has taken this position at this time, that she will be decided."

"I hope so, too," said Mrs. Johnson, "I see there is some decision about her."

I tried to be cheerful, and indeed I was. I felt I had done my duty, and, although some scorned me, I felt that God loved me, and he was drawing nearer to me as I tried to draw nearer Him. I felt that the people of God were praying for me at the camp-ground, and that was a consolation to me. I knew that Mother Johnson and my own dear mother were praying for me, and I felt like going to some quiet spot, and there praise the Lord for the comfort I felt in trying to take up my cross and follow Him, and beseech Him to give a greater manifestation of love to my poor heart. I retired to a glen, in the meadow not far from the house, where I had often been to gather flowers. I fell upon my knees on the clean grass; the hollow was not very deep, but sufficient to conceal me from observation; and there poured out my soul to Him who seeth in secret, for an evidence of acceptance. He gave it to me; I felt that He was mine and I was His. A sweet peace pervaded my whole soul; I felt that God was love, and that He loved me, unworthy me. I felt that I loved everybody, and Jesus, the lover of sinners, loved me, not me alone, but that he loved and interceded for those dear ones who seemed so indifferent about their precious souls. It seemed to me I almost heard him say, "Father, forgive them, they know not what they do."

About sundown I went to the house. There was a sweet calm on my countenance. Every one saw the change, and it seemed to make a deep impression upon the minds of all, and especially my cousin. She had to struggle hard to keep from expressing her feelings. Had she given expression to her thoughts, it probably would have been something like this: "I feel I am a sinner, undone, without the pardoning grace of God." There were others who felt as deeply as she, but there was no one there who dared to say to them "Come to Jesus just now," "Repent and believe in the Lord Jesus, and you shall be saved." I believe if there had been a suitable person, a minister or class leader, there to have held a prayer-meeting, there would have been a number converted that night. My mother and Mrs. Johnson were very timid naturally, and had never prayed in public, and I felt too timid to say anything.

We went to bed, but I could not sleep. I felt so happy in meditating on the mercy of my Heavenly Father, I felt my Saviour very near. I seemed to be in an ocean of love. Soon after we retired, there was a severe storm, (I always was very much alarmed in a thunder storm,) the lightning flashed, the muttering thunder rolled over our heads, so near that the house trembled, the wind blew, and a tempest seemed to be abroad. But for the first time in my life, I was not afraid. I felt that my Saviour's arms encompassed me, and I was safe, come life or death, my soul was happy. I felt a sweet assurance that God, for Christ's sake, had forgiven my sins, and I doubted no more; no, not for one moment have I ever doubted my conversion to God at that time, although it has been almost fifty years since. Oh! what seasons I have seen since I felt this union with the Father, Son and Holy Spirit, blessed three in one, and one in three, and the children of God.

  Happy day that fixed my choice
   On thee, my Saviour, and my God,
  Well might this loving heart rejoice,
   And tell its raptures all abroad.

  'Tis done, the great transaction's done,
   I am my Lord's, and he is mine,
  He drew me, and I followed on,
   Charmed to confess the power divine.

  Happy day, happy day, when Jesus
   Washed my sins away;
  He taught me how to watch and pray,
   And live rejoicing every day,
  Happy day, happy day, when Jesus
   Washed my sins away.

CHAPTER V.

RECOLLECTIONS OF EARLY MARRIED LIFE.—DEATH OF MY FATHER, BABE, BROTHER AND MOTHER.

I went home from camp-meeting a new creature, and everybody seemed to realize it. The news spread far and wide, that I had got religion at the camp-meeting. My friends who had opposed me so much seemed to give me up as a lost case, only occasionally tempting me, or trying to do so, with some new style of dress or some fancy jewelry; but they always found me firm in my purpose. Some said, "She is crazy;" others said, "Let her alone, and see what it will come to." I tried to live near the Lord by reading the Scriptures, as well as praying much in secret. I read the New Testament through on my knees, and fasted every Friday. And oh, what sweet communion I enjoyed with my blessed Saviour! I still attended meetings at Father Reed's, and found the class there most interesting. The class increased rapidly, and in due time a nice hewed log church was built. It was located about two miles from Father Reed's, in a lovely grove, near a nice stream of water and a large spring, and had a camp-ground laid out around it. Oh! what precious seasons I have enjoyed there—at circuit preaching, class meetings, quarterly meetings and camp meetings. I have witnessed the conversion of very many souls on that sacred ground; most of whom have long since reached the climes of glory, but there are a few of us left, looking over to the promised land, feeling that we are fully able to go up and possess the land when the Master shall say, "It is enough! come up higher." I resolved by the grace of God to cheerfully perform every known duty and to do all the good I possibly could.

My mother had for many years been in the habit of visiting the sick and with her own hands administering to the wants of the poor and needy of the neighborhood, both black and white. As she grew older her health failed, and she gave up this work to me. I enjoyed it very much, rest assured. I had often accompanied her on these errands, assisting her with the baskets and bundles, but to have it to do alone was a delight to my heart, as I did it in the name of my Master, remembering that He said, "Inasmuch as ye have done it unto one of the least of these, ye have done it unto me." I can never forget how it cheered my heart to hear the hearty "God bless you!"

I well remember one circumstance. On a pleasant afternoon a keel-boat, bound up the river, landed at the wharf. While assisting the deck-hands in loading, a colored boy belonging at my father's, happened to pass the cabin. As he did so he heard a feeble moan, and looking in saw a very distressing spectacle. There were two men, three women and a number of children, all prostrate on a few dirty quilts spread upon the cabin floor. One of the women was very old. She asked him if there were any Methodists in the town. He told her there were not many, but that he knew some. "Well," said she, with a trembling voice, "will you tell some one of them that there is an old Methodist lady here on the boat who is suffering almost unto death, and would like very much to see some brother or sister."

The boy ran home and told me. I at once consulted with my mother, who told me to go to my brother's store, acquaint him with the circumstances and ask him to go with me and learn the particulars of the family's distress. I did so, and we learned that there were a number belonging to the family, brothers and brothers-in-law, who had gone down the Mississippi to carry on a wood yard to supply the steamboats which were then running, with fuel. They were in quite comfortable circumstances when they started in the business, but in a short time, one after another were taken sick with bilious fever, and could get no help until everything they had brought with them and all they had earned was gone, even to the last feather bed, which the doctor had taken from under the old lady a few days before they left. The captain of the boat had taken them on board under these circumstances, bringing them thus far, and now he thought the people ought to take care of them. Some of them had not eaten anything for several days, and immediate help was necessary. Brother said he would provide a house and have them removed to it if I would get some nourishment for them. This was no sooner said than done. While I went to get some food and clothing, he had them carried to a nice house, and we soon had them as comfortable as possible under the circumstances. Oh! how often did that dear old lady lay her hands on my head and say, "God bless the child." She was very aged, and had been a Methodist for over forty years. She had heard the Wesleys (Fletcher and Cook) preach. She was very intelligent and communicative, and I spent many pleasant and profitable hours with her and her pious family. Both the daughters were devoted Christians and the son-in-law was a local preacher, all Methodists. They proved to be a very useful family in our village. We had prayer meetings at their house, and it was there that I for the first time prayed in public. Well do I remember what a cross it was; but right under the cross the Lord blessed me, and I felt more assured than ever by His assisting grace to bear the cross. This dear old lady lived to see me very sick, after my mother's death, and her trembling hands tenderly administered to my comfort. It was then my turn to to say, "God bless you, my dear old Mother in Israel." And I did it most fervently, I can assure you, my dear reader. I have no doubt the old lady has won a bright crown in glory long since.

During the summer of 1820 I became acquainted with Dr. John Roe, who was born in Pennsylvania, near Philadelphia, August 20th, 1800. He was a very pious young man, and had been converted at a revival in the neighborhood where he was born, through the labor and influence of Rev. William Hibbard, when about nineteen years of age. Father Hibbard was a great revivalist. The spirit of the Lord attended his labors, and the reformation spread greatly among the young Quakers, some very singular demonstrations resulting, such as jumping and falling prostrate on the floor and lying for hours as though they were dead. On one occasion a young Quaker lady fell on the floor and lay so long that many thought she was really dead, and they finally called a doctor, who said, "She is dead. Yes; as dead as she ever will be." "I think," said a whole-souled Methodist, "she is only dying to sin, and will soon live to righteousness." Just then she bounded to her feet and cried, "Glory to God! Hallelujah! Praise the Lord! 'As far as the east is from the west, so far hath the Lord separated my sins from me!'" Then there was a shout in the camp, and the doctor was put to the blush. But the blessed work went on and Sarah was converted, for the Lord was in it. Mr. Roe was under Quaker influence and had strong prejudices against the Methodists, but in this revival he was powerfully converted and took a decided stand in the Methodist church, for which he was severely persecuted. But in a short time many of his associates were also converted, most of his brothers and sisters, and many of his cousins being brought into the covenant of grace and joining the M. E. Church. A short time after this he emigrated to the West. He took his letter of membership with him, uniting with the Church wherever he found it. He stopped a while in Maysville, Ky., on the Ohio river, traveled through the southern part of Indiana and Illinois, and finally went to the southern part of Kentucky, where he settled in the village of Eddyville on the Cumberland river. It was here that I became acquainted with him, and we were united in marriage on the eleventh day of November, 1821. My friends opposed this union very much, not because they did not respect Mr. Roe, for they thought very much of him, but because he was poor, and they did not consider me fit for a poor man's wife. I knew nothing of hard labor or house-keeping. I had been taught habits of industry, but knew nothing about hardships. My mother, when consulted on the subject, said that she had no objection whatever to him, but regretted very much my inexperience in house-keeping, and if I would stay at home a year longer, she would instruct me in these mysteries. But we thought experience a pretty good school master, and so we were married and went to house-keeping. I made many blunders, such as trying to make light bread and forgetting to put in the yeast, then having to throw it away; churning a great while and not getting any butter out of the cream, then having to feed that to the pigs; making pie crust and forgetting to put in the shortening; burning the beef steak; making bad coffee; and not washing the clothes clean after rubbing the skin nearly all off my hands. There were no washing machines in those days, and I never saw a wash board until after I was the mother of three or four children.

Thus I labored under a great many disadvantages for not having been taught house-work. I think it the duty of every mother to teach her daughters to work. It is an easy matter to neglect, but hard to acquire habits of industry without instruction. The good Lord only knows what it cost me. My dear mother intended to teach me some time, but had no idea of my marrying so young. It is far the best to acquire habits of doing house work while young, as early habits are lasting, whether for good or evil. I strove to learn, and by degrees, with the aid of divine grace, overcame many difficulties which I met with. My friends were astonished at my progress, and my mother often said, "It is the grace of God that enables her to do so; she could not get along so well if it were not for religion." How truly I felt this. We erected the altar of prayer in our house on the day of our marriage, and by the grace of God we have kept it up ever since—forty-five years. We lived humbly, and tried to do our duty in everything. My husband was appointed class-leader of the little class in our village, which prospered nicely and a number of precious souls were converted. The Circuit Preacher received us into his charge, and his labors were blest of God to the building up of this Church, and the old "camp-fire" never went out, though burning feebly at times, until there was a church built and Methodism firmly established there.

We remained in Kentucky for a number of years, during which time my father died, away from home, but not without leaving us some hope of his having made his peace with God. After my father's death, my mother and youngest brother came to live with us while he was preparing a new home for them. During this time the Lord had blessed us with a dear little son, whom we named Matthew Humphrey, after his two grandfathers. This made a very pleasant family. Mother, husband and myself felt a great desire for the salvation of my dear brother. We labored with him in love, but his heart's warmest affections seemed centered in little Matthew, or "Little Joe," as he in a fit of pleasantry named him the first time he saw him. He almost idolized the little one, and a play with him was the first thing in the morning, and at night he would spend hours with "dear little Joe," as he called him. A few months after my brother and mother had moved to their new home, "dear little Joe" was taken very sick with croup, a very sudden and dangerous disease in any climate, but particularly so in the South. A physician and nurse were sent for in haste, and everything that was possible was done to arrest the disease, but to no purpose. My brother was also there, and was greatly distressed. "Oh! dear sister," he said, " I fear we are going to lose 'dear little Joe.' And what shall I do? I feel as though I could not give him up; how can I live without him? I can't bear to see him suffer such excruciating pain!" And he left the room weeping as though his heart would break. In a few hours the suffering of our little one ceased. He was ten months old. Oh! how he had twined around our hearts. We did not know how much we loved him until the tender cords which bound us so sweetly together were broken. But we knew that he was with us no more, for God had taken him to Heaven; for He said, while on earth, "Suffer little children to come unto Me, for of such is the Kingdom of Heaven."

Then some kind friends dressed him so neat and sweet in his white baby dress, and laid him on the stand in the parlor, folding his little white hands on that breast that never knew sin. Oh! how silent and solemn that beautiful Sabbath morning, July 10th, 1823. Then we felt that we had a new tie in heaven and fresh impulses to press on upward and toward that beautiful world where the inhabitants never say, "We are sick." Well do I remember the deep flood of sorrow that welled up from my dear brother's heart when he called that morning, and said, "Dear sister, the little sufferer has gone to be an angel, and I shall go soon. This is a great trial for you, and you must try and bear it bravely. May God help you!" His remark, "I shall go soon," went to my heart like a shock of electricity, but I scarcely conceived how soon his words would come true.

The funeral sermon for our babe was preached by our worthy Circuit Preacher in charge, Brother Robins, from the words of the Prophet to the Shunamite woman, "Is it well with thee? Is it well with thy husband? Is it well with the child? And she said it is well." The sermon was consoling to our hearts, and we felt there, under that cloud of sorrow, the comforting influence of the grace of God. I felt that He was the rock of my salvation, and that my feet were on that rock. How I realized the force of the words of the poet:

>   The dearest joys and nearest friends,
>   The partners of our blood,
>   How they divide our wavering minds,
>   And leave but half for God.
>
>   The fondness of a creature's love,
>   How strong it strikes the sense,
>   Thither the warm affection moves,
>   Nor can we call it thence.

Well do I recollect the kind sympathy and love manifested towards us that day while we moved slowly to the graveyard and committed the little tenement of clay to its mother dust. Well do I recollect the impression those sweet smiling features made, when I gave the last look, and how lonely the sound as the clods fell upon the coffin; but ah! well do I recollect the sweet assurance I felt in my heart, that if I was faithful to the grace given we should have a happy reunion in the morning of the resurrection. Bless the Lord, O my soul, for redeeming grace and dying love.

We were preparing for a campmeeting which was to commence in about ten days on Father Reed's campground. The time arrived, and we moved onto the grounds in Methodist order. No one said anything against it. Mother and brother went with us. All ate and slept on the same campground. It was the first time I had been accorded that privilege, and I assure you I enjoyed it. O, what a privilege to linger as long as I wished in the prayer circle, there to wrestle, Jacob-like, until my heart was filled with the joy of believing, and then, in my feeble manner, direct the mourner to the Rock that was cleft for them and me, and see them take the cup of salvation and hear them praise the Lord. O! it was joy unspeakable. This campmeeting was a great blessing to me and mine. My dear mother was much blessed; she arose to a higher state of grace than she had ever enjoyed before. My husband was commissioned anew for the important duty that involved upon him—he was steward and class-leader. A little colored girl and a young man, who lived with us, were both converted and joined the church, and many precious souls were saved. My brother was very much awakened, and began to think of his future state and the interest of his precious soul. I think this work in our family commenced from the death of our dear little Matthew, and fervently did we pray that what seemed to us an affliction might be sanctified to the good of our family. One night our tent was very full, and my brother thought he would sleep in a barn near by on some hay. Unfortunately the hay was damp and he took cold and it settled on his lungs. We went home without his being converted; but there was quite a change in his conduct and conversation; he read the bible and prayed in secret. His health failed gradually but very perceptibly to those that loved him. He was very fleshy—although not quite twenty-one years of age, he weighed over three hundred pounds. His appetite failed, and he complained of a pain about the region of the lungs. The best medical aid was procured, but none could define what was the matter. I was with him about three weeks; most of the time he felt as though he could not have me leave his bedside. He said from the first he should never recover. I often felt like talking to him on the subject, but his physician would not admit of it; he said it would impede his recovery. At length he was pronounced out of danger.

About this time I was taken very sick with billious fever; my life was despaired of; no one thought it possible for me to recover. I was for twenty-four hours insensible to all around me, and then revived, to the astonishment of all my friends. My brother was so much better it was thought best for him to ride out, and he did so, but told mother it was a forced effort, he was really no better. He said he wanted to visit me, and he and mother came up and were permitted to come into my room, but with great caution. I could speak but a few words at a time. He appeared much gratified to see me, spoke of how he had missed me at his bedside, and as he was just ready to start he took my hand and said, with all the warmth of a brother's pure love, "Dear sister, be cheerful, you will get well, but I never shall." I was trying to say something to him in my great weakness, when he drew his hand out of mine and was gone. Two days after, while preparing to visit a brother, who lived a short distance from our place, he took a chill. He had been very anxious to go before he took this chill, then said he, "Mother, I shall never go now." Mother encouraged him to think he would be better, and then he could go next day, but while she turned to the stand to get him some wine and water, he raised up on his elbow to take the drink, his head fell forward, and his soul passed into the the spirit world. It was on the 22d of Sept., 1823. Then it was decided that there was a tumor formed on the mucous membrane of the lungs, and it had broken and suffocated him. The physician came and tried to restore him, but to no effect; thus the hope of a fond and aged mother, and the joy of a loving sister, dropped into the grave of the youth, unexpectedly to many, for most of his friends thought him out of danger. He gave mother many evidences of a change of heart. He loved the word of God, and the society of religious people; was often heard in prayer, and we have hope at least that he died a humble, penitent seeker of the Savior, and he never turns any such away. I regretted then, and have all my life, and do now, that I did not labor more faithfully with him; that I did not tell him more about the Savior, and help him learn how to believe on Him, and claim Him as his present Savior.

We cannot be too importunate with our friends. Any one reasoning according to the natural heart would say, "my cup was full." Yes, it was full, but it was mixed by a skillful hand, He who doeth all things well, and it was sanctified to my present and future good. But the Lord still spared my dear mother to me, and how dearly I loved her; what sweet counsel we held together. After the death of my brother she came to live with me again, but before I recovered so as to take care of her, she was taken sick—very sick—but the Lord, in his mercy, restored us both, so that we were both able to ride out and visit our friends and attend public service.

There was a funeral about the latter part of January that we were very much interested in, and we attended, although it was a very unpleasant day, and from this exposure my mother contracted a cold, and was violently attacked with pleurisy. The best medical aid was obtained and everything done to arrest the disease, but to no purpose. But O! how loving, kind and patient she was under the severe suffering she endured, and how thankful for every kindness she received; how submissive to her Heavenly Father's will. "Come life or death, I am prepared," was the feelings she expressed. She had but one wish to live a little longer, and that was, that she might see my husband, who had gone to New Orleans, and whose return was anticipated every moment. She would often say, "I hope Dr. Roe will arrive to-day." But she was not permitted to enjoy this privilege. She died in great peace on the 7th of February, 1824.

Thus I lost my darling babe, my dear brother, and now my sainted mother, in less than seven months time, and my father and a dear sister a year previous. My husband being absent at this time was a source of great grief to me, but I felt while I stood by the bedside of a dying mother, that the grace of God sustained me.

While her hand clasped mine with a gentle pressure, and her splendid blue eyes, beautiful in death, were turned upward, and a sweet smile rested on her features, 'twas then I truly realized 'tis religion that does supply solid comfort when we die. Then I felt that my Heavenly Parent had chastened me thus, that I might learn to love Him more and serve Him better. This trial was sanctified to my good; it taught me the happy grace of trusting God for present grace and future good, and I was enabled to say truly, "Thy will be done."

My husband arrived just as we were returning from the cemetery. I was truly thankful for this mercy in the deep affliction I was passing through. He exhorted me to trust on Him "who doeth all things well," saying, "Mother had gone to that rest prepared for those that love and serve the Lord, and if we were faithful to duty and followed her example, we should one day enjoy that rest with her."

That cousin, spoken of in a former chapter, who tried to divert my mind from the subject of religion, was with us during mother's sickness. I said she was amiable, and truly she was; how kind and affectionate she was through that season of affliction, and how closely she criticised our conduct, feelings and expressions. More than once she said to me, "It is good to know the Lord in affliction. I wish I had embraced religion when I was young, as you did." I endeavored to guide her to the Savior then. She left us a few days after the funeral, and I never saw her again, but learned that in a long protracted illness, which closed her probation here on earth, that she manifested a Christian spirit, and I hope, passed into that better world.

Under this severe trial I felt sensibly that while my Heavenly Father afflicted with one hand, he sustained with the other. I enjoyed constantly a sweet communion with my Savior, and prayed fervently to the Lord, that if it was consistent with His divine will that I might have an interview with the departed spirit of my dear mother, and I often felt that through my Savior I communed with her; often I felt as though she was permitted to be a guardian angel around me, and she seemed to beckon me on to that better world.

One season, I recollect, it was a beautiful Sabbath morning, I was alone at my quiet little home—the home where my dear brother died—(it became mine after his death)—I was walking to and fro beneath a shade tree in the front yard, a beautiful spot. I was praying, meditating and enjoying a hope that sometime I should enjoy a Sabbath that would never end, with my blessed Savior and those loved ones who had gone before. Such a sacred halo was shed over me that my soul, spirit and body were all absorbed in love. I felt those words of the poet applied so sweetly to my heart:

> See the happy spirits waiting
>   On the bank beyond the stream,
> Sweet responses still repeating,
>   Jesus, Jesus, is their theme.
>
> Hark, they whisper—lo they call me,
>   Sister spirit come away,
> Lo, I come, earth can't retain me,
>   Hail the realms of endless day.

I asked the Lord to take me to that better world, that I might sin no more, but I was reminded that I was a probationer, and that there were many duties and trials before me, but I felt assured that His grace would be sufficient for the day. And I have always found it so for nearly fifty years. When I have lived by faith on the Son of God, I have ever triumphed over every trial and temptation. When I keep everything on the "altar," and in the path of duty, and can say with truth, "Thy will be done my Heavenly Father," then I am safe. To God be all the glory.

I gained many victories while I lived in Kentucky, and oh! how many of the "salt of the earth" I was permitted to associate with. There was Bishop Morris, our Presiding Elder for two years, from whom I learned those beautiful verses just mentioned, of his own composition, I think. Often has he reposed under our roof. He always imparted to us some good instruction, with a great deal of information, cheered our hearts and strengthened our resolutions to press on Zionward. He has long been spared to build up the church of his early choice. May his last days be peaceful and his death triumphant.

There was Father Holliday, another veteran of Kentucky—much good has he done for the salvation of souls, and for the building up of the Methodist Episcopal Church in Illinois—and the sainted Valentine Cook, the noble Marcus Lindsay, the words that fell from their lips burned as they went to the hearts of their hearers, and filled them with the Holy Ghost. I say blessed be the memory of all these holy men, and I think it well that we should call to mind and reflect upon the character and example of those who have labored so zealously to build up and sustain our beloved Methodism for the past century. Who will do it for the next? Who will be able to sustain and preach its wholesome doctrines from century to century, until the whole length of time is used up in bringing the whole ship's company safe into the port of Zion?

I must bring to notice here the humble, though noble, John Johnson, whose words were ever powerful. Why? the reader may ask. Because he was chosen by the Lord to preach. When first called to the ministry he could hardly read a hymn, or a chapter from the bible, but close application to study—while traveling—he, in the course of six or eight years, acquired a perfect knowledge of several languages, and became so noted for his deep piety, usefulness and scholarly attainments, that he was sought after by many who lived in important places, such as Frankfort, Russelsville and Nashville, where he was instrumental in bringing many souls to God, besides aiding in building up the M. E. church. Now with all honor to brother Johnson's memory I will (not intending to offend) relate an incident in his life. While traveling the Princeton circuit in Kentucky he became acquainted with Miss S. Brooks, an old Quaker's daughter, who was converted at a great revival under his influence. He thought he would go and see her. He rode up to her father's gate one evening, took off his saddle-bags, a pair of which all Methodist preachers used at that time to carry their books and clothing in. In a cool, shady grove was their cottage, and Miss Susie met him at the door, took the portmanteau and placed it in the best room, seated him politely, and went into the room where her father was. "Susie," said the venerable old gentleman—he was a very pious old man, if he was a Quaker—"I tell thee thou had better give John Johnson his portmanteau and send him away, for thee shall not marry John Johnson; if thou art not mad send him away—I tell thee thou shall not marry John Johnson if I can keep him away from here. Thee may get over thy Methodist notions, but I tell thee thou shall not marry John Johnson." And as he stepped toward the portmanteau Susie caught it up and made for the door, and John Johnson followed her. But in a few months they were married. Susie made Mr. Johnson a good, loving Christian wife, and Mr. Brooks a very kind father-in-law.

Brother Fowler made a visit to Illinois the summer

after my mother's death and on his return visited us. He traveled through the middle counties of this state, Morgan and Sangamon in particular. He called on Father Cartwright's family on their beautiful farm, situated within fifteen miles of Springfield; said he thought "Methodism was going to spread over the Prairie State," and advised us, if we wanted to make a "new home in a new state," to move there at once, remarking by way of encouragement, that "were it not for his missionary engagements he would willingly go with us." This advice inspired us with new views and plans to make arrangements to move. We were now anxious to be on the way to our new home, but circumstances would not admit of our starting at once, and we were desirous of making the journey in a comfortable manner.

My husband thought he would make another trip to New Orleans, notwithstanding he was unsuccesful on his first visit. We wished to retain our comfortable little home where we were, in case of Illinois not suiting us, for it might be possible that the climate would not agree with my delicate health—for delicate it was then. I had suffered from many attacks of billious fever, and had taken so much blue mass pills and calomel that I had become a fit subject for consumption, and many of my friends thought me a confirmed consumptive, and thought I would not live a year if I went to another climate, and were very much opposed to our moving at all, but if we did, were anxious that we should keep our home. But Dr. Roe thought he would have a home independent of this one, and thought there would be no better way of accomplishing this than to go to New Orleans with his pork, corn, etc. He therefore went to work with a will, bought a boat, loaded it with produce, and was ready to start by the first of November. When he was pushing off from the shore a gentleman offered my husband $2,000 for his cargo, but he thought if he could only get into market in time he could do better, and expected to realize as much as $3,000. But how uncertain are the calculations of man. He returned after making the trip with barely enough to pay expenses, and feeling very much discouraged.

Had we not made a sale of our cows and household goods in the fall, we would not have been able to start for the north. But we had suffered so much on account of our religious views and opposition to slavery, that we were anxious to depart for a country where the latter was not tolerated, and where we could enjoy our religion without persecution. As I was the only sister left near them, my friends were very much opposed to our leaving.

My oldest brothers were men of wealth and influence, in a worldly sense. My sister had married a wealthy man, and moved away some distance. Her husband was a graduate of West Point, and was a surgeon in the war of 1812, at the close of which he returned home and practiced medicine and surgery in our vicinity with great success; was preparing a farm for a residence when he died. He was an atheist in belief and went to his last long rest in that faith. Two years after his demise my sister died, so there was but my two brothers left in the country. The influence which the doctor exerted over my sister caused her to believe that this "Methodist religion," as she called it, was all fanaticism, and would wear off after awhile. They had some very pious servants, who prayed very fervently for their "master and mistress," especially for my sister; they could not bear the idea of her dying as "Master Henry" did, without a knowledge of the Savior. Her health was poor, and we all realized that she could not long survive. My mother's heart was constantly going out to God for her salvation, and I used to even mingle with the servants in their own little dwelling to pray for her; I would read a chapter in the bible, sing a hymn and join in prayer with them, and the Lord blessed us with the sweet assurance that she would be brought into His fold, and before her death the spirit of God awakened her, and she cried for mercy and called in the servants and requested them to pray for her. She also sent for Father Reed, that he might pray with and for her; and we have good reason to believe that she was saved, and I hope to meet her in that better world.

The elder sister was powerfully awakened, I believe, in answer to prayer. Her husband was an infidel, and was opposed to everything like revealed religion; but the spirit of God found her out and taught her that she was a sinner, and also revealed to her what she must be by grace to inherit eternal life. She began to inquire, "What shall I do to be saved?" There were no religious people with whom she could associate, except Baptists; she attended their meetings although forbidden to do so by her husband, and more than once upon his learning that she had gone to meeting did he send after her and had her brought home and treated her very unkindly; told her if she did not give up attending those meetings, she should leave his house and be cut off from all communication with her children; he said he was not going to have his children "carried of with their wild fanaticism." He would not allow her to keep a bible in the house if he knew it. She kept her bible in the cellar for months, and there read and prayed. The spirit of God led her into the light of His countenance. She told her Baptist friends her experience, and they thought it proper that she be baptised—she felt it her duty. There was a day appointed on which she supposed her husband would be absent; he was from home and she did not anticipate his return, but he came while she was in the congregation. They were near a stream for the purpose of administering the ordinance. There were a number of converts present, and there was a good revival among them. He heard what was going on, and taking his carriage went immediately to the congregation, took her home and shut her up and subjected her to very unkind treatment, and told her, as he had done on former occasions, that if she made a public profession of the religion of Jesus Christ he would discard her as he would a culprit, and debar her from any intercourse with her family. This he knew would be worse than death to her—there never was a more devoted mother. For a time this deprived her of any means of grace. She felt anxious to be baptised, but she knew it would not do to have the ordinance performed publicly. She consulted the minister and he performed the ceremony privately, so that no one knew it but his family and some of the elders. And now she knew she was a member of the Baptist church. It was a comfort to her, although she had not made a public profession of the Savior. Her husband did not live long after this. He had been in a decline for several years, and expired suddenly. She then made a public profession of religion, became acquainted with other religious ladies, and discovered that she was a Methodist in principle and doctrine, and united with them. Her family mingled with the Methodists in a revival, and a number of her children professed religion, joined the church, and so on, one after another until they all became members of the church with her. She lived many years an acceptable member of the M. E. church, died in triumph of the Christian faith, and has gone home to glory.

This gives me a new impetus for the kingdom. I hope the Lord will give me grace to conquer and take me to rest. All this, I believe, was in answer to a mother's faithful, fervent prayer. Courage, praying mothers.

But with all the opposition we met with, we made our arrangements and started for Illinois almost without money or scrip, scarcely knowing whither we were going. We felt a deep sorrow at parting with our classmates and many dear friends we had made there; they expressed the warmest wishes for our welfare. Well do I remember the feelings manifested when we parted; there were a great many present, some wept, others persuaded, many upbraided us for leaving the home where I was born and raised, to go to a new country that we never saw; others said we would not live out half our days in such a sickly country as Illinois; not a few prophesied that we would be back to our old home in less than a year, and the colored people were so grieved at our leaving that one said to me—the one who was my nurse—" Now indeed, if I had a bag of gold as big as my body, I would lay it at your feet if you would stay.

But we were satisfied that it was our duty and for our best interest to go to Illinois, and started on the eighteenth day of February, 1827. My husband drove a two-horse wagon, while I drove a one-horse buggy with a babe in my arms and another dear little boy two years old at my feet. The Lord had blessed us with two fine healthy boys to bring with us to Illinois. We met with some trials on the way, but nothing more than was reasonable to expect while traveling in such a new country. We camped one night, however, near a house where the people bore the appearance of thieves and outlaws. They would not let us stay in their house, and were most unaccommodating; would hardly let us have food for our horses or water from their well. I had heard so many hard stories of Illinois that I was much afraid for our lives, but through the mercy of God the beautiful morning sun rose on us in perfect peace and safety and we went on our way rejoicing.

We got along very well until we got within fifty miles of Edwardsville, when we had to take the prairie. The frost was just coming out of the ground, and such splashing and miring as we had in the black mud of the " Prairie State," none know but those who have been through a like experience in early times. The last day we traveled my husband had to get a team of oxen to draw us out of the mud three times in traveling eight miles. We concluded that it was best to stop and wait until the roads dried up. We succeeded in getting a small log house near the main road. We had not been there long until we received a number of calls. The news had spread rapidly that there was a family who had just arrived from Kentucky and they hastened to learn something, if possible, of their old Kentucky home and friends; some of them we had known in our southern home, others we had not, but we received a kind welcome from all, telling us what a beautiful country they had, and what rapid strides Methodism was making through the country; what great revivals; who their circuit preacher was; his name was "Folkes," and "Father Thompson" was their presiding Elder, of Lebanon, and many interesting occurrences, and urged us very much to remain with them, at least call on them before leaving. We told them we thought we might go further north. We were *en route* for Morgan or Sangamon. I had a sister living in Morgan county who had a large family, and we were decided to make our way there if possible.

The gentleman and lady who owned the house we were occupying, called to enquire if there was anything they could do for us. We told them we would like to buy some vegetables and meat. They said if we would come and see them the next day, they would give us all the vegetables we needed, and sell us some very nice bacon. We gladly accepted their kind offer and went up the next day, had a very pleasant visit with them, learned with pleasure how the Methodists were prospering and spreading all over the land. In conversation with them we learned that they were acquainted with Mr. John Messenger, a brother-in-law to the husband of a half sister of mine, who lived near Belleville, the county seat of St. Clair county, Ill., and that we were not more than forty-five miles from their home, and he thought he could direct us to a prairie road that we could travel with our buggy. The thought of seeing a sister whom I had never had the pleasure to know was very delightful to me. The arrangements were all made, and we were to start the following day. We were to leave the double wagon at Mr. Hunter's until the roads dried up a little, and then come and get it, and make the journey to Morgan county, where I had another half sister I had never seen. We had written them we purposed coming. They lived seven miles from Jacksonville, the county seat of Morgan county, near Alison's Mound. Every arrangement was made, and we were on our way by two o'clock.

We had not traveled far when we were overtaken by a very singular looking old gentleman; he was quite small in stature, light complexion, blue eyes, and a very large Roman nose. He wore Jeans clothes; his hair was very white and hung in heavy ringlets over his shoulders. He was well mounted on a noble looking horse. He rode up to my husband—who was on horseback, myself and children being in the buggy--and accosted him in a very formal manner, and inquired where we were from, where we were going, etc., etc. Rather inquisitive I thought, for a stranger. I thought of all the robbers and murderers I had ever read of in Illinois, and began to think our time was coming. At length I heard him ask my husband where we intended to stay that night. He replied that he wished to go as far as possible, in order that we might reach my friends the next day. "My reason for asking," said he, "is this, if you go past my house, which is a mile ahead, you will not find a house you can stay at short of ten miles. I entertain people as well as I can at my place, and I think you had better stop with me." Well, thought I, that beats all, that he should want to decoy us to his own house to do the deed. I gave utterance to a deep sigh, and my heart went pit-a-pat, and the uneasiness I manifested caused my husband to rein his horse near the buggy and ask me if anything was the matter. I then made some excuse to stop the buggy, and the old gentleman rode on. I said to my husband, "Why on earth don't the old man go along about his business; I believe he wants to entice us to his house and rob and kill us." "Oh no," said he, "don't think of such a think; I think he is a good old man, and we had better stop by all means." "Then," said I, "we wont get the chance, for I see him going down under that bridge; I believe he intends to kill us there in these gloomy woods." Said he, "Oh, dear no, I think the old gentleman is all kindness; he has just gone down the bank to water his horse." "You will see," said I. "I hope you are right, but pray don't stop until we see what the house looks like; but I fear we shall never live to get over that bridge." Just then my husband saw the old gentleman ride up the hill, then said he, "I told you so; all will be right; come, let's go along and see how things look." "Well," said I, "my trust is in the Lord, if we are slain." We crossed the bridge, ascended the hill, and there stood a large, substantial farm house, surrounded by shade-trees, a great large orchard on one side, and commodious barn on the other, and the old gentleman was just riding into the yard. "Now," said my husband, "don't you see, all is right." "I hope so," said I. "but I have my misgivings. Robbers may live in all kinds of style away up here in Illinois and nobody know it."

My heart beat double time as we drove into the yard. We were met by a fine looking old lady who spoke kindly to me, and invited us to come into the house, which was as neat and clean as a bandbox; everything in order and a first rate supper on the table, of which we were invited to partake, and we did justice to it; but all the time I was eating, the thought was in my mind that this might be the last meal we would ever eat; they are kind, but this may be done to gain our confidence and keep us off our guard. The old lady tried to draw me out in conversation, but I could not enjoy it. As night came on, a number of rough looking men came into the sitting room while the old lady was busy about her cares. I was left to my own meditations when these men came in. Now, thought I, they are to help do the deed. While thus ruminating, the old lady placed a candle on the stand and invited me into the room. On the stand I discovered a bible; I was thankful to see it, but the thought came into my mind, robbers may keep a bible for a disguise. Just then the old gentleman arose and stepped up to the stand, opened the bible and remarked, "I suppose it is so dark and muddy that there will not be many out to-night." He read a chapter, and we all united in singing a hymn, after which the old gentleman led in prayer. Before he was half through, my face was bathed in tears, and beseeching the Lord to forgive me the thoughts of my heart. Another led in prayer, and another, until they had all offered a prayer. We had an old-fashioned Methodist prayer-meeting, and realized that prayer is appointed to convey the blessings God designs to give.

After the meeting every barrier was removed, and what a change in my feelings. I realized that God was there, and that I was among his people. I could not rest there; I felt like confessing to the old gentleman, but thought it not best. I learned a lesson that has done me much good; I learned not to give way too much to suspicion, and not to be governed too much by first impressions.

We had a good chat with the old folks; learned that they, too, were well acquainted with my friends I intended to visit, that they were among the earliest settlers who had helped to plant Methodism there, and God had blessed their labors, and that there was a large society there, and the work was still going on. We had a good night's rest, a choice breakfast, and found it rather a hard task to take our leave of them. The old gentleman was a veteran, and the old lady a mother in Israel.

They gave us some instruction about the road, and with difficulty we prevailed on them to accept a small remuneration for the trouble they had been to, and we bid father and mother Planter farewell. We have never seen them since, but I hope to meet them in glory, where all are free from imperfection.

We had a very rough ride over a large prairie. The frost was still in the roots of the grass so that it bore us up. We saw numerous droves of deer that seemed to have an undisputed right to gambol over the level prairie, the heritage their Maker had given them, without the fear of the rifle. We passed over the prairie, entered a strip of timber, and came out at that beautiful Methodist village, Lebanon, so famed for its literary privileges. It had but just got started in its useful career. How many young men have grown up there under the sacred influence of its sanctified literature, and gone out to bless the world, eternity will only reveal.

We went on with only a passing view of the surroundings; suffice it to say that it was beautiful, and gave credit to the church and the community that sustained it in that early day. I hope it may share liberally in the centennial offerings. God bless the institution and water it with Thy grace.

At eleven o'clock next day we arrived safely at my brother-in-law's, Mr. John Messenger, a few miles from Belleville, to the great joy and surprise of my sister and family. We had a pleasant visit; found sister a warm-hearted Baptist. None of the other members of the family were religiously inclined, but possessed of merit, and were industrious and intelligent. We spent a number of days with them, attended Methodist meeting with them, where there was a large society of excellent members, and the Lord was still carrying on His work, and there was a spit of perseverance among them. I visited Rev. Edwards' family at Belleville, a nice little village. Then I called on a number of their Methodist neighbors, and a number of them called at my sister's, and urged us to stop with them. Oh! what a warm-hearted brotherly love there was among the Methodists at that early day; it was enough to know you were a Methodist, and you were welcome to all their hospitalities, their sympathy and their prayers. But we thought we must see Morgan county before we settled down.

We lost one of our horses while there, and we did not see how we could pursue our journey. We felt that we were in the pathway of duty and the Lord would provide for us, and He did. One of the neighbors offered to go, as he wished to visit his aunt in Morgan county. One of my nieces offered her horse, and Charley said, "Uncle, it is all right, when you are ready I will accompany you." I truly felt, "The Lord is my shepherd, I shall not want."

We prosecuted our journey, and arrived safely at my sister's, Mrs. Cadwell. She was the widow of Dr. Cadwell, of early memory, of Morgan county. I think he was one of the first physicians that settled in that county. He died the summer before we arrived, with a disease that prevailed there, which was very much like the cholera. He was an excellent physician, and had a very large practice through that country around him. More than once he was elected to the Legislature, and gave the casting vote that settled the slavery question in Illinois. He was rather skeptical in early life on the subject of religion, and quite indifferent, until a few years before his death, when he became deeply impressed with the importance of religion and the interests of his soul, sought and found the "pearl of great price," and died in great peace. A few years previous his oldest daughter professed religion and joined the Methodist church, for which her parents almost disowned her; they said they did not want that fanaticism in their family, but soon after this she married a class-leader by the name of Charles Harril. He was a faithful steward of the cause of God, and with her help did much to plant and sustain Methodism in Morgan county. Her next oldest sister would visit her, although much against the wishes of her parents, and she soon became a Methodist, too, and married a very fine gentleman by the name of William King, a Methodist of the real old stamp from England. They, too, were very useful in sustaining Methodism in that new country; they were wealthy, and spared neither time nor money to promote the cause of God and the good of souls.

They gave us a hearty welcome, and said they hoped we would enjoy all we had anticipated in the society of the Methodists in Illinois. But my sister still retained her skeptical views, although very kind in her social relations, and more than once she gave me to understand that she wished me to keep my religious views to myself. She had several daughters at home, and did not want them to be influenced by my religious views. I cannot say that I regarded her wishes on this subject. I soon learned, to my great joy, that one of her daughters, the next to the oldest, was under conviction, and was seeking the Saviour with a penitent heart. I encouraged her, telling her to put her trust in the Lord and Savior, who had died to save a sinful world.

It was not long after this that the two oldest girls found the Saviour in the pardon of their sins, and united with the Methodist church. My heart was troubled for my sister, who would not repent and seek the Lord. She was intelligent, strong in argument, and I feared to approach her, but I had faith in prayer, and felt that my Heavenly Father would hear and answer me by converting my sister. Her "Methodist children" and myself, prayed without ceasing for her conversion. We felt that nothing but the spirit of God could do this work, and knew by experience that His spirit could change and soften that hardened heart of hers. I soon thought I could see a difference in her manner. When I talked with her on the subject of experimental religion—and once she replied, "If I could feel the same as you tell me you do, I might believe in religion." I told her that this peace was secured only by belief, and to believe, then she would receive joy, and faith, through which we were saved. Having strong faith that she would yet be brought to the knowledge of this truth, I left them, with the promise that I would come and see them again.

We moved to Springfield, now the Capitol of our beautiful Prairie State. It was then but a small village. The houses were built of logs, daubed with the black mud of the prairies, there being but three frame houses in the place. The Court House was built of an inferior quality of brick.

I shall never forget the first class-meeting we attended at Springfield. When our names were recorded on the class-book, the number of names thereon was forty-two. Brother Joseph Tartington was minister in charge, and Father Cartwright was Presiding Elder. Services were held in the Court House twice a month. The class met at private houses, and weekly prayer-meetings were also held. Our excellent local minister, John Kirkpatrick, called on us a few days after our arrival, and told us where to find the class-meeting. It met in a little log cabin, and we found there a large class of warm-hearted brothers and sisters, who welcomed us to their circle. We found that the Master was in the midst thereof, and we were made to rejoice in the hope of a blessed immortality, and realized that we were in our Father's house and among His children, although we had never before met with any of them except Brother Kirkpatrick. There we learned that Brother Cartwright was going to have a quarterly meeting in the Court House two weeks from that time. My heart rejoiced at this news, for I should then see one whom I had known in days gone by—whom I loved and revered and claimed as a spiritual father. I could trace the influence of the spirit of God on my heart at seasons ever since he administered the ordinance of baptism upon me and said "God bless the child." To think of seeing such a friend there in a strange land, where I knew no one, was calculated to inspire a great anticipation; and it did, I assure you. I counted the days, the hours, and almost the moments as they passed. About a week previous to the quarterly meeting I was sitting at the door of our little cabin, which was situated on a street which is now one of the main streets of the capital of our noble State. I was thinking of the time when when I should see this friend, and I saw a gig pass the door with a load of wool lashed to the back of it, and I very readily recognized his venerable features. I arose to my feet, clapped my hands and cried out to a young lady who sat with me (a Miss Dobbins who had came to the country with us) "There is Father Cartwright, it is, it is; how can I let him pass and not speak to him!" "Are you sure it is he?" said she. "I am," said I. "Well, then," remarked my companion, "sit down and write him a note, inviting him to call, and send it to Mr. Stiles, the proprietor of the carding machine, and he will give it to the elder, for I know he is going up there to get his wool carded, and I will take it."

We had became a little acquainted with Mr. Stiles' family—it was only a block from our door. I seated myself to pen the note, but hearing the rattle of wheels, I looked up and saw that he was passing swiftly by, and I called out, "Father Cartwright!" at which he reined up his horse at the fence where I stood—I did not wait to go the gate. He raised his hat very politely, and said, "How do you do, Madam?" I said, "Father Cartwright, don't you know me?" "Indeed, Madam, your countenance looks very familiar, but you have the advantage of me, I cannot call you by name." "I do not wonder," said I, "a few years has made a great change in my appearance, but can you not recognize in me Elizabeth Ann Lyon?" "Ah, I do, I do!" said he, and jumping from his gig, he clasped my hand, saying, "I am happy to meet you in Illinois; I hope you are well." "I thank you, I am, and very much rejoiced to see you. Do come in and have some dinner with us, wont you?" "Indeed I will, with pleasure. I am engaged to Brother Matheny, but I will send him an apology." He brought his horse and gig into the yard. I sent for my husband, and we were soon seated in the best room in our little cabin, enjoying an interesting, social and religious conversation. We related many interesting circumstances that occurred in early days in Kentucky; we told him of our conversion, and many incidents in relation to it, and spoke of our desire to make Illinois our home; our purpose in coming to the Prairie State; our misfortune in preparing; our resolve to make the journey, if we did have to come poor. "That was right," said he, "this country is the poor man's retreat. If there is any place where the poor man can rise to influence, wealth and prosperity, it is in this new country. I am glad you have come, and I hope you will enjoy all and more than you have ever anticipated in social and religious society here. Methodism is taking a gracious start in Illinois, and God is blessing the Word wherever it is preached, and that is pretty much all over the settled portions of the State. We have a very promising conference, and we are to have a quarterly meeting here in the Court House one week from last Sabbath, and I will bring Mrs. Cartwright to see you then—no preventing providence."

We told him we had heard Brother Tartington preach, and had been to class, and liked the appearance of our surroundings very much. "Yes," said he, "we have some noble veterans here, and their motto is:

'True to Methodism.' We are going to have several camp meetings this summer at different points in the district," (then embracing what is now a Conference) "and I hope you will attend as many of them as possible." My husband told him we had a nice horse and buggy, and would attend all meetings we possibly could, as we desired to see the country and get acquainted with the Methodists of Illinois. The venerable old gentleman took dinner with us, returned thanks and asked God's especial blessing upon us, and we parted, really feeling that we had had a very interesting interview.

The time for the quarterly meeting arrived, and Brother and Sister Cartwright were present. They were our guests, although the hospitalities of ministers, doctors, lawyers and judges were extended to them. When they were solicited, their reply was, "Please excuse us, we must stop with our old Kentucky friends this time." We were very thankful for this marked preference and respect. The quarterly meeting commenced on Saturday, with preaching at twelve o'clock noon, and at early candle-light. This was the manner of giving out evening meetings, as there were but few people in Illinois at that early date who had clocks. The mantle clock was not in use then, and the old-fashioned ones with long wooden cases were difficult to move, and were left behind.

Brother Cartwright preached at twelve o'clock, noon. The quarterly conference occupied the afternoon, and Brother Tartington preached at candle-light, and the services closed with a devotional prayermeeting. The preaching was food for my soul. I had not heard

Brother Cartwright preach since I had been converted, except on this occasion.

Sabbath morning at nine o'clock we assembled without the tolling of a bell, in the upper room of the Court House, to enjoy a Love-feast. The room was filled, and the door closed, and oh! what a precious hour it was, as one after another arose to speak of the mercy of God; the love of a precious Savior shed abroad in their hearts; the victories they had gained since their last quarterly meeting or love-feast, and of the blessed hope of immortality and eternal life through Jesus Christ, our Lord. Many shouts of glory went up from hearts that were filled to the overflowing. The walls of the court house fairly rang with the melody. The house, for the present at least, seemed to be sacred on account of the presence of the Lord. It appeared to me something like the love-feast, or classmeeting the disciples enjoyed when doubting Thomas made one of their number, and our blessed Savior permitted him to put his finger into the wounds, and Thomas cried out, "My Lord, and my God!" I do not think there was a person in that house but who could say, "I know my Redeemer lives and intercedes for me; I shall see Him as He is. Praise the Lord for the hope set before us."

At eleven o'clock we had public service in the lower story—quite a large room—and it was filled, and every door and window was crowded with attentive hearers. Father Cartwright discoursed, and seemed endowed with the power and demonstration of the Spirit of God. Some were awakened to a sense of their sins, and others were converted. It was a time long to be remembered, and will be remembered in glory.

"Well," said I to my husband, "if this is the way the Methodists enjoy religion in Illinois, I am glad we came here." "So am I," said he, "and I hope we may enjoy some good camp-meetings this summer. Brother Cartwright informs me that there will be one on Indian Creek, about thirty miles from here, in about four weeks from now; we will try and go, won't we?". "Yes," said I, "if all is well."

The time came, and as our babe was unwell, we thought that we should have to remain at home with it, but my husband and a number of our class-mates went. The grounds were beautiful, and the water excellent, and oh! such lovely surroundings. A very large congregation was present, including many ministers, and Father Cartwright was a faithful Moses. The Spirit of the Lord attended the preaching of the Word, and it was borne home to the sinner's heart, and many cried out: "Men and brethren, what shall I do to be saved?" They were directed to Him who has said, "Come unto me, ye who are weary and heavy laden, and I will give you rest."

The Spirit of the Lord was manifest in every sermon, exhortation and prayer meeting, and great good was done. I think there were about one hundred united with the church before the close of the meeting, and those who went, returned with clear and undisputed evidence that they had been with Jesus—you could see it in all their deportment. My husband was wonderfully blessed, and there seemed to be a sacred halo surrounding him; the same was true of Brothers Cartwright, Smith, Cormack, and their families. This Spirit diffused and was strengthened in our class, and we had a revivlal all summer, and Brother Cartwright thought he would have a campmeeting just after the close of the Annual Conference, which was in session somewhere in the southern part of the state, and he thought that as the preachers returned northward from the conference to their regular work in the northern portion, they would stop and assist him in the labors of the meeting.

A beautiful spot was selected on Brother Smith's farm, three or four miles from Springfield. The announcement of the meeting was given out, our camp built, and we moved onto the grounds. The preachers came flocking in from the conference to the number of eight or ten. The grounds were well settled by Thursday, and a deep feeling pervaded the congregation. The ministers discoursed with power, and the members were working energetically for an outpouring of the Spirit of the Lord, but there seemed to be no especial demonstration of mercy until Sunday night. There had been a few conversions and much good wrought. Still there were two young ladies who had been under conviction since the Indian Creek campmeeting, and they had been forward at every prayermeeting for prayers, but had not found peace up to the time of this campmeeting. One of these young ladies was Miss Sarah Cormack, the daughter of a local preacher who lived in Springfield, and belonged to our class, the other was a Miss Smith who came from Morgan county with my Methodist friends, Mr. and Mrs. Hurd, and Mr. and Mrs. King, who came up to attend the meeting. They were very much interested in Miss Smith. She had accompanied them to the Indian Creek meeting, and was first awakened there. (The Methodist people thought nothing of going forty or fifty miles to a campmeeting those days.) Those young ladies were almost in despair. They and a few others made a covenant that they would pray and wrestle all night until the Lord should bless them.

When the evening came we went out to the woods. A number of the sisters prayed to the Lord in behalf of these earnest seekers; others came away rejoicing, but these two seekers were sad, but still sought for mercy. The horn sounded for public service at the stand, and we had the pleasure of enjoying an excellent sermon by Brother House, our new minister, a very promising young man. After this there was an exhortation and a call for mourners, and those two young ladies made their way to the altar and there prostrated themselves, with the resolve that if there was mercy for them they would struggle until morning but what they obtained the blessing. The prayermeeting proceeded as usual, and quite a number were blessed, but those young ladies were mourners still. Brothers Cartwright, Cormack, Tartington and my husband, Sister Kirkpatrick and myself had covenanted to pray with and for them as long as they desired to stay there. First one and then another prayed with them, and the Lord seemed to draw near and still nearer to us, and while Sister Kirkpatrick was praying, mercy came in such great power that we were all overwhelmed in an ocean of love. The mourners shouted, "Glory! glory to God!" The rest of us fell prostrate on the ground in that leafy temple, while the orb of night shed its silvery rays upon us, and the language of each soul was, "glory, glory." It was then about twelve o'clock, and the people had nearly all retired to their tents, and many were asleep, but this shout roused them, and they came to the stand in scores, and as soon as any one touched us by shaking hands they fell to the ground and cried out, "Glory! glory!" This seemed to be the language of every soul; many said they had never been blessed so powerfully before. Father Cartwright heard the sound; he was in bed, and said to his excellent wife, "Come, Frankie, let's get up and go to the stand, there is something more than usual going on there; Brother and Sister Roe are not in the habit of making such a noise; the power of the Lord is there, I feel it." "So do I," said she, "I hope those dear girls have been blessed."

They made their way to where my husband and I were, and he said to me, "Sister Roe, the Lord is giving you a great blessing, as good measure as Benjmin got: pressed down and running over; religion is as good in Illinois as in Kentucky." "Yes," said I, "I never had such a blessing in Kentucky as this," and taking hold of one of his hands with one of mine, and Sister Cartwright with the other, they both fell prostrate to the ground, exclaiming, "Glory! glory to God in the highest!" Then the great backwoods preacher and his dear wife lay there for some time drinking from the well of salvation, while no language could express their feelings, but "Glory! glory!" By this time, those who had first fallen under the influence of the gracious shower were able to walk about and exhort. And oh, what language! It certainly was inspired by the Holy Ghost. I think it was something like the Pentecostal shower. Every one seemed to hear and understand. There was not one well person left in the tents. Saints and sinners alike rushed to the stand, and sinners were prostrate all through the congregation crying for mercy. Many new converts just born into the Kingdom were crying, "Glory! Glory to God! For as far as the east is from the west, so **far has** the Lord separated my sins from me!" This state of feeling continued until the light of the morning appeared in the east, when Brother Cartrwright dismissed us by singing the doxology, and we set about preparing some refreshments for the inner man. But while this was going on, the sound of "Glory!" could be heard all over the camp ground—in the tents, at the stand, in the woods and around the fires, while we were cooking and setting tables. And while at breakfast, I saw a number stop eating and cry out "Glory!"

The sound of the horn summoned us to the stand to hear a farewell sermon or exhortation from Father Cartwright, as we were to separate soon. I do not remember whether he took a text or not, but I do know that every word was clothed with divine power. At the close of his remarks he said, "I wonder if there is a sinner left on the ground or one mourner who is not converted." "Yes," said Brother Cormack, "here is one;" pointing to a young man who stood leaning against a tree, and who had stood out against all the sacred influence of the Indian Creek campmeeting. He was a young lawyer who thought it would be disparaging to his professional character to be a Methodist. I am glad that the world and the church have outgrown that kind of thinking, for there are many excellent lawyers at this day who are devoted Christians and worthy members of the Methodist Church. He had come up to this meeting with two praying sisters, all starched up, with a ruffled shirt and breast pin, and imagined he was cutting quite a dash when he first came on the camp ground. But he had been slightly awakened the night before and fell to the ground, groaning and crying for mercy. He had held out well, but now he was looking sad and dejected, and when Brother Cormack pointed at him he started for the woods with Brother Cormack after him. He just reached the edge of the woods when he fell prostrate to the ground and cried out for mercy. Brother Cormack prayed with him a while, and soon he was able to receive the truth and believed with all his heart. He came back to the stand rejoicin his present salvation, being willing to unite with the Methodist Church, as were many others. The meeting closed with the best of feeling on the part of all. As we left that sacred spot, many, very many of us felt the sweet assurance that we, if faithful to the grace already given us, should have a sweet reunion in our Father's Kingdom to go out no more. Many of those dear brothers and sisters I have no doubt are shouting in glory; while some still linger on the shores of mortality, battling with the cares of life, looking over to the Promised Land with the anticipation of one day there entering into rest.

At this meeting I first saw Jerry Walker, first missionary in Chicago. He cheered our hearts by relating the bright prospects of the great Northwestern mission. Immigration poured in from all parts of the earth, and the people were of the enterprising, intelligent, religious class. Wherever a Methodist family was settled, there our ministers would make a standpoint, there raise the banner of Emmanuel, and cry, "Behold the Lamb!" **They** would preach in log cabins and in the leafy groves until a school house could be built, which building would serve for both until a church could be erected. The circuit was enlarged and district after district **was formed**; then one division after another of **our Conference came,** and the word ran **and was** glorified.

We moved **that** fall to Spring Creek, about seven miles from Springfield. There was no class formed in our immediate neighborhood, but about **two** miles from us, on the opposite side of the creek, was a large log house, owned by a widow lady—Sister Ferrell. We got Brother House, the circuit minister, to make an appointment to preach at Sister Ferrell's, and we soon had a class organized, with my husband as class leader. Another appointment at Lick Creek, three miles above, resulted **in** the formation of another small class. When **the** latter class was formed we thought best to join it, but the members of the first were unwilling to spare us unless my husband would remain as leader, which arrangement was made and our names **remained on** the books **at** Sister Ferrell's. Here **we met our** much esteemed brother, James McKain. **We did** all in our power to encourage and strengthen this class. The members increased in grace, although we had no revivals. Another class was formed four miles below us on Sugar creek, at Simon Peter's house, where we visited, obtaining strength and encouragement. Still farther down the same creek, in Father Royal's neighborhood, where Father Cartwright held meetings, (Oh! what a good sermon I heard him preach in a grove on "Baptism.") a great revival was held. Father Royal lived here and carried on a pottery shop, and was also local minister at that time. He was a very spiritual Christian. We became intimately acquainted, and found him great help in the divine life. He often preached to us at Sister Ferrill's. We also became acquainted here with Brother James McKain, who was then our circuit preacher, and afterwards our missionary in the Rock River Valley. We formed an intimate Christian friendship that lasted till his death.

About three years after this we moved to Island Grove. Here there was a large society, and we found great comfort and took great pleasuse in serving the Lord. This place was fifteen miles from Springfield. While living there we attended a camp meeting at the old Spring Creek camp ground near Father Walter's. This meeting was attended with great power. The Lord poured out His spirit in a powerful manner. There I heard the lamented Bankston preach a great sermon from Job's words, "I have heard of thee by the hearing of the ear, but now mine eye seeth thee; wherefore I abhor myself and repent in dust and ashes." Oh! what a sermon; and what power attended the word. There were more than one hundred conversions at that meeting, and the people went home rejoicing in Him who ever liveth and keepeth those who trust Him. Father Cartwright was still our "Moses." Oh! what a baptism of the Holy Spirit he received at that time. There we also became acquainted with Brother Henry Summers. My husband was a member of the quarterly conference that licensed Brother Summers to preach the Gospel. He preached an excellent sermon for us while on the camp ground. I shall never forget the untiring efforts made by the preachers and their wives, and the class leaders and their wives, to persuade his wife to give her consent to his joining the conference. Why will women be so selfish? Think of the good that noble man has done in building up our Zion. She became fully converted to the work and was a great help to him. If she had persisted and hindered him from joining the conference, who would have done the work that he has done? I do not know but he is laboring yet.

Time and opportunity offering, I went down to visit my sister and her family in Morgan county, and attend a camp meeting on Mr. Harril's farm, still in Father Cartwright's district. When we arrived at my sister's I thought to stop and stay with her the first night, for I had no idea she would attend the meeting at night. But, to my astonishment, I learned that she, with her whole family had moved on to the camp ground, to remain until the close of the the meeting. It was quite late when we got to the camp ground, and the evening meeting had begun. Our friends manifested great joy on our arrival, and I can assure you I felt happy when I learned from one of her daughters that my sister was under conviction. Rev. Peter Acres was there and had preached several of his searching sermons, and they had found way to her heart, and the daughters said to me, "Behold! she prayeth." They knew and were satisfied that she had been to the grove alone, and that they had heard her praying. "Oh!" said I, "girls, we must pray without ceasing, and I do believe we shall see her safely converted before the meeting closes."

The camp ground was in a lovely spot, plenty of good water, beautiful shade, and every convenience that could be expected on a camp ground. A large congregation and some of the best preachers of our conference were in attendance, and everything conspired to make the occasion interesting and profitable. There had been a good many conversions already. My sister was a very attentive hearer, and we thought prayerful, although she had not ventured in to the altar. The next day, when they called for mourners I went up into the altar and tried to labor with the mourners, and I was much blessed. While there were shouts of new-born souls all around me I began to raise my voice and cry "Glory!" My sister was very much surprised to see me, as she expressed it, so excited. She said, "Oh! girls; you must go and get her out of there. She will die." "Oh! no;" they replied, "she is enjoying herself. We would not disturb her for anything." "Well," said she, "I will go and get her out of there. Where is Brother Roe? I should think he would be crazy about her." Then she found the Doctor and said to him, "Are you not afraid sister will kill herself? Why don't you go and get her out of there?" "Oh! no, sister," said he. "I would not disturb her for anything. I want her to enjoy herself. Perhaps she is doing some good." "I don't think anybody ought to kill themselves to do good," she replied; "I will go and try to get her out of there myself." She made her way into the altar near me and reached out her hand to touch me. I clasped it and said, "Now, dear sister, won't you here and now give your heart to the dear Redeemer, and let Him mould it into His image." Just then she fell, like a dead person, on the ground, and cried, "Lord, save me or I perish!" She lay for three or four hours in that situation, and many who came to look at her said, "I do believe she is dying." Many of the preachers came and prayed for her and exhorted her to believe and trust the Lord. She did not speak. There was no uneasiness in my mind, however. I believed the Lord was doing the work in His own way. I sat by her and held her hand in mine, trying to exhort her to believe. "Believe, sister, and the Lord will reveal Himself to you in the pardon of your sins." She uttered a loud groan and said, "Can the Lord forgive such a great sinner as me?" "Yes, yes; sister. It was for sinners Jesus died—just such sinners as you and I. Can't you believe?" "Yes," said she, "I do believe. Dear Lord, save a trembling sinner;

> 'Whose hope still hovering 'round thy word—
> Would light on some sweet promise there,
> Some sure support against despair.'"

Just then my husband held up some of the blessed

promises, such as, "Come unto me, ye heavy laden, and I will give you rest;" " Believe, and through Him ye shall be saved;" "Son, or daughter, give me thy heart." Just then her countenance changed from an agonizing expression to that of cheerfulness, and she exclaimed, "What mercy, that God should forgive such a sinner as I. I do believe, dear Lord. Accept the offering of a broken heart. I do believe the Saviour loves me and died to redeem me." Just then the light of joy was shed abroad in her heart and she expressed herself thus: "The great transaction's done. I am the Lord's and he is mine!" From that moment we felt that she was saved—saved through faith on the Son of God. Oh! what joy there was in all the circle of her friends. From that moment she was a different person, so meek and lowly, and such a decided Christian. She united with the church, erected the altar of prayer in her family and traveled with her children on the way to Zion. She passed into that better land a number of years since.

This camp meeting was a great blessing to many. There were many conversions. I do not know the the exact number converted, but there were scores and scores. The church, was greatly strengthened, the ministers newly commissioned and the work still spread on and on. We went home much encouraged to do our duty and trust in a prayer-hearing God.

About this time Brother Royal came to our house and said he wanted us to go with him and make a new home in a new town on the east side of the Sangamon river. He said the proprietors were offering two lots to each settler. They wished to have a

Methodist town established, and he thought we could do better as regarded business than we were then doing. He wanted my husband to go and practice medicine there. He had studied medicine in Kentucky, and wished to practice when he first came to Illinois; but I opposed him so strongly that he had not given his entire attention to the business, but had practiced to some extent among his most intimate acquaintances. After coming to Illinois he adopted the botanical system of practice, and was very successful, but I could not think of his making it a business for the reason that he would be away from home so much, leaving me with the great responsibility of raising our family of boys, for we now had four and the oldest not quite eight years old. I finally consented to move to the new village. It was called Athens, lay in the east part of Sangamon county, four miles from the Sangamon river. It was pleasantly located in the edge of a grove, bordering on a beautiful prairie. North east of the village two miles there was a log meeting house, and west of us two miles there was another. There was but a small class at either of them, but there were some excellent members in each. One in the west class, Father Stringfield, was an old veteran in the service in Kentucky. He had traveled mostly in the upper part of the State, and I was not acquainted with him there; but I love to think of our acquaintance with him in Illinois. Our names were placed on the class record at Brother (or Father) Stringfield's. We moved into a house in his yard. He lived on a farm that lay near the church or meeting house. We lived there until we built a house in the village, for there were no houses there except one dwelling house, one store, one blacksmith shop and a horse mill, which made it necessary for us to build a house. Brother Royal had built a stable and moved into it before we got there, and had commenced his house. We all had to build of logs. They were near by, and were the best material that could be had for the purpose. The men had to go six miles to get a tree that would make clapboards to cover the houses. My husband went eight miles to a saw mill to get some slabs, such as they saw off the outside of the logs. We were too poor to afford a floor made of proper boards, they were so high, and cost so much. We soon got our house up, the floor down, the roof partly on, and moved in.

Our circuit preacher was the lamented Asahel Phelps. He was young in the ministry and his health was rather delicate. He had just recovered from a severe and protracted illness in the southern part of the State, and was just able to attend Conference when it met, and they thought best to send him north. He came rather reluctantly, but was very acceptable. He was a host on doctrinal points, but proved a great revival preacher; that year he preached at both of these meeting houses, and we soon became acquainted with and strongly attached to him. He appointed a prayer meeting and also left an appointment for preaching at our house. Some one in the congregation said, "I believe Brother Roe's house has not got all the roof on it yet." "Well, said he, "Brother Roe, I suppose you will be ready in time, will you not?" "Yes," he replied, "I will try and have it on by that time, no preventing Providence." Brother Roe worked with all the diligence possible, and the day the prayer meeting was to be at night, he went for the last load of boards, getting home just in time to nail them on. But he lacked a few boards, so that we held our first prayer meeting in a house without an entire roof. The house was full, and we had a real old-fashioned shouting prayer meeting. And that was the commencement of one of the best revivals I ever enjoyed. Brother Phelps preached in the power and demonstration of the spirit; Brother Royal had great liberty in preaching the word; Brother Stringfield preached alternately with Brother Maclemore, and the house was repeatedly filled with people. The Lord blessed the word, and it was carried home to the hearts of sinners. Many flocked to the Saviour, sought for pardon, and found peace in believing.

We had preaching every Sabbath at the churches, and at our house in the village in the evening. The spirit of the Lord attended the word, and it proved the power of God to the salvation of many. There in that humble dwelling I have seen the hoary-headed sinner who was steeped in sin, the middle aged and the youth, kneeling together, pleading for redemption through the blood of the Lamb, and heard them rejoice in a sin-pardoning God. The work went on and on, until there was such an awakening spirit all through the country, that the official members could not get one night's rest in the week.

Brother Catterton, who afterwards became the father-in-law of Brother Phelps, was very useful in this revival. He was a licensed exhorter and circuit steward, a bricklayer by trade, and lived just on the edge of the village on a small farm. Oh! what power there was in his exhortation. Two of his daughters sought and found the Saviour in that revival. The oldest, Charlotte, afterward became Sister Phelps. The second one, Rebecca, when she approached the mourner's bench, had on a very nice bonnet, and kind Sister Sackett approached her and was about to remove it, when her father spoke up, "Never mind, sister," said he, "let the bonnet go. I can lay brick and get her more. I had rather see her there than riding in a coach and six." Brothers Catterton and Royal and my husband were going night and day among the mourners. They would be sent for from miles in the country, saying, "Come and pray with us. We are lost and undone if we can't get religion." In one instance, where they were sent for, a man and his wife were converted before they got there, and were shouting and happy; so they had nothing to do but rejoice with them.

One day Brother Royal, my husband and several of the brethren were talking about the mercy of God in the salvation of the people; how the work was spreading; who was converted last night; when they expected Brother Phelps and how much they needed his help; hoped he would remain with us during the next week, etc., when some one remarked, "Brethren, I love the work, but it will not bring bread and butter." "Never mind," replied Brother Royal, "I have one load of every kind of potter's ware left, and we will live while that lasts." Every kind of business was stopped and the people stood about in groups in the streets of our village and in the yards and houses, reading the Bible and talking about the great work. Singing and prayer could be heard from some direction at almost any hour of the day or night. We had a pleasant female prayer meeting, which was a source of much good, and there were many souls converted. It was conducted by dear old Mother Rogers, who was our leader. She exhorted powerfully, and oh! what a near approach she would make to the Lord in prayer. It did seem as though the Lord denied her nothing she asked for, as she did truly ask in faith, nothing doubting. She was a power in that revival, and has long since gone to the climes of glory. Methinks there must have been some bright stars added to her crown during that revival. Most all who labored at that time, as well as many who were converted, have gone into our Father's kingdom, — Brother Phelps, Father Stringfield, Father Maclemore, Brother Shepard, Sister Sackett, and Sister Royal. Oh! Sister Royal was a host in that revival. Blessed be her memory. It is right to think of the venerable dead who lived and labored to sustain our beloved Methodism all along the century and say, "Blessed be their memory." For many do claim them as the instruments in the hands of the Lord to bring them to the fold. Oh! my heart kindles with a desire to pass over the river and enjoy that rest. But all my time will I wait patiently till my Lord shall say, "It is enough; come up higher." And with hopeful trusting heart we may believe whoever may live to see an hundred years, will see Methodism clothed with that power there is in a sanctified literature. May the Lord ever keep us as a Church humble and holy, and may it be a power to tell to earth's remotest bounds that God is Love and died for a sinful world. For He hath said, "Come unto me all ye ends of the earth, and be ye saved." Bless the Lord, Oh! my soul, for a full and free salvation.

Brother Cartwright was still our Elder. He left an appointment for a quarterly meeting, and Brother Phelps thought it best to have a camp meeting at that time, as neither of our meeting houses would hold half the congregation. He consulted the stewards and class leaders, and Brother Cartwright sanctioned it. The meeting was located at Father Stringfield's, a very convenient spot. We did not think of holding the camp meeting more than two weeks before the time appointed, but everybody seemed ready for a camp meeting, and when the time came we were there in Methodist order. Everything conspired to make the meeting interesting, and it was. Much good was done. Here I first saw the lamented John Sinclair. He was traveling some circuit near, and so it was convenient for him to come and help Brother Phelps, who was very thankful for his assistance. He was the means of doing much good there, and many souls were converted and the church much blessed. There was a great baptism of the Holy Spirit. If I recollect right, it was the last night of the meeting, after the meeting closed at the stand, a group of those veterans came to our tent with two or three mourners. They sang and prayed with those mourners until they were enabled to realize by a living faith that their sins were forgiven and the love of God shed was abroad in their hearts. "How streaming mercy flowed to every heart." Well might we say we sat together in a heavenly place, while His glorious presence here our earthen vessels fill, and we could antedate the day when we should meet around the Father's throne and sing halleluia to Him who loved us and washed us in His all-atoning blood, and gave us His spirit to bear witness with ours that we were the children of God. Oh! how we loved one another; how we loved a Christian ministry; how we loved a world that lay in wickedness, far from God by wicked ways. There were a good many of them there, and it seemed that the preachers and exhorters were commissioned anew to cry "Behold! behold the Lamb." They did so, and went from tent to tent and preached Jesus and the remission of sins. And Oh! what a time of the outpouring of the spirit of the Lord. What a gracious farewell we had next morning when we parted. My heart is imbued with the same blessed spirit while I write. Glory to God for his redeeming and sustaining grace, and for the hope I have to-day of soon meeting those dear Fathers and Mothers, who were Fathers and Mothers in Israel to me, and those dear Brothers and Sisters who helped us to bear the standard of Methodism and unfurl the banner of free salvation in those days.

We remained in the village some time, nearly three years I think. During this time we became acquainted with old Father Mitchell, the old pioneer minister, who was one of the earliest standard bearers in Illinois. There was a gracious power attended his preaching. He held a two-days meeting in our village during one of his itinerant tours. I think he was the soundest man on the doctrine of the Trinity that I ever heard preach. He, too, has entered into the harbor of rest long since.

While living there we attended another camp meet-meeting at the Walters camp ground. A great many of our classes went to this meeting, and there were many souls converted and wonderfully blessed. I say classes, for the three classes were pretty large. I think the one in the village numbered about ninety-five persons, and we began to think of building a church—long since our log house had become too small, and we had worshiped in a large school-house. Our village had grown very much, and truly it was a Methodist village. I have heard Brother Phelps say he had "often stopped when he had been walking out in the morning or evening and listened and heard eight or ten families at prayer all at the same time."

Here we became more acquainted with Brother I. H. Sinclair. He came over on our side of the river to perform the marriage ceremony for Brother Phelps. and we had a two days' meeting appointed on the camp ground near Father Stringfield's, and he preached in great power while there, and the Word was like bread cast upon the waters, it could be gathered many days hence.

That fall we attended a conference campmeeting at or near Jacksonville. The conference was held in the town, and the campmeeting was conducted as usual, except that we had a greater number of preachers, and of course, a greater variety of preaching. There we became acquainted with John and James Mitchell, very promising young men. It was there also that we became acquainted with Brother Beggs. In early days his labors were much blessed in building up Methodism in the northern part of the State of Illinois.

I think that Bishop Roberts presided at the conference. There was a great Sabbath-school demonstration. On Sunday, all the schools in that section were invited, and met at Jacksonville, and marched up to the campground in a double column. Never shall I forget what a beautiful sight it was to see them march onto the campground and take their seats; oh! I felt then that was the way to plant Methodism (and I feel so now.) We had a very appropriate address from Brother John T. Mitchell, and well do I recollect how young he looked; how genteel and commanding was his appearance, and how his words burned in the hearts of his hearers, when he encouraged us to look forward to the time when that army of Sabbath-school scholars would grow up and take our places in the ranks of the Methodist army, and battle for the right. This encouraged our hearts to hope that some great good might result from our labors in the Sabbath-school in our village. From sixty to eighty attended regularly. My husband was superintendent, and he had a good number of faithful teachers, and the school prospered beyond our anticipations; but with all our prosperity, we felt, religiously, like living and dying there together, but the Lord decreed it otherwise, and we were willing to be led by Him, knowing that the path of duty is always the path of safety.

CHAPTER VI.

DOCTOR'S ADVENTURE ON THE FARM.

The young doctor bought a good deal of corn one fall, and got it hauled to him for one shilling per bushel, and he also bought about one hundred fine young shoats. He kept a trusty man who took good care of them, and I had a few of my own. In the spring we fenced in a forty-acre lot for them which cost over one hundred dollars, enclosed a reservoir made by a buffalo wallow in a ravine, and then made a dam below it for the hogs to drink from and wallow in; built a nice shed for them to sleep under, as well as for shade; and this cost him fifty dollars more. He laid in enough corn, as he thought, to last until the new corn would do to cut up and feed green. He thought he had his plans nicely arranged, pitched his crops, got in his wheat, oats, barley and corn—nearly an hundred acres of corn on which to fatten his hogs. The season was very favorable; plentiful showers, gentle breezes and a rich sunshine brought on the crops early. By the 10th of July the barley and wheat were harvested and in stacks, and the oats nearly all down and bound; corn nicely cultivated, and well cared, and nothing could look more promising than the whole crop. They closed up the labors of the week Saturday evening all feeling cheerful and hoping to finish harvesting on Monday.

We had a beautiful garden of vegetables also, but Sunday afternoon it became a little cloudy, or rather hazy, so as to dim the beautiful sunshine of the morning. Some of the family had been to Crab Orchard to attend meeting, and as they were on their way home they discovered something flying everywhere in the air, but they could not ascertain what it was. One says to the other, "See how thick they are getting; I wonder if it can be grasshoppers? I fear it is." They seemed to come nearer and nearer until they began to light on the ground, and then they knew that it was that greatly-to-be-dreaded scourge—grasshoppers. We who were at home had discovered them also, and they came down like great clouds and settled all over the farm and garden, except a little plat where we had lettuce and onions, and on the peach trees which were not far from the house. We had quite a number of them, and they were loaded with fruit, and the seeds were just hardening, and I heard pa say just before his death, "I never saw such nice peach trees before; I should not wonder if we should have fifty bushels from them next year." "Oh pa," said I, "that is too much to expect; that will be only three years from the setting." "Well," said he, "they bear in this country the third year from the seed, but those were raised in a nursery and set here, and that will put them back a year—it will be three years next spring since they were set out." "Well," said I, "there are a few of those seeds we planted come up, and we will see if they bear." They did bring forth peaches three years from the sprouting, nice large peaches, but few on a tree. They ripened nicely, and the trees were then loaded with fruit. We felt sad to see those grasshoppers eating the fruit right off the seeds and leaving them hanging to the limbs. They ate all the leaves off and devoured the bark of the small limbs, there being hundreds on quite a small twig.

They destroyed our sweet corn in a few hours the first day, and still they came—the earth was literally covered with them, many being as large as a small finger, and shaped just like any other grasshopper. They commenced their destruction on Monday—they settled down on the ground Sunday night and did not eat anything—(they do not eat at night, but cuddle up in a pile like a swarm of bees.) Tuesday morning I saw heaps of grasshoppers as large as a wash tub. Numbers of these swarms could be seen all through the garden, and if I had thought to have poured hot water on them I might have saved our four hundred head of nice cabbage that was just heading. But I did not think, and as a consequence the cabbage was destroyed. They ate the lettuce and beets, but to my great joy they had not touched the black seed onions. I gathered some of those onions for breakfast and went in with great joy to tell the doctor's wife that the cabbage and onions had been spared as yet. She ran out to see if her plot was safe. She said, "Ma, mine are all right." I hoped that they might be spared, but the 'hoppers took them as they made their way to the cornfield. Before ten o'clock there was not an onion or cabbage left—we had planted a great many onions. They commenced on a forty-acre field of corn, which we could see from the house, about ten o'clock, and before night there was not an ear of corn or green leaf to be seen, and the stalks looked as though they had been boiled. All was over; the potato bugs had taken our late potatoes, and now the 'hoppers our garden, corn and fruit. I assure you it was sad, but it was so all over the country.

CHAPTER VII.

REMOVAL TO ROCK RIVER—PROGRESS OF METHODISM.

Brother Wm. Royal was recommended by our quarterly conference to the annual conference at its session in Jacksonville, Morgan county, Illinois, in the fall of 1831, and was appointed to a mission extending over several counties, embracing the town of Bloomington, Illinois, and the surrounding country. There he labored to plant the standard of the great Redeemer, and lay the foundation of Methodism. He worked in great suffering and want, but his heart was fired with zeal for the salvation of precious souls and the cause of his Master. Himself and family endured hardships as faithful soldiers of the cross, and the Lord abundantly blessed their labors. Sister Barbara Royal was a great help, through the grace of God, in sustaining her husband in the then arduous duties of the Gospel ministry.

How many circuits, churches and charges were then a mission? It would be impossible for me to tell. If some of those faithful standard-bearers, such as

Bros. Royal and Gaddis, with others, were permitted to view the landscape they would cry out, "Praise the Lord! nothing but the grace of God and our blessed itineracy could have done this great work, and to Him be all the glory."

Brother Phelps grew rapidly in spiritual life and ministerial influence, and was soon ordained presiding elder, and was sent north in the year of 1832-'33.

Brother **Maclemore**, Brother Overstreet, and Mother Rogers were soon released from their service and passed over the river Jordan in the sweet assurance of that rest that awaits the faithful. Mother Rogers was very useful at the Athens revival. She was the leader of our female prayer-meetings.

Brother Sacket moved to Rock river and settled near Elkhorn Grove, about twelve or fifteen miles west of the river. There were but a very few families located in the Grove then. There they labored faithfully to plant Methodism in all its simplicity and truth, and it flourished and grew, watered by the showers of divine grace. One revival succeeded another until there was a large class formed. Dear Father and Mother Ankeny were among the fruits of these revivals, and have long since gone home to receive their reward, with many others whose names I cannot give.

Brother Sacket wrote to my husband, telling him of the beautiful country that was open for settlement, and urged us to come. Brother Catterlin had sold his nice little farm and had moved north and settled in Hennepin, Putnam county, on the Illinois river. He also wrote the doctor, urging us to come. So, in the fear of the Lord, we left our home and friends in the village with regret, but felt it our duty as well as interest to go, so we took our departure in November, 1834, for Rock river.

We had a family of five boys, healthy, promising children, and felt it our duty to try and get us a farm, as we thought it the best and most prudent place to rear our boys. My husband told me that if I would come to this new country he would discard the practice of medicine, and would turn his attention to farming. This pleased me. I was willing to endure any privation that could be expected in moving to a new country, if I could only rear my boys on a farm.

We traveled as far north as Putnam county, and there we met some friends who advised us to stop. They informed us that the Indians had not, nor would not go until spring, and perhaps not until the spring following, and that the few settlers there had not raised more grain than they could consume, and that the late settlers had came there to buy grain, paying a high price for it, and if we went on we would have to supply ourselves in the same way. This news brought us to the conclusion that we had better take their advice, which we did, and remained there for some time.

In December, 1835, my husband came to Rock river and selected a claim, that being the mode of securing a farm. He erected a cabin and returned to Putnam county for his family. We were almost ready by the time he returned for us, yet regretted to leave our home, although it was temporary. We had found kind neighbors and Christian friends, to whom we had become very much attached—some Methodists, others Presbyterians; the latter had a large church, and we often worshipped with them.

Brother Phelps had resigned his office as elder, and was traveling the Hennepin circuit, and he would come to our house and preach every four weeks, as most of them were divided into four week circuits at that time. He and his horse, "**Tom**" by name, had a hard time of it traveling through the mud and sloughs. We did not have much of a congregation, but Brother Phelps said he would come "if he had only **our family** for **an audience.**" And he did so, much to our comfort and instruction, until we came to Rock river valley.

We left our home in Putnam county **in** 1836, early **in March.** At the close of our first day's journey we had arrived at Hennepin, and **there** we had a **good** visit with Brother Catterlin, **his** wife and interesting daughters (they had no sons.) The weather was very unpropitious for traveling, as **the frost** was just coming out of the ground, and **the ice** was beginning to **break up in** the streams. But we were obliged (through **fear** that **some one** might take our claim from us in **the** absence of my husband, **as** was often done) to proceed **on** our journey. The night we stopped with Brother Catterlin's family it rained very hard, taking the **frost out** of the ground and softening **the** ice in the river so that our team could not cross on the ice. Brother Catterlin informed **us** that there was a ferry about eight miles above Hennepin, and that he understood **the** river was open **up** there and boats running. So we started for the ferry, and got along nicely for a few miles—we were driving oxen, as we dared not start with horses, it being so very muddy, and there being no grain on which to feed horses. After traveling about half the distance, we turned into the timber, making our way to the river. We found that the road had not been worked much, if any, since it had been made, and the rain had washed away all the bridges, which were many. It seemed as though we crossed a creek, that wound through the Illinois river bottom, at least five or six times, and had to build a bridge at every crossing. It took us till near sundown to accomplish this.

Brother Catterlin had told us that a suspicious set of people lived at the ferry, and advised us to drive on a few miles from the ferry to stop over night. Well, there we were at the ferry,—sundown, and the wind blowing a tempest of snow and hail, the ground freezing under our feet. My husband called again and again for the ferryman, and it seemed as though some one answered, but we could not understand anything, the wind blew so hard, and my husband concluded he would have to go ahead and see what he could do. He could see a hut plainly on the other side. The ice seemed to be strong in the middle of the stream, but near the shore it was broken away, and the water was rushing along in a strong current, some four feet in width, between the ice and bank. A small tree had been felled by some one, and this indicated that they had crossed over to the ice, and the doctor was resolved to try and get over. I begged him not to make the venture, but instead, build a fire by a log near the road and stay there all night. "Oh!" said he, "you and the children would perish here." "You will perish," said I, "if you attempt to cross that river, and if we must perish, let us all perish together." But he was resolved to go, and taking a long pole in his hand, climbed upon the **tree**. I cannot describe my feelings, for I never expected to see him return; but soon he was safe on the strong **ice**. "Now," he called out, "dont feel uneasy, I will not venture on the weak ice," and with the remark, "I will often call out 'all right,'" proceeded. For a while we could hear him, and each token of his safety **was** received with delight, and the little **boys would** smile, while their teeth chattered with the cold, when they heard their pa's voice. At length we could hear the welcome sound no more, and we could not tell whether he **had** gone down into the deep or not, and perhaps it might be the storm **or** the rushing, roaring water as it passed us that prevented **us** from hearing his voice. **Oh!** what suspense I suffered **for** an half **hour** or more. If ever I trusted and prayed earnestly it was then, and I felt that His everlasting arm would sustain me, and no harm would befall us. Pretty soon I heard him say, "All safe!"

On his arrival on the other side, the doctor learned that the ferry had been opened, but the ice had floated down into the channel, and that they had run the boat through and had closed it up, but men were at work half a mile below cutting another opening through the ice, but it would be impossible for us to get across that night. "Well," said I to my husband, "the Lord will take care of us, and no harm will befall us."

There seemed to be no other alternative but for us to remain where we were, as we could never grope our way back over that miserable road and shattered bridges, to a house six miles back. This psalm came to my mind, and it fell deep into my heart: "I will both lay me down in peace and sleep, for thou, Lord, only maketh me to dwell in safety." So we concluded to build a fire by the log and get supper, and then make our beds in the wagon and try and get warm, and sleep if possible. The gale had passed over, and it was now more calm.

The doctor went about cutting some wood from the limbs that had fallen from a tree near by with which to build a fire, while I took the things out of the wagon to get supper with.

Just then a man approached us in haste, saying. "We have got the boat over on this side, and will take you across the river yet to-night; we had to make a landing about half a mile below here." We hurried our things together and went along down the bank of the river about half a mile, and there we found the boat and several strong men. We had two yoke of oxen, one cow and a dozen small shoats. They thought it best to take the stock over first, and then return for myself, the children and wagon. They run the wagon near enough to the river so that they could, on their return, get it on the boat. My husband and the two oldest boys went over with the first load to assist in getting the stock ashore. I was now alone with my three smallest boys, and wrapped them up and kept them as warm as I could in the wagon.

While I sat there in the front of the wagon—which

was fixed up in emigrant fashion, with bows and cover—meditating upon the goodness of God, who was about to deliver us from this exposed situation we were in, the little boys were saying to me, "Ma, we will soon be where there is a warm fire." Just then I looked down upon the water above the opening they had cut for the boat to pass through, it being only of sufficient width to admit the craft, using poles by sticking them into the ice to propel it along. Near the shore the ice had thawed, and the water was running. In the river I could see the body of a dead man, with his face just protruding out of the water, and it was dreadfully mangled, and looked as though the ravens had been picking at it. It was twilight, and as I looked upon this scene, a cold shudder ran over me. I recalled what Brother Catterlin had told us, and his words of warning, to "drive on a few miles from the ferry, before stopping for the night," and the rumor afloat that a man had been killed at this place during the winter.

At that moment the men cried out, "All safe over." They soon came back again, and with the shout, "all aboard," pulled the wagon onto the boat. We were soon safely landed on the opposite bank of the river. The oxen were soon hitched to the wagon, and driven with all haste possible up the hill, the men following and often hallooing at the team, and one of the men remarked with an oath, "That woman and the children will freeze to death before that team will get them to a house." We soon halted at the door of a miserable cabin. They had been kind enough to build up a log heap of a fire for us to get warm by, and the woman remarked, with some embarrassment, "I should have had some supper for you had I anything to get." "Dear woman," said I, "do not feel unhappy about that, we are thankful for the comfort affored by your fire, we can soon get supper for ourselves when we get warm." But we did not get very warm, for there were cracks all around the house large enough for a dog to crawl through. The door was made of clapboards, and they were so warped and sprung, that it was but little defence against the pitiless wind. After awhile we got a little warm, and I prepared some supper and made our beds on the floor and retired. I had sought in vain for an opportunity to tell my husband what I had seen in the river.

Soon after our arrival at the cabin all the men left except the owner. He furnished us with some cut-up corn with which to feed our team and then retired, his bed being near our own. After all was quiet I tried to tell the doctor of what I had seen in the river, and found that I had been overheard by the other occupants of the house, and they seemed to be uneasy, and were whispering to each other. I then told them all about it, and asked them if anyone had been "drowned near that place." They said "No," but thought the body "might have floated down the river." After this they seemed to be more restless and uneasy, and shortly afterward the man got up and went out to a hut of a stable, got his horse and rode away. I did not sleep any through the entire night, for I feared I had done wrong in telling them. I thought it possible they might fear exposure by my telling about seeing the dead body, and this might bring harm to us, and perhaps cost us our lives.

I learned from the woman that the men had gone to a tavern, as they called it, up at the usual ferry. I thought that her husband had gone up there to let them know of our discovery. I awoke my husband and told him of my fears, and when he learned that the man had actually gone, he felt a little alarmed, and we concluded to get up and go to some other place where we would feel more secure. It was Sunday morning, and we thought if we could get out on the prairie we might find some church-going people.

When we started from home we expected to cross the river at Hennepin and get to Knox's Grove by Saturday night, and spend the Sabbath there with some of our friends. But having met with so many misfortunes, we were then twenty miles from there.

We packed up our effects on short notice—we could not think of spending the Sabbath in that place—and started on our journey, the woman directing us which way to go. We traveled about six miles in a northwesterly course when we arrived at a house. We stopped and inquired if we could stop there until the next morning. They told us that most of the family had gone to meeting, but gave us permission to stop until they should return, and thought it likely that we could stay over night. We found the people of the house very pious, pleasant and intelligent. We told them where we had put up the night before, what we had seen, etc., and what our fears were. They said they had every reason to believe that our fears were well founded, as those people at the ferry were a shiftless, drunken set, and being in such an out-of-the-way place, they could carry on all sorts of mischief without being found out, and that there was strong suspicion of a man having been killed there in the winter for his money, and they would inform the neighbors and see if anything could be discovered in regard to it. They thought those men would be likely to make an effort to recover the dead body, and if that was acomplished there could be no discovery made. We took our departure early the next morning, and never heard anything more concerning the mystery.

We traveled along pleasantly but slowly, and night found us about a mile from Knox's Grove, a beautiful little grove situated in Bureau County, and about sixteen or eighteen miles from Princeton. As night came on it grew very cold. There was a very little snow on the ground, and it was frozen enough to bear the oxen up, but they slipped and slid about a great deal. Just before we got to the grove we had to cross a slough and then quite a stream. The oxen went into the slough a short distance, and then stuck. After whipping and coaxing and tugging and striving and unloading, my husband got discouraged and gave it up. I said, "My husband, let me take some corn in my hand and go before them, I think they will certainly pull to get to it, they are so hungry." "Well," said he, "try it." I did so, and they pulled it out, and soon we were on solid ground. But just beyond us was the stream. We found that it was frozen over, and the oxen, not being shod, could not stand upon it. What to do we did not know. Finally we concluded to take the oxen off the tongue and tie them to the wagon and feed them, and walk to the Grove. My husband was a good skater, and he took first one child and then another, until he had taken them all safely over, and then he told me to take hold of his arm and he would take me over. I did so, and we were soon on our way. As we approached the Grove—it was now quite dark —just across the road lay a large prairie wolf. I had never saw one before although I had lived so long in the Prairie State. I was very much frightened, and thought it would jump up and come at us, but when we approached nearer we found it to be dead, and then the doctor had quite a laugh at me.

We found a house near by and enjoyed a good night's entertainment. Our kind friends went out with my husband the next morning and scattered hay on the ice, then wet it and let it freeze, and thus they brought the oxen over in safety. We pursued our journey and arrived at Washington Grove, on Rock river, in what is now Ogle county—there was no county organized then, nor for nine or ten months afterward.

The Indians had taken their departure two or three weeks previous to our arrival, and their tracks were yet fresh in the Grove. Our family made maple sugar—caught sap in the troughs the Indians had made, and boiled syrup with their remaining camp-fires. The frames of their wigwams were still standing in the grove. The maple trees are still plenty in Washington Grove, and I am astonished that the people have abandoned the use of them for making sugar.

At the time we arrived there, only three families lived in the Grove—at that time the emigrants settled in and just around the Grove to secure the timber. There were two families on the southwest side, and a bachelor's hall, kept by a Mr. Fay just across the creek that runs through the Grove. There lived another family with a bachelor brother, Hyrem Leonard, in the Grove.

The Grove looked delightful to us, after traveling over a prairie of eighteen miles without seeing a fire. The weather was extremely cold, and we suffered very much. Mr. Blackmore gave us a cordial welcome to all the hospitality their little log cabin afforded—sixteen feet square. The doctor boarded with this kind family while he was making his claim and putting up the body of his house. This family had lived near us in Putnam county, and had moved to Rock river the year previous. They were anxiously looking as the time for our arrival had expired. The doctor had made arrangements with them for us to remain until he could make our house comfortable enough for us to move into. The family consisted of an old lady, a widow, one son, a bachelor, one sister, a maiden lady, and another, a widow with three children, seven in all in the family. Our family numbered seven, five boys and ourselves, the oldest ten years and the youngest three years. There we were, fourteen of us in a little cabin sixteen feet square—a little over a foot apiece —with a fireplace made by building a mud wall against one end of the house, leaving an opening at the top of the roof, forming a funnel on the top of the boards, with sticks and mud, to make a draft. Oh! what nice log fires we would build up, and I assure you the cabin presented an appearance of comfort, with our big fires on our broad mud hearth neatly swept, our beds made up on our scaffold bedstead, all around the log wall well daubed with mud." "Jack Frost" dared not to make his appearance. On one side was the door, and on the other was a four-light window, and under that stood a four-legged table made of clapboard, hewn out of an oak tree by a tool called a frow, well known by settlers of a new country. On this table we ate our meals; six could be seated, and sometimes we crammed in some of the small children. Oh, what comfort we enjoyed, I never enjoyed such comfort in a richly furnished parlor, as I did in our log cabin.

Mother Blackmore was an old Revolutionary Methodist. Her maiden daughter was a devoted Christian. They brought their certificates of membership with them. The widowed daughter was a back-slider, although a fine woman otherwise, with one of the warmest hearts ever placed in its casket. She loved the Methodists, and believed in their doctrines. The brother was a decided friend to Methodism, but knew nothing of experimental religion at that time.

In that cabin, under those circumstances, we had divine service the first Sabbath after our arrival; preaching by Rev. J. Noe, a local Methodist minister who had moved there a few months previous. He had been preaching alternately in the log cabins around the Grove, and had formed a small class. The Missionary, Brother Joseph McKeon, of former acquaintance in Sangamon County, Illinois, had arrived a few weeks previous. The mission was called the Buffalo Grove Mission, attached to the

Galena District, Rev. Alfred Bronson Presiding Elder. When Brother McKeon came to the mission, Brother Moe handed in the names of the members to him, and he organized a class properly, appointing Father Isaac Rosecrans as class leader. There were fifteen, besides our families, in attendance, and nearly all stayed to class. We had an excellent class meeting. I never shall forget it. I expect to recall it in the better world, if I am so happy as to get there. To one who had been for some time without religious privileges, especially that of class meeting, it was precious. True, Brother Phelps had class with us when he preached at our house, but there was seldom any but myself and family present. Of course I expected to live in this new country without religious privileges for a while; but now the first Sabbath found me so delightfully situated, here to meet with some of the old pioneers who had stood the toil and burden of earlier days and helped to plant the standard of the Cross and sustain Methodism in Ohio, Vermont, and other places, and hear them tell of the wonders of Emmanuel; how wonderfully the grace of God had sustained them mid all the trials of life; and then speak of their hopes of an eternal inheritance in the better world, and their hopes of seeing this wilderness blossom as the rose. They hoped the gospel seed would be sown all over those prairies, and that it would produce "an hundred fold," and in the end, everlasting life. Well do I recollect how my heart was filled with the love of God, how near my Saviour was, how strong the emotion of Christian love was toward that little group. There were

Christian ties formed there that day never to be broken.

I met there for the first time Father and Mother Rosecrans, Brother and Sister Clark, Brother and Sister Dorset, Sister Chloe Benedict, who is now the worthy consort of our much esteemed Brother Barton Cartwright, and others, who have entered into the heaven of rest. And then to realize that the missionary of the Cross was there before us, and that he was our own familiar friend. He had been our minister in the Sangamon Circuit. He had visited at our house, and we had enjoyed sweet Christian counsel with him. This increased our joy. I had always known our Methodists to be a working people, but I did not expect to find them here, so close on the track of the savage, and so near the emigrant path. But it was even so, and it was a great comfort to me.

Father and Mother Rosecrans stayed and took tea with us, and we talked over our past experience in regard to the success of the Methodist church everywhere we had lived. The old gentleman remarked, "One reason of their success is, that they are all and always laboring to scatter its sacred influence. I hope it will be so here, and if so, there is not a doubt in my mind but it will be the power of God to the salvation of the people here as elsewhere. Now, brethren," he continued, "we must have a church, even if a small one and built of logs. We must have a place to worship. The Lord does not despise small things." With one consent the brothers and sisters resolved to make an effort to build a log meeting house, and our interview closed with good feeling.

On the 4th of April, a few weeks after our arrival, the doctor said to me, "Mother, I think we had better move into our new home to-day; I could get along much better with my work if all were there." I was much pleased with the idea, and in a few hours we were packed, loaded and on our way, the distance being about two miles, and our friend Blackmore said he would go and help us that day. We could not hire a man for any price, but occasionally the neighbors would go and help each other, and thus our friend Blackmore kindly offered us his assistance that day. We arrived at our new home safely, found the house built of round logs and the roof on; the upper or chamber floor laid with clapboards. The logs were neatly hewn down, the clapboards shaved smooth with a draw-knife and nailed over the cracks, all of which was very neat and comfortable. Only part of a chimney was built, no floor below, except what was made of the large chips that the doctor had hewn from the logs, and they lay promiscously over the ground inside.

Every one of us went to work heartily, the doctor to finishing up the chimney, friend Blackmore to hauling some stone with which to fix up the fireplace with back and jams, so that the fire would not burn the wood work. The little boys and myself busied ourselves with laying those large chips smooth and regular, and it made quite a temporary floor. Pretty soon we had things so comfortable I got dinner, and friend Blackmore partook of our frugal meal and then took his departure, with his best wishes, saying that some member of his family would be up soon to see how we got along at our new home. After our friend had left, the doctor and I went to putting up some shelves, made of clapboards, for a cupboard, some temporary bedsteads; made a table out of a drygoods box, and by night we began to feel quite at home at our own fireside.

Our cabin was just within the edge of the grove, which made a nice shade in summer, and a good shelter in winter. As evening approached we felt a little lonely so far from neighbors—two miles to the nearest neighbor; twelve miles to Dixon; fifteen miles to the nearest neighbor northeast of us, and two miles to Rock river. There were a number of families settled on the west side of Rock river, but there was no ferry near us, so it was rather a lonely place.

As we drew near the fire—it was a little cool—I meditated thus: "Now, if I could hope that my husband would remain at home, as a farmer generally does, with his family, I could bear this lonely feeling, but I know not how soon he may be called away, and I left here with my dear little ones, without a door to protect us from an attack of prairie wolves, or any other wild animals which might be roving through this new country." I asked the doctor if "he had ever seen any wolves in the grove." "Oh! no," said he, "they stay on the prairie, that is why they are called prairie wolves. They will not hurt us, but they may pick up some of our pigs or chickens; they will not attack a person."

The hardy pioneers, with the approval of the missionary, went to work, and in a few weeks they had a nice, sound log meeting-house, hewed down inside, and the cracks battened up with clapboards. This made it look white and clean. The floor and seats were made of puncheons, as they were called, the door of clapboards, and after being neatly brushed out it was ready for dedication. The next thing was to have a two days' meeting and dedicate it to the Lord.

Brother McKean went for Brother Thomas Hitt, (of early memory) of the Illinois conference, who had moved and located on the west side of Rock river, about six miles distant from the stream, in the suburbs—now—of Mt. Morris, to assist him in the dedication services. It was given out all round the mission. When the day arrived we were astonished to see the congregation. How our hearts glowed with gratitude to the Giver of all our mercies, for this blessing. Never did the hearts of any society, who were about to dedicate a church, worth ten, twenty or thirty thousand dollars, throb with such emotion as did ours. There was no anxious thought as to who would make up, by subscription, or otherwise, the remainder due on the church, for all was paid.

Brother Hitt preached a very appropriate sermon, and the people listened with delight, and with astonishment realized that there, on almost the same ground where the Indian wigwam stood but a few months since, and only the yell of the savage was heard, now there was a Christian church reared, and the sure sound of the gospel trumpet echoed and re-echoed in our hearts, and in the groves (the church was between Lafayette and Washington Groves.)

I think I shall ever recollect the sweet, sacred feeling that pervaded the congregation as they sang those sacred verses, composed by the divine Watts:

> "From all that dwell below the skies,
> Let the Creator's praise arise;
> Let the Redeemer's name be sung,
> Through every land, by every tongue.
>
> Eternal are thy mercies, Lord;
> Eternal truth attend thy word;
> Thy praise shall sound from shore to shore,
> 'Till sun shall rise and set no more.
>
> Your lofty themes, ye mortals bring,
> In songs divinely sing,
> The great salvation loud proclaim,
> And shout for joy the Saviour's name.
>
> In every land begin the song—
> To every land the strain belongs—
> In cheerful sounds all voices raise,
> And fill the world with loudest praise."

The benediction was pronounced and the services closed.

Thus began our acquaintance with the lamented Brother T. Hitt. He was very useful in the settling of this country. He preached nearly every Sabbath, and with great acceptability. He attended all the quarterly, two-days and campmeetings, and labored with much love for the good of precious souls, and a lasting memory should be kept of his untiring labors in founding, building and sustaining the Rock River Seminary. It cost some effort to build and sustain such an institution at that time, I assure you, and had it not been for the sustaining grace of God in our hearts, and his filling our hands with his benefits, we never could have done it. Many a hard day's work did my little boys do hauling lumber from a small water mill, on Kite creek, with which to build. Oh! what labor, what untiring energy it took to accomplish it; but thank and praise the Lord, it was done.

I well recollect the year and day that the corner-stone of that institution was laid; it was on the 4th day of July, 1840—the same year that the Rock River Conference held its first session, commencing Aug. 26, and continuing till Sept. 2d. It held forth in a large tent a few miles from Mt. Morris, on a camp-meeting occasion, two sacred and long to be remembered incidents in the history of the Rock River Conference. I hope it will not be forgotten when the history of that conference is written.

Well do I recollect Bishop Waugh's sermon on that memorable occasion on Sabbath morning—what power there was in that sermon, the spirit of the Lord overshadowed the congregation, the presence of the Most High rested upon us. Many who may read this may remember, with me, that sacred occasion. Bless the Lord for all his benefits, and may He ever abide with the Rock River Conference. Well do I recollect how small that body was then. There are but a few of that venerable company left, although it is but forty-five years since. A few years hence there may not be any left, all having gone over to possess the promised land. But how that body has increased; it now numbers about one hundred and eighty-seven men of talent, men of noble acquirements; oh! may they know what it is to live in the depths of humility, and rise to all the heights of love.

What a power they may be in the salvation of the world if they live at the foot of the cross, with an entire consecration of their all to God and his cause; and oh! what a crown they will have in that day, when He cometh to make up his jewels.

How many of this noble body of men have obtained the better part of their early education at that dear old Rock River Seminary!

Great good has resulted to the church, individuals and community in general. All through the Rock River Conference you will find men of talent, whose characters have been moulded there. Also physicians, lawyers and business men **have received** their education at that Rock River Seminary, and are scattered all through our community. And well may we say that while dear Brother Hitt, and may of his co-laborers, such **as Rev. John** Clark, John **T.** Mitchell, **A. E.** Phelps, and other of the first trustees and agents, have ceased **from their** labors, yet **their** works do follow **them, and** this noble old institution has struggled through many hard waves that threatened its ruin, as a Methodist instiution, **and** through **the** untiring efforts **of its worthy** trustees and noble friends, now stands on a firm **basis,** and is manned with a noble faculty, and bids fair to be more useful in its latter than in its former days. Long may it live to shed its influence over the rising generation.

I remember when we, **a few** Methodists—a handful in comparison to what there is now in the Rock river valley—laid our offerings on that altar, and the Lord accepted and sanctified them, and our children have grown up and shared in its benefits, eight in all, six sons and two daughters, have received the best part of their education there, and have gone out to do battle with the cares of the world, all the better for the kind instruction they received there. Well do I recollect when the noble Mr. Pinckney came to the institution. He was just fresh from the classic hall, his heart warm with the love of God, and deeply imbued with the worth of precious souls; was well calculated to be useful, and nobly did he do his duty. The Lord blessed his labors, and many souls were brought to the knowledge of the truth through his instrumentality. I recollect a sermon he preached in the upper hall, before it was divided up into rooms. Great power attended his words—what a crowd at the altar of prayer; what an earnest struggle there was to enter into life, that is hidden in Christ with God.

We will now call the attention of the reader back to the little log meeting-house. We soon had a day-school and Sabbath school organized, and we all felt quite at home. Brother McKean was faithful to his work—hunting up emigrants who were Methodists or inclined to be, putting them into classes, encouraging them to be faithful, visiting them once in four weeks, that being as often as he could possibly get around. I think there are several districts now, composed mostly of what was "Buffalo Grove Mission." About September, 1836, I think, Bro. McKean had a camp meeting at Elk Horn Grove. Brother Bronson, our presiding elder, preached the Word in powerful eloquence, and many souls were converted; many believing and were sanctified. The conversions were mostly confined to the class of young folks, averaging from ten to fifteen years of age. Some of the brethren were talking to Brother Bronson on the subject, and said they were afraid those young converts would fall out by the way; and some of the brothers and sisters thought the younger children ought to be taken out of the altar. The elder said, "No, no, brothers, that would be wrong. I fear you would grieve the spirit of God if you did so." Just then we heard the shouts of the new-born souls. "That work is of the Lord," said the elder, "I feel it, it comes like electricity to my heart." "Would you let them join the church?" asked a brother. "Yes," replied the elder, "there are ten chances to save them in the church, to one out of the church. Take them in and nurse them, and they will grow up men and women in Christ Jesus. Don't lift your finger against it." Among the converts were my friends the Blackmores, who welcomed us so kindly on our arrival. The son and widowed sister each got religion, and went home rejoicing in the Lord. This added two more to our little class. There were a few more families who moved in, and among them were some Methodists who joined with us. I think the class numbered about twenty-five or more persons at this time.

A few weeks after the camp meeting we suffered the misfortune of having our little church burned down, and for awhile we were compelled to use our little log cabins again, and often they were a blessing to our souls. And we rejoiced in the hope that we would some day enjoy a mansion in our Father's house, where fire could not consume it. By the following spring we had another church built upon almost the same ground. Now there was a small saw mill started in Washington Grove, and we had the logs sawed this time. The church was built of frame, the shingles were made by hand for the roof, and soon Brother Hitt was called to dedicate another church, and still the only one in Rock River Valley.

When we moved to our new home there was not a house in sight, no road except the one we had made traveling from Washington Grove. We named our home "Light House," because it stood upon an eminence, and from the circumstance of our taking in those who were traveling on the "Old Indian Trail," running from Rockyford, (now Rockford) to Dixon, where there was a trading post and a fort. Many travelers would have perished the first winter we were there had it not been for the light I kept in the window, when it was stormy, to direct my husband, and others who might be out in the storm, to the house. There is a strip of timber running up from Rock River, forming a beautiful little grove. This stands on a bluff, and just below it in a large hollow is one of the loveliest springs that ever ran out of the earth. All around it there was a grove of small trees, but now they are large and majestic. Many times have I gone to the top of that bluff, and casting my eyes over that beautiful prairie, I could not see a single human being. I could occasionally see a deer bounding swiftly along, or a wolf skulking—the birds flitting amid the tall grass and lovely prairie flowers. I would reflect thus: Dear Lord, who will settle this beautiful prairie? It will be settled some day without doubt. And then I would kneel and beg the Lord to send some intelligent Christian people among us. This was the constant yearning of my heart.

In the spring of 1837, there came three excellent men from Canada, Brother John Martin, the father of our worthy brothers—Jas., Henry, and J. W. Martin, of the Rock River Conference; the other, Bro. Nathaniel Brown, the brother of Bro. S. Brown, of Light House Point; also Bro. Anthony Wood. They were hunting for a Methodist home. We were glad to welcome them; they found locations to suit them, and then they returned to Canada for their families. In the fall they returned with their families, with Bros. Philip Plants and Amasa Woods accompanying them. About this time Bro. Enoch Wood and Brother Henry Farwell moved in from New York state. They came in Methodist order, bringing their letters with them. The following year brought Bro. Nettleton and Bro. Richard Martin, from Canada. Bro. R. Martin was a local minister, strong in doctrine, very exemplary and useful among us.

Brother Moses Nettleton brought a large family with him. They have grown up to be useful men and women among us. The oldest daughter was married, and I think it was the first wedding in our colony. They now reside at Light House Point, and they have done much to sustain Methodism there. Their home is a resting place for the itinerant and weary pilgrim. Their hearts and hands are ever open to receive and administer to the wants of the friends of Zion. Brother J.

Martin had four sons and one daughter. They were dedicated to the Lord in infancy, and the three older children were converted in Canada. William, a very pious young man, died at the age of 21 or 22 years— the first death in our colony. It was hard to give him up, there was so much promise in his character, and his loss was deeply lamented. Brother Luke Hitchcock preached the funeral sermon at the new frame church. I don't think I ever saw so much deep-felt grief manifested on a funeral occasion. Some who read this may no doubt remember this sad occurrence. Yet they sorrowed not as those who have no hope of immortality and eternal life through our Lord, Jesus Christ. Two were spared, and two more sons were born in Illinois. And now there are three of the sons co-workers and ministers in our Zion; James is in California conference, Henry in Rock River Conference, presiding elder of the Rockford district, John W. in the Minnesota conference.

Brother James Nettleton, youngest son of Moses Nettleton, is a useful member of the M. E. church, and of the official board of Light House Point, ever ready, he and his good wife, for every good word and work.

And still the friends came in from Canada. Soon Brother John McKenney and several of his brothers, and dear old Father and Mother McKenney came with them. Brother John Edmonds came in early time, and settled on a beautiful farm near the large spring and camp ground, and he still lives there, getting rich and doing good. He has done much for the cause of Zion, and has long been a faithful superintendent of the Sabbath school, and prays for its success everywhere. He brought his mother, three sisters and a brother with him. His mother was a pious, devoted Christian, a good tailoress, and was very useful in our colony. The sisters were very good housekeepers, and often did they come and help me, much to my relief, when burdened with labor and care; they always came in the dignity of the lady and the spirit of a Christian. Two of those young ladies were converted soon after they moved to our neighborhood, and joined our class. Sarah, the younger, is the worthy consort of Brother Jas. Nettleton, before mentioned, of Light House Point.

Brother Edmonds and his excellent wife, have raised a large family, have taken a great deal of pains to educate them, and the Lord has converted them, and they bid fair for great usefulness. In their pleasant family I found kind entertainment.

While attending a camp-meeting, on the dear old camp ground, in July, 1869, I formed a brief acquaintance with Doctor and Sister Palmer, the great revivalists. They were very useful, while with us on this camp-meeting occasion, and we hope the Lord will permit them to visit us again.

In the year 1837, Brother Robert DeLap was sent to our charge, but failing in health, he had to return home. Brother Henry Summers was our Presiding Elder, and succeeded in getting Brother Barton Cartwright to supply us; he came, and was acceptable and useful among us.

That fall Brother Isaac Paul was sent to our circuit and he thought there had better be a class formed at our house. This was very congenial with our feelings. He preached and made an effort, and there were twelve united in a class that evening, and John Martin was our class leader.

We had enlarged our cabin that year, and we offered the use of it for a meeting house, and it was gladly accepted, and our humble dwelling was honored with the preaching of the gospel and the presence of the Lord for more than two years. Many precious souls were converted there, and our little class gradually increased.

The next summer Brother Paul thought we would have a campmeeting in the grove, near the spring—I used to go there to do my washing, and under those little trees I had knelt many, many times, and prayed the Lord that there might be a campmeeting there, as the place was so well fitted for it; such excellent water and such a beautiful grove. And now the Lord was about to answer my feeble prayers, and I rejoiced in hope that my children and friends would be converted there. Our oldest son sought and found the Lord at a campmeeting the year before at Elkhorn Grove, on the west side of the river. He had been faithful and joined the class at his home. But there were others of my children who were old enough to know the joys of salvation; and while I was thankful for this token of mercy, I was anxious for the rest of my children.

Brother Paul gave out the announcement of the campmeeting all around the circuit. It was then a four-weeks' circuit, and there was great solicitation and anticipation in regard to it. The time drew near, and the spot was selected for the meeting.

There was a family living in our neighborhood who had been to Michigan on a visit, and came home with the smallpox. They lived near the place selected for the campmeeting. This news flew, as it were, round the circuit—although we had no telegraph then—and the people were much alarmed, and Brothers Rosecrans and Martin, and all the official members thought no one would come to the meeting, and so no preparation was made. Brother Paul came on Monday, and finding this condition of things, went to my husband and inquired of him what he thought, as he had been in attendance on this family through their illness, and he replied that he had "vaccinated all through the neighborhood; that the family was almost well, and the house could be thoroughly cleansed, and he would warrant that no harm would come to anyone." "Well, if you will do that," said Brother Paul in reply, "I will push the meeting." He sent the news by letter, and on horseback, all round the circuit, and himself remained at home and rallied the brethren. He labored intensely, and by Friday evening there were the usual tents on the ground, and the campground well arranged. Brother Summers safely landed, and we had a gracious meeting that night. On Saturday a number more settlers came in, and then we had quite a large congregation. Brother Summers preached and prayed in the spirit. Brother Lumery was there and gave us some of his old-fashioned spiritual preaching, so spiritual that some of the wicked ones called him the "Holy Ghost

Preacher." The spirit of the Lord was upon the people, the place was sacred on account of it. What attention, what religious zeal was manifested there!

But there was another difficulty. The country was overrun by Blacklegs, some called them,—a set of horse-thieves who were stealing horses and cattle, robbing houses, and doing all sorts of mischief, and many of the people feared they would be there, at least on the Sabbath, and do some mischief. Sabbath came, and early in the day the "ring leader" of this set was seen to walk on the ground with a number of suspicious looking characters with him. The ministers kept an eye on them, as they kept pretty closely together; but they were attentive listeners to the preaching, and appeared civil. Many of the congregation were alarmed, but I was not; and told the brothers and sisters if we treated them kindly they would do us no harm, and perhaps the Lord would convert some of them. Brother Summers thought so too. I was acquainted with several of them through the Doctor's practice in their families. I had reason not to fear them, as they respected the Doctor, and would treat me and my friends kindly for his sake, although he was not present, being off visiting the sick. After we had been at dinner at our tent the "leader" came to me and said, "Mrs. Roe, a number of us would like to get some dinner with you if you will take the money for it." "But," said I, "that would be wicked, and I don't think I could do it." "But," he said, "I feel that would be imposing upon you to eat without paying for it, as there have been more than fifty eaten with you already. We shall go away without our dinner unless you will accept something for it." "Well," I replied, "Brother Summers, our elder, is here, and if you will give him something you can leave it on the table by your plates, and I will give it to him as a present from you." Said he, "We wish to give it to you, and you can dispose of it as you see fit." "Well, well," I said, "sit down and eat your dinner." They did so, and when they left I found several dollars on the table, and I gave it all to Brother Summers. They lingered that evening till the meeting was about closed, and then left without doing any harm but taking a saddle off our tent, having seen Brother Law put it there while they were taking their dinner.

The meeting commenced at early candle-light. Brother Lumery preached in the spirit. Brother Paul exhorted, the power of the Lord was in every word, every prayer. What an easy access the child of God had to a throne of grace! Brother Paul called for mourners, the altar was soon crowded, and the cry from the gray haired sinner down to the youth was, "Men and brethren! what shall we do to be saved? God be merciful to me a sinner!" They were directed to believe on the Lord Jesus, and the promises held up to them, and many claimed those precious promises, and found Him of whom Moses and the Prophets did tell. The next morning we had a love feast at the stand, and it was a love feast indeed. There were quite a number who found peace in believing while in the love-feast. Among them were three of Brother Henry Farwell's sons. They were quite youths then. Jackson, the oldest;

Charles, the next; and John V., the third. The two younger now reside in Chicago, and this sacred leaven that was hidden in their hearts that beautiful morning in that little grove has diffused its influence all along their lives.

Brother Summers gave an opportunity to any who wished to join the church, and there was rising of forty united, and most of them joined our class. Among them my second son, F. M. Roe, and Brother Farwell's three sons, Brother Martin's only daughter (Sarah Jane). She lived a faithful, exemplary life, and a few years ago died a happy Christian death, and has gone up to possess the goodly land before her aged parents. But their prospects are bright for an inheritance there. I have kept a Christian watch over that happy group, and never knew but one to willfully and wickedly backslide. That was John Carr, Jr. But he was mercifully reclaimed on his death-bed, I believe in answer to a mother's prayers, and died in a sweet hope. Some others have gone to rest, but many still remain, and are pillars in our church.

Our meeting closed with the best of feelings, and from that time we had a continual revival for two years. And our class increased till it had to be divided, there were more than a hundred members. By this time we had got a frame school house, and held our meetings there. Brother John Clark held the first quarterly meeting in our school house just before he left for Texas. It was a gracious revival. Then we held a protracted meeting for several weeks after. Many souls were savingly converted there, and we were worshipping there when some of the leaders of the desperado gang were captured for murdering one of our best citizens, who was shot within two miles of our school house.

The year before we built our school house Brother Luke Hitchcock was sent to our circuit, and oh! how useful he was in building up our Zion. I recollect he preached his first sermon in our log cabin. Some said he was too proud for our "log cabin Methodism," but they were mistaken in the man. There was a dignified bearing in his appearance and deportment, but oh! how humble, kind and polite he was in all his social relations. I never think of our early acquaintance with him and his excellent wife but with the greatest pleasure and earnest Christian feelings. He was then a young man, but long has the Lord spared him to labor among us. Many long years has he traveled our prairies to preach the everlasting gospel. I often think what a rich reward awaits the veterans of the Rock River and Illinois Conferences. Such laurels as they will wear when He cometh to make up his jewels. Father Cartwright, Jesse Walker, S. H. Thompson, John Sinclair, A. E. Phelps, John Clark, J. T. Mitchell, Hooper Crews, S. H. Stocking, R. Haney, I. Paul, B. Cartwright, L. S. Walker, Jas. McKean, R. R. Blanchard, A. Bronson, Father Mead, Brother Summers, and all such, with many others too numerous to mention here. I think Brother P. Judson traveled our circuit after Brother Hitchcock. Some revivals took place on the circuit, but none in our class. That year we built our parsonage. A good state of religious feeling existed, but no revival this year, as the subject of building a church was under consideration.

The next year Brother L. S. Walker was sent to our charge. The parsonage was finished, and he moved into it with his excellent wife and family. The first donation I ever attended was at the new parsonage. We were glad that we had a home for our preacher, and wished to make a demonstration, so we appointed a day, and as many as could get into the house assembled, and each family that attended took some refreshments for themselves and friends. We had a very pleasant time, had prayers, returned thanks, and retired to our homes, leaving the preacher and family some better off than we found them. That year we had a good revival at the "Old Church," as we began to call it, now that we talked of having a new one. And we talked in earnest; the Doctor offered a lot of three acres, large enough for a church and a burying-ground, and other subscribed liberally, and soon there was enough to justify the building committee to commence. The friends at the old church approved our action, though they could not help us; but after the revival there they were a little more generous, and helped us some. Brother Walker was with us two years, and then Brother Brooks came to our charge. He labored with us acceptably, but we had no revival that year. The church building moved slowly. It was not then as it is now; no iron horse running all over the country. The lumber had to be drawn from Chicago, and the wheat had to be sold for fifty cents per bushel to purchase the lumber with. We expected that things would move slowly, but the hearts of the people were fixed to build a new church, and where there is a will and that will is to the glory of God and the good of souls, there is a way. And it was so in this case. The first builder became discouraged and gave it up, but the contract was then let to our much lamented Brother Woodcock, and it was pushed to the completion, and dedicated to the Lord. There have been many good revivals within its sacred walls. There is a large membership there now, and the officials are mostly made up of our early converts.

Our worthy Brother, Barton Cartwright, who labored with us in those early days, is now the preacher in charge on the Light House circuit. After his arduous labors as Chaplain in Gen. Sherman's army, his family is now living in the little brick parsonage—built more than twenty-four years ago. He has been very useful in that circuit, and I hope the Lord will water his labors with showers of grace, that he may be more useful in his latter than former days.

Our mission is now divided up into several districts, and a great many towns are scattered over the land, and in almost every one you can trace the fruits of Methodism, and I think if the veterans were permitted to view the landscape o'er, their language would be, " Glory to God in the highest!" And what may we not hope for in the next century, if the church continues humble and faithful to her trust!

CHAPTER VIII.

RECOLLECTIONS OF METHODISM IN CHICAGO.

In the fall of 1836 my husband thought it best to move to Chicago, as he was very much worn down with the practice of medicine. Instead of coming to Rock river to be a farmer as he anticipated doing, he had run unavoidably into a heavy practice—there were scarcely any physicians in the country—and it was impossible to get rid of it. He practiced with great success, while the little boys and myself managed to open and improve a large farm. The little log house at the edge of the grove that had answered for kitchen, parlor and bedroom, as well as for a meeting house, for years, had given place to a nice frame house on the broad prairie.

Everything had prospered for us since we came to our new home, and it would take a great while to tell of all the mercies in temporal things, as well as religious, while there, but let me say: "The Lord careth for those who put their trust in Him."

We then owned a half section of land, and everything that was necessary for our comfort on a large farm, but we were both much worn down with the cares and duties of life, and thought it best to rent our farm, move to Chicago, put our children in school and try to rest for a year or two. Our oldest son had studied medicine for two years, and had attended medical lectures at Cincinnati, and he would take up the practice of his father, and we could rest and recruit our health. But contrary to our anticipations or calculations, my husband went into a large practice, but his health improved, and the last year of our stay there his practice was worth $2,500.

We moved to Chicago December, 1846, and there were but two M. E. churches in the city at that time. The great city of the west was then in its infancy, and of course Methodism was weak. The old Clark street church was then in its youth, just finished. Brother Ryan was there, and they had a large number of excellent members such as Brother and Sister Shaw, Bro. and Sister Wheeler, Bro. and Sister Shaddle, Bro. and Sister Lyman, Bro. and Sister Lunt, Bro. and Sister Whitehead, with many others whose names I cannot recall.

Brother S. Bolles presided over the old Canal street charge, and labored with all his untiring zeal and energy. There was a large membership there also, some of the excellent of the earth, such as Brother and Sister Shermen, Bro. and Sister George, Bro. and Sister Wisencraft, Bro. and Sister Hagan, Bro. and Sister Webb, Bro. and Sister Kettlestring, and dear Sister Brown, her husband having passed over the river of death, and entered the Church Triumphant a few weeks before our arrival in Chicago. Brother and Sister Brown were the same (of early memory) at Light House Point. Our names were attached to the Canal street charge. I was placed in Brother Wisencraft's class, and he was a faithful leader. My husband was installed as a leader, and placed on the official board. And indeed we were a live church. alive to duty, and how sweetly we lived and worshipped together.

The old Fort still stood in Chicago, and how I felt when I looked upon it and thought of the time when Father Walker visited us in Springfield (he then had charge of the mission there) and remembering how deeply he was impressed with the importance of planting gospel seed there, and especially of planting it through the instrumentality of the M. E. church, and the deep interest he manifested while he told us about his visits to the old Fort, and his anticipations in regard to the place becoming a great city, and an important point for Methodism, and of the sermons he had preached in the old Fort, while all around was an uncultivated prairie; and while I stood there I looked over the beautiful young city, and I cried out, "What has God wrought here since Father Walker traveled to this mission in 1831? how He has watered the seed that has been sown here; how abundantly it has produced, not only an hundred fold, but a thousand. Behold what a great matter a little fire kindleth!" I would say to the gospel minister, "In the morning sow the seed, and at noon withhold not thine hand," but cry, "Behold! behold the Lamb!"

We had protracted effort and revival influence every winter while we remained there, and the work deepened and spread every year; it could be seen and felt through all the walks of business life, the merchant, lawyer, physician, mechanic and day laborer demonstrated by their daily walk and conversation that they had been with Jesus, and we enjoyed sweet Christian communion at the old tabernacle of a church, and it was made sacred by the presence of the Lord.

Our classes and prayer meetings were such as will be remembered through eternity. I have heard many testify at the love feast to the pardoning mercy of God, and speak of Brother John Clark as being the instrument in the hands of the Lord, whereby they were brought to a knowledge of pardoned sin; others of Brother H. Crews, and of Brother Ryan, and one I heard speak of the first class meeting ever held in Chicago, his name I cannot recollect. He told me the particulars in regard to the meeting, and of many incidents of the mission, the Indians, etc. He had lived in the Fort at the time he spoke of. Well might we say, "What hath Lord wrought in that beautiful city since 1850!"—that was the year we left it.

My husband and four oldest sons left for California while I and my four youngest children started for Mt. Morris, Illinois. Oh! that unfortunate year, how many broken hearted mothers and orphaned children it made! how many sacred family ties were sundered! how many characters and constitutions were ruined! and how much money was lost in seeking after sordid gold eternity only will reveal. But I am thankful to say, my husband and sons, (although they lost everything in worldly goods) came home better men for having been to California; they learned valuable lessons there that they could never have learned anywhere else. They seemed to have a more abiding trust in the Lord. I have never heard of so many going out of any one family and all returning alive.

Among the many tokens of kindness and comforts that I provided for them, I made up a suit of burial clothes, and while I was putting them up and bedewing them with tears, I recollect of offering up a fervent prayer to Him who doeth all things well, that they might not be under the necessity of using them, and they brought them back to me without having undone them, and my husband said to me, "Mother, here is the bundle you gave us, and said we must be careful of them. I am thankful we did not need them." "Oh!" said I, "I am so thankful; I had much rather you would bring them back, and know you did not need them, moneyless as you are, than to have had one of your bodies enrolled in them, and brought me a bag of gold instead." I never had faith to pray for their success in getting gold, but I did have faith and did pray fervently that the Lord would spare their lives and bring them safely home, and this prayer was answered.

Praise the Lord! I am thankful that it ever was written that "if ye ask in faith ye shall receive." Oh! how comforting the grace of God is to my heart in all this trial. The oldest child left with me was a son, John H. Roe, about sixteen years old, and he sought and found mercy at a revival at the good old seminary, and was a devoted Christian, growing in grace every day. There were two daughters and one son son younger. We kept up the family altar, and we surrounded it and poured out our hearts to God, our Redeemer, in fervent prayer morning and evening for sustaining grace and their safety, he (John) leading in prayer one time and I the next, and O, how the Lord blessed us. Oh! what a comfort that child was to me in that season of trial. Can I ever cease to love him, or to praise the Lord for giving me such a child? No, and I hope to praise Him in eternity.

CHAPTER IX.

RECOLLECTIONS OF PAYNES POINT.

When they returned, it was thought best to locate on a farm on the east side of Rock River near Paynes Point, about seven miles from our first home in Ogle County. Fifteen years previous, my husband helped to build the first two log houses which were put up in Paynes Point. They still stand comfortable houses yet, and were tenanted by some of our best citizens when we came to the Point in 1851, one by Brother Augustus Austin.

About two miles east of the Point, on the old road leading from Oregon, seat of Ogle County, to Chicago, we built a comfortable little stone house, and moved into it November 6th.

Our old friends welcomed us back. My husband commenced practicing, with his usual success, the boys to improving the farm. When we came to the Point there was a small class there. Our names were attached to it. We met in a school house, with Brother L. Hitchcock presiding elder, Brother Wing, preacher in charge, Brothers Sovereign, Wadsworth and Campfield, local preachers who preached alternately, so we had preaching every Sabbath. Here I have heard the worthy old veteran Father Puffer preach. He was strong on doctrinal points. Here I heard Brother Campbell preach, then a local preacher, but formerly a preacher on Light House circuit. I heard him preach a powerful sermon at Paynes Point two or three years previous, when Brother A. Phelps was preacher in charge. I think that Brother L. G. Walker took the Point into the itinerant work when he was traveling Light House circuit. In answer to a request from Sister Taylor, George Taylor's wife, I have heard Brother Sharp, of Canada Conference, then local preacher, who afterwards moved to California,—preach in sister Taylor's cabin in early times. Sister Taylor was a woman of strong faith, very exemplary in life, lived faithfully and died a happy death. She used to attend meetings at our log cabin at Light House. She was anxious to have her house taken in as a preaching place then, the circuit was so large, but the circuit was cut up and changed so afterward, that Brother Walker took it into the charge.

There was another family by the name of Taylor who were useful in those early days in planting Methodism at the Point. Mother Taylor was a humble, exemplary Christian. Her prayers went up like holy incense to Him who heareth prayer, that there might be people there whose hearts were fixed to serve the Lord, that there might be a church erected there. And her prayers were answered. She lived to see it and enjoy its privileges in her last days. She was nearly ninety years of age. I saw her not long before she departed, at a quarterly meeting, she was exulting in redeeming grace and dying love. She spoke of the comforts of religion along the journey of her long life, and her prospects of entering into rest, and a few months afterward she fell asleep in Jesus.

I think the first revival influence at Paynes Point was through the instrumentality of Brother Wing, the winter previous to our removal there. There were a number of converts, among whom was Sister Eleanor Gray Taylor, George Taylor's only daughter, who afterwards married my third son, Giles B. Roe. She was received into full connection after we came to the Point by Brother L. Hitchcock, at quarterly meeting held in the grove. She was a faithful Christian until her death, which took place on the 10th day of January, 1863. She left her devoted family to unite with her sainted mother to praise the Lord through eternity.

Brother Wardsworth, a local preacher, mentioned before, was a very early settler. His life has been mostly devoted to the local ministry of the M. E. church. In his house the itinerant has always found a welcome home, made so by the kind hospitality and Christian spirit of him and his devoted wife, Mary Wardsworth. Their names were attached to this class when it was first organized, and faithfully have they labored to build up and sustain the church of their early choice. They were formerly from New York State. They were anxious to do all in their power to build up Methodism around them; but now there was a time that called for all their liberality and energy. There must be a church built at Paynes Point, the little school house would not hold the congregation any longer.

Brother Wardsworth signed liberally and circulated a subscription paper. There were more than a thousand dollars subscribed, a building committee appointed, Bros. A. Austin, J. Butterfield and Wardsworth, being the members of that body, and they went at it with zeal and energy. The lumber was to be hauled from Rockford, the stone to be dug for the foundation, and a great deal of hard labor to be done; but they had some faithful co-workers, and it was accomplished, and we had a nice large church standing at the edge of a beautiful grove, looking so dignified—a credit to the builders, to the neighborhood and the Methodist church—and now it was to be furnished. Sisters Wardsworth and Butterfield took a horse and buggy and went from place to place, until they secured the means to do that, and the church was dedicated, the whole cost being about fifteen hundred dollars. The remainder was raised the day of the dedication, and the church was free.

Brothers L. Hitchcock and H. L. Martin were the preachers in charge. There was a protracted meeting continued from the dedication, and Brother Martin labored faithfully, and with the help of the local brethren the meeting continued six weeks. It was good sleighing, and the people came from a distance. The house was crowded, and there were scores of souls brought to the knowledge of grace. My fourth son, M. C. Roe, among the rest, was savingly converted and united with the church.

Most of these converts are living and faithful. Some of them have gone to glory, and others have gone forth to bless the world, with an orderly walk, and a Christian example, while others remain there holding up the Christian standard, hoping and praying for another shower of mercy.

CHAPTER X.

RECOLLECTIONS OF ROCKFORD AND OUR NEW HOME ON THE PRAIRIE.

In June, 1856, we sold our new home at Paynes Point and bought some new land farther east about five miles, and a piece of land in the suburbs of the beautiful city of Rockford, and built us a nice house, and thought we would settle down there and enjoy social and religious life in our declining years, as we had battled long with frontier life.

When we first knew Rockford it was nothing more than the Rocky ford of Rock river, with a few log houses near it, but now it was a beautiful city. But I remember that those log houses, some of them, were built and occupied by praying people, one by Brother and Sister Samuel Gregory, another by Brother and Sister David Beers. Another faithful servant of the Most High was Sister Enoch. Long and fervently did she pray and labor for the prosperity of Zion, and especially the church of Rockford, and the Lord permitted her to see it bud and blossom as the rose, and she passed over in triumph to the Promised Land.

Those five persons constituted the first class organized at Rocky Ford in 1836. It was formed by Bro. Wm. Royal, then traveling on the Fox River Mission. If I mistake not he formed a class at Belvidere, and Brother and Sister Mason formed a part of that class. How faithful and diligent were our frontier ministers in hunting up the lambs of the fold, forming classes, and appointing leaders who, like good shepherds, led them to living streams and into green pastures, while they inspired them to faithful endurance, amid all the difficulties and hardships of frontier life, and together they were enabled to hold up the standard of truth, which is mighty, and will always prevail. Great will be their reward.

These dear brethren at Rockyford had their family altar erected in their little log cabins, and had their weekly prayer meetings. They poured out their souls to Him who heareth and answereth the fervent prayer of faith, and sent them a preacher. Brother Royal sought and found them, and left them an appointment: this encouraged them very much. The first I learned of them, as a regular charge, was in 1838, then it was embraced in the Chicago district, Brother John Clark, presiding elder, L. S. Walker, preacher in charge. These brothers did much to sustain Methodism in Rockford that year. I have heard Brother Gregory speak of them and many others of the early Methodists of Rockford.

The preaching of the Word was blessed, the class increased rapidly, and when Brother Bolles had charge of the circuit they had a gracious revival, and they were enabled to build a nice brick church, and there are still many of the standard-bearers holding on to the faith once delivered to the Saints.

The first winter I lived in Rockford was a season of great revival in the First Methodist church, as yet the only one there. There were scores of souls brought into the fold of God that winter; many are now pillars in the church. Brother Reed in charge, preached in the power and demonstration of the spirit. Every word seemed to be seasoned with grace and sanctified to the hearers' benefit, saint and sinner, and the work prospered, and the people devised great things, and soon the Court Street church was built, and then the Third Street, and now another in South Rockford, and their membership now numbers about twelve hundred persons. Soon they will need another.

These churches have been blest with seasons of revivals. May the Head of the church still be with them, and the heralds of grace preach the pure old Methodist doctrine "Salvation by faith on the Son of God," and there will be a sacred hallow shedding its sacred influence over the surrounding country, from the Rockford station. It is a beautiful growing city, and I attribute much of its prosperity and success to the piety of its early inhabitants. To God be all the glory!

After we got settled in Rockford, we did not feel altogether satisfied. We felt as though we were not occupying the right ground exactly, and concluded to come out and improve our new land. It was situated in the southeast part of White Rock Township, about six miles north of Lane Station, and one mile from the road leading from Lane Station to Rockford. We built a small house and moved into it. There were but a few neighbors, no class, and not even a school house to worship in. At Lane Station there was a small class but no church, they worshipped in the district school house. We were again on missionary ground. We handed our letters back to Paynes Point charge, and the friends gave us a warm welcome. I told the Doctor this looked like frontier life again. "But," said I, "we will have a church here some time." And he replied, "It does not look much like it now." "I have seen worse chances than this for a church," I again said. "Oh! ye of little faith, believe and ye shall receive."

That fall there was a school house built in the adjoining district, and in the spring we prevailed upon Brother Wardsworth, whom I mention in the preceeding chapter, to give us an appointment and see if we could get a congregation. He left an appointment, and the seats of the school house were comfortably filled, and they manifested so much interest that Brother Wardsworth left another appointment, although he had to travel thirteen miles. The congregation increased, and he continued his appointments, once in four weeks. In the winter following, he labored in the revival at Paynes Point. In the spring he sent us another appointment, and by this time there were a good many moved in, and our school house was filled. Brother Wardsworth was quite encouraged, and said he wished some of the circuit preachers would take us into their charge, either the Lane charge, or Lynnville charge, which lies still north of us.

The doctor saw the preachers on both charges, and urged them to come and preach for us, but they thought it impossible. Brother Wardsworth would say to us sometimes, "Well, Brother and Sister Roe, this seems something like your early pioneer life, does it not? away out here, without any church or any of your classmates?" I replied, "Yes, it does, but we are on the stepstone of better days; we shall have a meeting house here sometime." He and the doctor would laugh at me and say, by way of encouraging me, "It is a long way ahead; I fear we wont get one in Lane." "You'll see," was my reply, "I have faith to believe."

The first year we were here, Father Hayes built across the road from us. This was a comfort to us, for they were old and tried friends of ours in this new country, although we had lived most of the time ten or twelve miles apart. Brother Hayes was a member of the Paynes Point charge, and had given liberally to the building of the new church at that place, as well as ourselves. To live so near together was a privilege that we enjoyed. Their children were settled near, and made a good share of our congregation.

That fall the doctor and I went to our last quarterly meeting at the Point, and besought Brother H. L. Martin to represent us at the Conference and try and get us attached to the Lane charge. Brother Hannah was sent to that charge with an appointment for Roe's school house. He preached for us once in two weeks,

He formed a class, and there were twelve persons united. He labored with us two years with great acceptability.

Brother Wardsworth promised us a protracted meeting, and I think in the latter part of October he commenced the meeting. Brother Hannah preached and Brother Wardsworth exhorted and conducted the prayer meetings; he also visited every family within two miles of the school house, and there was a great turn out of attentive hearers, and the seed fell in good soil, and produced good fruit, and there was a general awakening and quite a number of converts, among them Brother and Sister Emory Hayes, Sister Elizabeth Hayes, Brother Hiram Hayes' wife, and one of Father Hayes' daughters who lived at home, Miss Minnie, and John Gilcrist, a young man who lived at Father Hayes', Brother David Hayes' wife, Mary Ann, and our youngest daughter, Frances Maria Roe, united with us, and we felt it quite an accession to our little class. Father Hayes was like the good old patriarch, ready to say, "Now, dear Lord, let me depart in peace, I have seen all my children converted." Oh! what joy we felt in this token of mercy; and now, when I talked about a meeting house, they were not quite so doubtful.

Bro. Hannah was with us two years, and labored faithfully in word and doctrine, and now the brethren began to talk of building a church in Lane—they had built a small parsonage.

Bro. Brookens came on the circuit and went to work with his usual zeal and energy, and had a protracted meeting at the school house that winter. It was attended with much good, there being several conversions. Among them were, John Conlin, Bro. and Sister Mills, who united with our class. The next year Bro. Brookens returned to Lane and had a protracted meeting in the basement of the church, that part of the edifice being completed—the upper portion was not yet finished. The meeting resulted well, there being a number of conversions.

The next year Bro. Plum labored with us, but there was no revival that year. The next year, lamented Bro. Crackeren labored with us, preached faithfully, but no revival. The year following Bro. Page was with us. He was a fine speaker and a strong reasoner. He commenced a protracted meeting in our school house. The weather was very unfavorable, yet much good attended the effort. There were three conversions, and four accessions by letter from the Congregational church.

During those years we had three quarterly meetings in our school house, the first, while Bro. Hannah was with us, Bro. Kease presiding elder. I well recollect a remark he made when we drove up with a two-horse wagon with a table and the preparations for the sacrament, quite like old frontier life. The doctor was away from home, and as he was steward and class leader, I felt it my duty to prepare and take those things.

The next was while Bro. Brookens was with us, Bro. Jewett presiding elder. He was there in due time. I saw him take his shawl, roll it up, and put it into the window opposite the stand where a pane of glass had been broken out. Oh! how mortified I felt.

I offered a fervent prayer to the Lord to open the way whereby we might have a comfortable place to worship in. He could not preach with that cold air rushing in upon him; but oh! what a sermon he did preach for us, with his blanket shawl for a defence. I then began to talk more earnestly about building a meeting house, but it was thought quite impossible, while they were building at Lane.

The next quarterly meeting was held while Bro. Page was with us, Bro. John Gibson, presiding elder. The school house was too small, and we went to a beautiful grove near by. Bro. Gibson preached in the spirit, and the Word was borne home to the hearts of some. Bro. Page called for mourners and there were a few went forward for prayers. This was the last quarterly meeting Bro. Gibson held on our circuit.

Previous to this meeting there was a subscription paper circulated for a meeting house in our neighborhood, as the Lane church was finished and dedicated. The doctor told the brethren and friends that he would give one hundred dollars and a site on the northwest corner of his farm if they would accept of it. and the subscription was circulated with the view of its being built there, and there were twelve hundred dollars subscribed, and a building committee appointed, but they concluded that the doctor's site would not answer; they would have to have a north or west front, and they preferred a south front. And now Bro. H. Hayes offered a site for a south front, and he being one of the building committee, he took the oversight of the building, and it was hurried to speedy completion.

The conference of 1864 sent our much esteemed friend and Bro. L. S. Walker (of early memory) to the Lane charge. He came on and we welcomed him with all our hearts, and it brought the fond recollections of former days, when the Lord was precious, and we enjoyed sweet Christian communion together, as well as social relations with him and his dear family when they lived in the little brick parsonage near our home at Light House Point. We prayed most fervently that the Lord would make them useful on our charge. He commenced his labors with a Christian confidence and a sweet reliance on Him who had been his shield and strength for lo! these many years, hoping and praying that the Lord would revive his work all through the charge. There were then four appointments.

Our church was near completion when he arrived, and he did all in his power to forward it, and it was finished and dedicated on the 12th day of January, 1865. The dedication services were conducted by Rev. M. Raymond, of Evanston. There was a power in his sermon that reached every heart. The house was crowded.

The building committee reported a deficiency of $1,200. This was in consequence of the rise in building material and the price of labor. It was made up in a short time, and the dedicatory ceremonies was conducted in the most solemn manner, and I felt that the house was the Lord's, and my heart said, "Amen; praise the Lord! I have seen the desire of my heart." And I felt in that hour that the Lord would revive His work in that sacred place.

Bro. Walker made an effort just then for a protracted meeting, but owing to bad weather, and other obstacles, it was not prosecuted, although there was some good done. We passed through that conference year with a good state of religious feeling, our congregation increasing all the while.

Bro. Walker preached many faithful sermons for us, and the conference of 1865 returned him to the Lane charge. He was well received and preached with great earnestness, and seemed to have the weight of souls on his heart. He promised us a protracted meeting in the fall, but there were hindrances with the farmers until about the 20th of January, '66, then our meeting commenced. The preaching and praying were fervent, the congregation increasing, and was mostly made up of the heads of young families and young people. There were many of the congregation who were powerfully awakened, but were not willing to come out and take a stand for the Lord. Bro. Walker told them from the pulpit, what he thought, and urged upon them the great responsibility that rested upon them while they stood in the way of others. Our beloved Bro. Begle was with a local brother who belonged to the Lane class, also Bro. Haymaker; they both labored with great acceptability. These local brethren had labored with great success in our other protracted efforts, and while Bro. Walker urged these responsibilities upon the congregation, having given the opportunity to kneel at the altar for prayer Bro. Wm. H. King walked forward to the altar, and said, " Now, my dear friends, I want you to pray for me, I am in earnest, I want to seek the Lord, I fear *I am* in the way of others, and if so, I want to get out of the way." And as he advanced still nearer the altar, he said, " Now, my dear friends, if you follow me, you will follow me to the good world, for by the grace of God I mean to find it." And he knelt down, and one after another and still another of his friends followed him, until there were quite a number. Then the congregation knelt in fervent prayer. Oh! what earnestness was felt and manifested there on that sacred spot which had so lately been dedicated to the Most High. Oh! what emotion filled the hearts of those who had watched every expression manifested by those dear friends and kind neighbors whom we had prayed for so long and felt so anxious they should come and taste the joys of pardoning love, and what joy we felt, as one after another they arose and spoke of the goodness of God in sparing them; to see that sacred sight and then speak of the joys of salvation and their resolutions to serve the Lord all their days. The cloud was broken, and victory was on Israel's side.

From that time on for as much as five weeks, the altar was crowded with mourners every night. We held noon-day prayer meetings, and they were precious seasons. There we heard the young convert tell of the joy in believing on the Lord Jesus, and hear one after another say, " The Lord has converted my children, my father, my mother, my sister and brother and my neighbor." And so on; and there wrestle "Jacob-like" until the blessing came, and the Saviour gave us His new and best name, Love.

The work went on and on, until every house in the

neighborhood became a house of prayer; and the accessions to our class were over seventy persons, and we hope they will live faithful and be triumphant in death. Some of the converts joined other churches. the Baptist and the Presbyterian.

Bro. Weller, the Presbyterian minister, came up from Lane, and preached for us several times, and when the meetings closed there were three classes formed and prayer meetings appointed for different places, where there were several conversions. Two years have elapsed and the most of them are faithful members yet, and to Him who hath loved us and washed us in His atoning blood, be Glory and Dominion forever!

CHAPTER XI.

VISIT TO NEBRASKA.

We left our new home, as we called it in a former chapter, situated on a beautiful prairie in Ogle county, White Rock township, six miles north of Rochelle, on the twelfth day of June, 1868—the next day after I was 63 years old, and the doctor in his 68th year, would be 68 on the 20th day of August. We got our tickets and were seated in a splendid car on the great Northwestern railroad leading from Chicago to Omaha, Nebraska, at six o'clock in the evening.

We had just sold our new home for four thousand dollars, and felt it our duty to lay out at least a part of it in land in Nebraska, and now started there for that purpose, and to visit two sons who resided in Iowa near Cedar Rapids. I assure you, kind friends, we did not leave that comfortable home where we had resided for a number of years without deep emotion. The last child had gone out and left us to battle with life's cares alone, while they made a home for themselves and families, and they were settled some distance from us, and we were lonely, and thought we would lay out a good part of the money we had in land, and part in improvements, and try to draw our children to a new country where we might all be united in our efforts to do good and derive good.

With this great desire we started, but not without a pang of regret at leaving the pleasant home where we had supposed we would most likely spend the remnant of our days; where we had seen the great wild prairie bud and blossom as the rose; where the Lord had converted so many of our dear kind neighbors, and the last one of our dear children whom we had prayed for so anxiously for years; where we had had many struggles with the enemy, always obtaining the victory through divine grace, all of which cost some effort, I assure you, and had we not felt that it was our duty to go forward we should have given it up. But we felt that we were in the path of duty, and that our Heavenly Father was leading and directing us.

Having learned by long experience that the pathway of duty is always the pathway of safety, we felt that we leaned upon the Arm that moved the universe, and we went forward. And I must say that while my dear husband and I walked around the place to take a last look at what was our once happy home, but which we had now sold to another, that there was such a spirit of thanks and praise and humble gratitude to our Heavenly Parent pervaded our souls that we scarcely felt a tint of sorrow in parting with it. My husband said, "Oh! mother, how good the Lord has been to grant us the desire of our heart in the conversion of our kind neighbors and children, and permitting us to see that neat little church built and honored with the conversion of many souls in it. And now, if we go willingly and happily to Nebraska we may see all there that we have here."

"But I fear not," said I, "we are getting old."

"But," said he, "many of our friends thought it impossible we would ever see this orchard bear, but see what lovely fruit we have, and we may live to have it there. The Lord always blesses the diligent hand, and I feel almost as willing and able to work as I did when we began here. So we will put our trust in the Lord and go forward."

"But," said I, "don't you regret to leave this nice farm where we have taken so much comfort and done so much hard work?"

"Oh, no; the Lord has blessed our labors here, and He will bless us there if we put our trust in Him. We have labored hard to make it comfortable; we have enjoyed it, and I hope they will."

"Pa," said I, "those are my sentiments exactly." And we never mentioned our nice home again. We got our business arranged, and started as remarked at the beginning of this chapter, and went on our way rejoicing.

It was thought best that our youngest son, Malcom C. Roe, who was practicing medicine with his father, should go with us, and we found it very pleasant to have him seated at our side in the car.

We traveled very pleasantly—the cars were heavily loaded—and safely through a lovely country; crossed the Mississippi river on the new bridge in safety although it creaked so we were somewhat alarmed; passed through Clinton, then a nice flourishing city, and many other pleasant towns, and arrived at the large and prosperous city of Cedar Rapids. They left some cars there, and we went whirling on to Fairfax station, eight miles farther on. We got off on the platform just as the clock struck two—there was no depot—and found our way as best we could by inquiring. There came up quite a severe shower just as we left the car, and we stopped under an awning in front of a store, and a dog rushed out and commenced barking furiously, and I was very much frightened for fear they would shoot us for burglars; but they heard us talking and calmed down. We went to the store in the morning and had a good laugh over our burglar scare. The shower ceased, and we found our children next door.

We were much pleased to meet them and find them well. The other sons lived but a few miles distant—the eldest U. C. Roe, a physician and local preacher, the younger, Mathey C. Roe, a carpenter by trade, but was just commencing on a farm—had just finished Fairview church. Since he came to the neighborhood he had formed a class and was its leader; had built a church, and had preaching regularly every Sabbath only about one year and a half. Well done for a new country, thought we. The oldest son preached for us Sabbath, and we had a good class-meeting, and we enjoyed the sermon very much.

Monday morning the train was on time, and we went on our way rejoicing. The weather was lovely; the fields were waving with grain, promising thirty or forty bushels to the acre. We were very much pleased to notice that in almost every depot town there was at least one, and sometimes two or three nice small churches, and one good school house. This spoke well for the enterprise and thrift of the people of our new country. Even Fairfax, although it was a small place, was struggling to build two new churches. I feared there would be some strife among them, but hoped that it would be nothing more than good religious zeal and energy, each aspiring to do the most good in the shortest time, and I prayed the Lord to help them in their efforts to promote His glory and save precious souls.

While at Fairfax we attended a Sunday-school picnic—this was on our return from the far west—as a celebration of our National Independence, that was a a credit to the new settlement. It was near the Fairview church, and was managed mostly by their class and Sabbath-school. They marched in a column from the church to a beautiful grove about half a mile from the church. Here we had the good old Declaration of Independence read by a young man of promising talent, Mr. Megar; a very appropriate speech by Rev. Gordon, of Cedar Rapids; good music by the Keystone choir, and a splendid dinner. Many scholars and teachers, and a large company of very intelligent people present, evinced the deep solicitude felt in the Sabbath-school cause, and this spirit seemed to pervade the whole country.

I would not fail to mention that Iowa has several splendid literary institutions to boast of. The Mount Vernon, the oldest, stands on a beautiful eminence, and is a splendid building. A beautiful slope from the railroad to the college pavement, I would say, is one of nature's beauty spots. Energy and enterprise have done much to beautify it, and the very scenery is calculated to induce study. Long may it live to bless this redeemed world! We also saw the State Agricultural College. This is a splendid edifice, and is located near the center of the state. The building displays a great deal of taste, and, as it stands on a beautiful eminence, we had a nice view of it from the train. It has done much for the culture of the state.

We also saw a small tribe of Indians near the Iowa river. It was a very broken, hilly region, such as we saw nowhere else in the State. Their dirty little huts or wigwams were huddled together in little groups on the hill sides, exhibiting filth, want and destitution. We saw a number of squaws hoeing corn in small fields or patches near the huts, while the Indians lay lounging on the ground or sitting on large stumps, covered only with a few rags and their heads all trimmed off with feathers. When the cars passed them they yelled like Indians. The car windows were crowded full to see them. Oh! how I pitied those poor squaws, and the whole tribe or tribes, as my mind glanced at the contrast. How thankful we should be that we live in a gospel land and among a people who fear the Lord. I earnestly pray the Lord that some means may be devised by which this great, and in some degree, a noble race may be brought under the influence of the gospel of our dear Redeemer, and into the covenant of grace. What a change it would produce in their relations to each other, to the world, and to that better world.

We passed on over nearly two hundred miles in that dark night, only knowing that we were passing over prairie country, over bridges, through strips of timber, and occasionally stopping at a depot to leave mail; but upon returning on the same road in the day time we found the country to be very similar to the northeastern part of Iowa, but not so well settled. About seven o'clock we came in view of Council Bluffs. We rode a good many miles in sight of these bluffs before we came up to them and arrived at the city. These bluffs are covered with a green verdure, composed of a fine, soft grass, looking much like velvet. The railroad runs near their base along the Missouri river bottom. Being covered with this velvity verdure makes them perfectly beautiful, oh! magnificent! I never saw anything in creation that proclaimed more clearly that the Hand that made us is divine. Such a continuous chain of them for miles, such beautiful peaks, such deep gorges and gulches—they seemed to vie with one another to see which would be the most singularly formed. I can think of nothing more like it than great banks rolling one against the other, and all covered with green velvet carpet. I suppose they do not look so magnicent when the green verdure has passed away. The anxious passengers, and there were a great many of them on board,—many of them land viewers bound for Nebraska,—were glad, very glad, to see the city, and hear the conductor cry out, "Council Bluffs," for it was now after eight o'clock, and the train was due a little after seven. We had had nothing to eat since we left Boone Station; there is a splendid eating house there, well arranged, well furnished with every comfort that could be found on any railroad, east or west, and we were all very glad to see a place where we could get refreshments. Immediately after landing upon the platform we were accosted by one of the proprietors of the Commercial Hotel, I. P. Bushnell, who politely enquired if we wished entertainment in a kind tone of voice, while the other men and boys ran around crying at the top of their voices, "This way, this way, right to such a place, or such a hotel." The doctor told the gentleman he would go with him. He drove the cab politely to the platform and helped us in very kindly, drove to his hotel, and then furnished a good warm breakfast, which we did justice to I assure you. We soon learned that we had missed connection with the train that would have taken us from Council Bluffs to Brownville, but at three o'clock another train went down on the St. Joe & Missouri Valley road.

After breakfast Mr. Bushnell spent some time in the parlor, and from him we learned some very interesting incidents connected with the early settlement of Council Bluffs. It was then a small place, and was overrun with Mormons, who had stopped here in their retreat to Salt Lake City, after having been routed from Northern Illinois. About this time a Methodist minister by the name of William Simpson came to the place in pursuit of horse-thieves, and he saw the great importance of establishing a charge there under the control of the Methodist conference and endeavored to do so. A Mormon elder by the name of Hyde felt that he was encroaching upon his influence, and opposed and persecuted him very much. But Bro. Simpson labored there for several years with success, subdued the Mormon influence and built a church costing a considerable sum, and established a regular charge there. They have had successive revivals, and in 1868 built another church costing $23,000, which was dedicated by Bro. Eddy, editor of the *Northwestern Chrtstian Advocate*. They now number 383 members. Other denominations labored and succeeded, and are doing well, and since the railroads have been built through that city it has grown rapidly, and there is a good religious influence there. Mr. Bushnell is a smart and intelligent young man; has had the advantages of an excellent college situated at Iowa City. He is well calculated for any business, but his aim was to become a gospel minister. My husband, son and myself were well pleased with his acquaintance. Long may he live to bless the world.

Three o'clock arrived, and we were quite ready to go, and our host conducted us safely to the cars—there was no depot—and we had to get off on some boards. The road was not finished, only worked down opposite Brownsville, but the train would not go to the terminus. That evening we got within seven miles of Brownsville, put up a splendid tavern which had just been finished to accommodate travelers. We found in our host an old acquaintance of Chicago; had a pleasant visit with the family; made an early start, and run down to Phelps, opposite Brownsville; there they helped us out on some boards and into a cab which awaited us from Brownsville, which was on the opposite side of the Missouri river. So I had the pleasure of riding on the first steamboat that ever run on the Hudson river, and the first steam passenger car that run on the Missouri River Valley road there at Brownsville. All the land hunters that went into Nebraska crossed the Missouri river. It was then thought the rearest route to the land office that was open for entry.

Mr. Brown drove us safely to the river, which was three miles distant, and when we got there we learned, to our disappointment, that the steam ferry boat had sunk a few day previous, and there was no way to cross the river but in an old scow—an old ferry boat they had used for years—and I shuddered at the thought— oh! that turbulent, muddy river—but the ferryman said it was perfectly safe. My husband said he "thought it was safe," and I told him that "One thing I knew, that we leaned upon the Arm that moved the universe, and duty called, and I hoped the Lord would preserve us." Myself and husband went onto the boat, and one after another came aboard until there were as many as ten men on the boat, and they loaded in several barrels of eggs and kegs of butter from a grocery near by, and we moved slowly from the shore, and oh! how my heart throbbed, but those beautiful lines came to my mind, "When through the deep waters I call thee to go, the rivers of woe shall thee not overflow." The ferry man was very cautious. The water was very still, and we moved slowly, and after some time arrived safely at the other shore.

A very genteel young man, who was proprietor of the Star Hotel, which was near the bank of the river, met us, took our satchel and politely conducted us to his residence, where everything was in order. As we passed through the hall to the parlor, we saw Dr. Molony, of Belvidere, Ill., whom we were quite intimately acquainted with. He came into the parlor and we had a very pleasant greeting. He had been out into Richardson county, Neb., to visit his farm of 5000 acres, where he had two sons at work, besides a number of hands improving the land; had a very large peach orchard, and would probably raise 500 bushels of peaches that year. The Doctor was anxiously waiting for a boat to come down the river, on which he intended going down the stream to some point, take the cars, and return to Belvidere. The Doctor was a great land speculator, and he, with many others, have bought up large tracts of the very best land in Nebraska—bought it up with college scrip which was sold only a few years ago by that State, thus shutting out the homesteader, and the country is not settled up around there yet. They held the land at $5 per acre, but had bought it for 60 cts. an acre with scrip.

Brownsville was a very prosperous town, made so by the new settlers in the country lying back of it; was the County Seat of Otoe county, which was bounded by Richardson, Johnson, Gage, etc. The settlers all hauled their goods, groceries and lumber from that place. It is the most romantic place I ever saw; churches and houses sit upon the very top of the Missouri bluffs, and were finished in the latest style, and looked as if they might be tipped over the steep embankment by the first storm which might strike them. But some of them have stood there for many years. It was long years ago a trading post for the Indians. There were some good buildings put up then, and many of the maret here still, and there are many enterprising men in Brownsville.

The land office was there for many years; my husband and son went there, as others did, to get some field plots to enter and buy. Our friend Mayberry met us there, and they found the gentleman in the land office very kind and polite. They got their field notes, hired a nice double livery rig, and went off to look for land. We traveled through a good deal of Richardson county, and went into the southeast part of Gage county; found our old friend and neighbor, Tobin, settled on a nice farm of half a section, one hundred acres of which was in nice wheat and corn. They had left our neighborhood in Ogle county, Ill., about fifteen months previous, but they still lived in their camp, which was made of logs at the bottom, and boarded up the sides and over the top, but it was somewhat shattered and looked dangerous to sleep in, so we took supper with them and then went on to "Pap Tyler's," as he was called by everybody who knew them, real kind-hearted old people, who lived on the east bank of the Big Blue river. They provided entertainment for all the traveling community. We were splendidly entertained over Sunday. We learned from Bro. Tobin and Bro. Tyler's folks that there would be circuit preaching at Blue Springs by Bro. Mann, on Sunday at twelve o'clock, and Sunday-school at half past ten, and were much pleased with this information.

Blue Springs was a little town just laid out on the west side of the Big Blue river, the largest stream running through that part of the country. Near this town are three large springs situated closely together, the water is very blue, which gave the place its name. There had been a severe rain while we were at Brownsville, and had raised the river so it was not safe to drive our carriage across; but Bro. Tobin said he would come up and bring his big wagon, and take us over to church and Sabbath-school. I don't think I ever saw a nicer stream than the Blue, it is like the springs, unusually blue, and glides over beautiful white rocks and has very steep banks. It takes an experienced person to drive safely through, but Uncle Tobin had experience, and he took us safely to the western bank of the beautiful Big Blue, and drove up to the double log house where the preaching was to be. In Blue Springs were found, on the bank of the river a saw mill, and grist mill, partly enclosed; one dry goods store, Hodge & Hanson, proprietors; one blacksmith shop; a shoe shop; two or three very small board houses, and in the log building where the preaching and Sabbath-school were to be, a family lived in one end, and the post office and a small grocery occupied the front end; and there were three or four traveling tents pitched upon the village green, which were filled with emigrants. After the sermon a small but interesting Sabbath-school was held. The congregation poured in till there was not a seat to be had; the natives gave away to the new emigrants and then stood up as long as one could crowd in; those who could not get in stood around the door and two small windows, until there was quite a circle. The preacher pressed in, and took quite a dilapidated chair which was set for him. He was a fine looking man, but any one could see from the expression of his features that he was very much depressed in spirits from some cause. He arose, stepped behind the chair, opened the Bible and read a chapter, read a hymn, and the congregation joined in and sang it with tones of deep-felt melody such as touch the heart. Oh! what an earnest, solemn rendering of thanks arose from the hearts of those people! What an earnest beseeching the Lord for continued mercy. And while on our bended knees we felt that the Lord overshadowed us, and every one felt that the Lord was present. We arose and Bro. Mann took for his text. "What will it profit a man if he gain the whole world and lose his soul," and preached a heart-comforting sermon. At the close he told us that that would necessarily be his last sermon, for awhile at least, that his family was suffering, and he must go down to the river and hunt up some work to supply his family with food; being a mechanic, he thought he might get some work there.

The class-leader arose and said, "Brethren, we are all so near Bro. Mann's condition that it will be difficult for us to do much, but it will not do to let him leave this work; we will pass the hat and see what we can do to-day, and the official board must make some arrangements for him and his family right away. It is even as he said; they are suffering. I was at his house a day or two since, and they had nothing but corn bread and wild gooseberries, cooked without sugar, to eat, and corn coffee to drink." The hat was passed and $8 were collected. Bro. Mann was in charge of what was called Club Creek Circuit, but now changed to Blue Spring Circuit. It is a noble circuit now, supporting three preachers well.

In after days, when we moved to that country, we found Bro. Mann at his post laboring for precious souls, and have heard him say more than once that that eight dollars seemed to do him more good than one hundred at many other times in life. He had a wife and four children. He preached twice and often three times every Sunday, and frequently through the week; a deeply pious man; has filled some important positions in that conference.

We succeeded in securing one eighty acre tract of land in Blue Springs neighborhood, went on from there to Sicily Creek, about twelve miles, passed over some nice prairie land, found some nice new farms near the stream; met Bro. Mann at Bro. Knight's; took dinner with them, and through their instrumentality, secured another eighty-acre lot of land near Sicily creek. They then had a class of twelve or fourteen, and many of the members were very intelligent, although they lived in log huts, and some in dugouts, and had an earnest of an inheritance above, a house not made with hands, eternal in the heavens —blessed hope!

I often think of our trip to Blue Springs on that blessed Sabbath morn, as we were seated in Bro. Tobin's nice large wagon driving down the creek valley to the ford, the beautiful stream gliding by over the large white rocks on one side, and the mountain range of beautiful building stone which rose in a solid mass as high as sixty or one hundred feet on the east bank, the bottom land spreading out from the stream, and all along the bank of the creek the large oak and walnut trees spread out their mighty arms to protect us from the rays of the sun, while the feathered tribe flitted through them, proclaiming that the Hand which made us is divine; and while passing down the road to the crossing in rather a meditative frame of mind, Mrs. Tobin looked up with a radiant smile lighting up her features and her black eyes glistening with joy—she did not speak very good English—while she said, "Tobin, Tobin, I did not think we should have the Doctor's folks here in this new country to go to church with us so soon when we parted with them in our nice new church. I am so glad, I am so glad!" "That is so," said Bro. Tobin. We rode along for a few minutes in silence, reflecting upon the singular Providence which had brought us together under such pleasant circumstances.

When we bid them farewell, the evening before they started for Nebraska, it was in the nice new church which both families had helped to build; where the Lord had converted each other's children and dear neighbors; and where, eighteen months previous, we had expected to remain the rest of our days; where we both had comfortable homes, and Bro. Tobin had just built him a splendid house just the year before; and now, on this beautiful Sabbath morning, we met in the wilds of Nebraska, glad to assemble in a small log room to worship the Lord, some weeping and others smiling, and I assure you, reader, there was deep feeling. The Doctor remarked, "Brother Tobin, if we are faithful to duty, do all we can to set up the banner of the Lord, we shall see souls converted and churches built in this country." Just then we arrived at the ford and the Doctor remarked, "Ma, here is the Big Blue river we have been told so much about." "And," I remarked, "the half has not been told." "It is surely so," said he. We drove up to the little log house, got out of the wagon and entered the little church, and truly the Lord was with us.

The next day, when we met Bro. Mann with a few other brethren, we felt and realized that they were children of the Lord. We left Sicily Creek with Bro. Mann, and he directed us to some land he thought nearer to the road than it really was. We found several pieces, but the doctor did not think they would pay to enter. But we lost our compass. There were but a very few roads here, and we lost ours. Bro. Mann invited us to go to his house to stay that night, but we did not make it, and so put up at a log hotel, or part log and part boards, on the Fort Carney road leading from St. Joe to Fort Carney, the road upon which all the provisions for the Fort, and over which all the Californian emigration passed. We stayed all night there, and early next morning the doctor and son and friend Mayberry took a scout around the country for about fifteen miles, but found no land to secure by entry. There was lots and lots of beautiful land and water and some timber, but all entered by the college scrip or at government price, $1.25. And the gentlemen came home to the tavern all discouraged. The doctor said he would go back to Iowa and pay $5.00 per acre for land before he would buy such land as he found there, and we loaded up and started for home. We crossed the Blue, and drove through Beatrice, and the land looked better and better every mile we traveled, and my husband would remark, "What splendid land." When we got within about ten miles of Beatrice, the doctor remarked, "Boys, if I could buy this land for two or three dollars per acre I would give it." Mayberry said, "Well, doctor I will take you to a man right off who has three sections in one body that he will sell. He has five hundred acres broke, and has twenty teams at work breaking." We soon began to see the teams, and soon saw the old gentleman himself mounted upon his pony, and riding to and fro among them. We drove up to him, and Mr. Mayberry gave us an introduction and told him that the doctor wished to buy a section of land. The doctor said, "Will you sell?" "Yes, sir, one or more sections if you wish," said the gentleman. "At what price?" "Two and a half for the sections which have no breaking, and five for those that have breaking, or two hundred and fifty dollars a section." We looked the land over, and the doctor told him he would take the unbroken section at $2.50 per acre. Mr. Newhall said he would come to the tavern where we were going to stay, and go with us to Brownsville and make out the deed, and we bid him good evening. At eight o'clock in the morning he was on hand, and we drove to Brownsville that day, distant about forty miles. The next day we had our papers made out, and on the morrow started for home. Mr. Walker took us over that dreadful river in a sail boat, there being no steamboat yet.

The last night we stayed at the Brownsville tavern there were nine states represented by emigrants hunting land. All had bought more or less, but most of them were speculators.

We had a very pleasant time at Brownsville; formed the acquaintance of quite a number of Christians, Mr. Dorsey, Methodist; Mr. Lett, Presbyterian, both of whom were very intelligent business men, and had held positions in the land office, and had been citizens there for twelve or fifteen years. They gave us a good deal of interesting information in regard to the progress of business and society in the community; they were acquainted with all the enterprises of the day and hour; they were there when there was nothing but a few log huts there; they had helped to build a splendid school house and several churches, a Baptist, a Methodist and a Presbyterian. They invited us out to a strawberry festival. There were some as fine residences in Brownsville as I ever saw, and each one of those gentlemen owned one of them. The Dorsey family were among the first residents in the town, and Father Dorsey died there a number of years previous.

I think we lift Brownsville the 28th of June on the Valley railroad, and while we had been gone they had put up a good depot and tavern, and we had a nice platform to get out on—quite an improvement for such a new county. We had a very pleasant ride to

Council Bluffs; got there just in time to get onto the Northwestern train for the east—about seven o'clock. We rode all night, and arrived in Boonsboro just in time for a splendid breakfast, and from there hurried on and got off at Fairfax about twelve o'clock; found our children all well; stopped a few days with them and then started for our home in Ogle county, delighted with our trip and the new country, and we had traveled all that distance, and had not heard one bit of profane language or seen a drunken man.

Our children prevailed upon us to stop in Malta, DeKalb county—two of them lived near there—and we concluded to do so, until they could get ready and go with us. We bought some property there, fixed us up a nice home, as we thought perhaps we might have to wait a year or two. But we were not satisfied, as we felt that duty called us west, and we felt as though we ought to influence our children to go west, as we believed it would be of great advantage to them, in a pecuniary sense, and they could also be so useful in that new country, and it would be so pleasant to have them settle near us—in the same county at least.

We spent the winter very pleasantly at Malta. We helped them build a church there, the first Methodist church built in that place. They had helped the Baptists build, and occupied their church every other Sabbath until they had boarded out their money, and then did the same with the Congregationalists and boarded that out. And now it was time to build for themselves. So they went at it in earnest, and built a nice church, and then they had a gracious revival.

Many precious souls **were** converted through Bro. Bunker's influence. **We** stayed there until spring, and then concluded that, as our children were **not** getting ready to go with **us, we** would have to go alone and drive the stakes. **We** hoped they would rally around our new home, and we offered each one who would go with **us** or follow after us 160 acres of land, but they all had comfortable small homes, and money was very scarce through the country and they could **not sell,** and so could not go, but we hoped they would come as **soon as** they disposed **of their** effects. We continued **to get** ready. Our youngest son, who went with us to **visit** Nebraska, had **just** returned from Bennett Medical College, Chicago, a few months previous, and was opening up **a nice** practice in and around the village, and his **friends urged** him **to stay** and his wife inclined **to stay with her** friends; so we found we were **to** go **alone.** One grandson, M. P. Roe, volunteered to go with **us, and** we hired another man, Michael Shelly. Chartered a car, loaded it with furniture, wagon and team, plows and harrows, five barrels of flour, barrel of pork, butter, pickles, forty bushels of potatoes, and started it westward, the hired man on board to take care of the horses and our favorite dog, Ponto. **The** doctor, myself and grandson left on the passenger train that night at three o'clock, sad to leave our dear children and many dear friends behind, but feeling that we were in the pathway **of** duty, that the Lord was guiding us, and hoping **that** good would come out of it, we were cheerful.

The doctor took considerable medicine with him.

He had been keeping a drug store in connection with a grocery through the winter while at Malta, had decided not to travel and practice any more, but to prescribe at his office. This he did a great deal, but frequently his friends would prevail upon him to go with them on the cars and prescribe for difficult cases, who were not able to come to him. He did not intend to ride and practice in that new country.

We overtook our freight car at Cedar Rapids all safe. They were to lay over there for the Sabbath, but we went on to Fairfax, and stopped with our children. We spent the Sabbath together, and attended two new churches—the Methodist in the forenoon and Presbyterian in the afternoon. They were both finished off in fine style.

Monday morning our freight car passed us under good headway all safe, and the hired man gave the signal. At twelve o'clock we boarded the passenger train and pursued our journey very pleasantly, and about dusk we overtook our freight again all right, and here they dropped off one passenger car, and the Doctor prevailed on the conductor to couple on our freight car. It was very gratifying to us, to know we were all on the same train and under good headway. We passed on swiftly and safely, and about daylight arrived at Council Bluffs; got our breakfast at a good hotel; found our friends whom we had known on our former visit all well, and they gave us a hearty welcome.

The next thing was to get our car shipped onto the Missouri Valley road. It cost us twenty-five dollars to do this, and it was to run down the road to a new station just opposite Nebraska City—I don't think they had named the station yet—but the freight would not reach there till the next morning at ten o'clock. We boarded the passenger train and went that far that evening, and when we arrived there we found that the depot agent had gone to Illinois to get married, and in his place was a cross, illnatured fop. We inquired for a tavern. "There is none, and you can't stay here," said he. The Doctor replied, "I guess we can stay; I see there are quite a number of folks who appear as though they are staying here; I see two or three houses here." "Well, they can take care of themselves," said the agent. "Well," said I, "we can stay in the depot." "No you can't," said he, "we do not let people stay in our depot."

Just then a very fine looking young man spoke up and said, "Grandpa, and Grandma, if you are not very particular, I think you can get pretty good entertainment at my boarding house; the house is not finished up, but it is pretty comfortable for this warm weather, and their board is good; there are also some nice old people stopping there, and you will enjoy their company." "Thank you, kind sir," said I, "we will go with you, and you must accept our gratitude for the respect shown us by yourself."

He advanced across the road and we followed. He showed us in and introduced us to the kind folks as some "travelers who wanted lodgings for the night." They kindly replied, "We will do the very best we can for them; we have one bedroom that is lathed, and we can finish another in time to sleep in," and, from the rapid tap, tap of hammers, it would seem as though their predictions would be fulfilled. There were two bedrooms with quilts hung around the lathes for the old folks, while the young men slept on the diningroom floor; and the hotel keeper and lady occupied the kitchen; thus we were all comfortably situated for the night—after having partaken of an excellent supper—and I assure you we were very grateful to those kind people for their hospitality. The unkind fop would gladly have seen us lie out doors.

We slept well and awoke much refreshed. The sun arose bright and cheerful, but soon went under a cloud, or the cloud went over the sun. We could hear the muttering thunder and see the lightning flash, and just as our freight train appeared on the track, the rain and hail came down in a perfect tempest, but our car was safely uncoupled and run onto the side-track. That cloud passed by, and then another, and so on the whole day and night. But those old people were very intelligent, and they done all they could to make it pleasant for us. Their children were very kind; gave us good board and plenty of it, and on the whole we were quite comfortable.

The next morning was calm and lovely over head, but oh! that Missouri mud, I never saw anything like it. The Doctor tried to get to the river, but it was impossible—mud knee deep, and in many places sloughs of water up to a man's waist. He came back and said we would have to be resigned to our fate, and went to unloading our car; had taken the horses out the day before and put them in a not very good stable, but they stood it pretty well. That day the Doctor looked around and tried to hire two or three teams with which to take us to the neighborhood where our land was situated, four miles from Crab Orchard, on the emigrant trail leading from Nebraska City to Fort Kearney, in Gage county; but they did not succeed very well, only secured one team.

They loaded up early the next morning and we bid farewell to our kind friends and started, I on top of our wagon load seated on the spring seat, while the Doctor acted as teamster; but we had not traveled but a few rods when I lost my balance and fell to the ground, but by a great effort I managed to light on my feet, and here the mud was ankle deep. I made my way to a knoll that was covered with old leaves, and drew off my shoes and stockings and waded through the mud to the river, which was about half a mile, through dense woods. The teams got there first, and they were a perfect daub of mud, and the men had to scrape the wheels several times while on the road.

We crossed the river in safety, and I was thankful to place my feet on Nebraska soil once more, after having washed them in the Missouri river and dressed them. The Doctor and I concluded to walk through the city that we might view the largest city in our adopted state, and what had been the Capital until within eighteen months, when it had been moved to Lincoln. We saw some very fine business blocks, nice churches, school houses and beautiful residences with lovely surroundings, and some of the nicest gardens and nurseries that I ever saw; we could scarcely believe it, although we saw it with our own eyes, all was so lovely; and all this was once a wild

Indian territory, but was now under such fine improvement, and families out of the city, on the Fort Kearney road, had their large farms and splendid buildings.

As soon as we got onto Nebraska soil we had good roads, except the sloughs, and there we had tugging, I assure you, yet the teams stood up pretty well under the travel. We expected, or hoped to reach a very good tavern that evening, in the edge of the DeKalb settlement, which located there three years previous, but about sundown we had to drive through a bad slough, and there got stuck. We worried for some time but to no avail. There was but one small house in sight, which was two miles from the tavern. The men concluded to go to the house and see if they could get a team with which to take me there, and see if we could stay there—the house was about a half mile distant. Both of our teams were in the slough. The kind folks said we could stay, but had but one bed, and no provisions but bread and milk. The gentleman got out his team and came to our assistance, and by this time it was almost dark. They concluded to drive in with the team and get some beds, bedding and provisions, and take me to the house, and the men would take off the teams and bring them up and leave the wagons until morning. I was thankful to find a place where I could sit down.

They had two or three chairs, and the lady, a kind-hearted soul, offered to get the supper; said she, "Grandma, you look so tired, you had better lie down." I was tired, sick and lame. I did lie down on the beds they had thrown down on the floor, and oh! how good **rest did seem to** me, and I soon became unconscious to all around me. Pretty soon the Doctor awoke me for supper. I took some refreshments, and the kind lady fixed her and me a very comfortable bed on the bedstead, and I went to bed, thankful that I was so well provided for. She fixed the rest of the beds on the floor as best she could.

I had not been asleep long when I was awakened by something falling on my face and hands, similar to fine hail. I called out to **the** Doctor, "Please get **a** light, there is something falling on my **face and** hands, and all over the bed." This aroused the lady, and she remarked, "It is only the dirt falling out of the sod which our **house is made of**, and when the wind blows, now **it has become dry, it** crumbles off, and **we are so** used to it that it **does** not disturb us." So the Doctor did not strike a light, **and the rest fell asleep**, but I could not sleep, for **I was** afraid every minute that the whole roof would fall **in on us**. But morning came; the roof was still **on the** house, and we were all alive and **very** thankful that we **were** as comfortable as we **were**.

The men folks went early and dug out our wagons and brought them to the house. We ate our breakfast, reloaded our wagons, bid our friends adieu, and went on our way, cheered with the hope of reaching our future home that day; arrived at Bro. Howard's, on Yankee creek, near the line between Johnson and Gage counties, on the Johnson side, about sundown— about four miles from our section of new land, with no breaking on it except the hedgerow. Never shall I forget the kindness we received from Bro. Howard's family. They allowed us to remain with them until we could get up a shanty to cover our heads so we could get some prairie broke up on which to raise a crop for the next year. Bro. Howard sold us some logs for sleepers for our house, grandson and the hired man, cut and hauled them up to our section the next day, while Doctor and Bro. Corbin, one of our Ogle county friends whom we were very glad to find in the neighborhood, went six miles to a small steam mill, where they ground corn and sawed lumber, and got some cottonwood lumber and hauled it up to our place. It was now Saturday evening. We spent the Sabbath with Bro. Howard's family very pleasantly. They had a large log house, in which were two large rooms below and some other rooms above; had two sons and two interesting daughters and a niece who made their home with them. One son, James Howard, and a son-in-law, Mr. Brown, who lived near them, came home on Sunday. We had some excellent singing and a prayermeeting. Oh! how we rejoiced to think we had found a people who feared the Lord. Those good folks had been there seven years; had just come when they had the great Indian stampede. It was something like this: There came a runner through the country purporting to be from Fort Kearney, crying, "Flee for your lives, the Indians have taken the Fort, and are killing every family they come to!" Bro. Howard had his misgivings about the report in the first place, but soon the settlers began to pour into their neighborhood on their way to Brownsville; every hour there would come a new recruit. Bro. Howard advised them to take a stand there and see what would be the result. They came pell mell, some without hats or shoes; some in their night clothes, with very little provisions, some without **any,** until there were two hundred or more men, women and children on the ground before sundown. Each family felt it their duty to communicate the news to their neighbors as soon as they received it, and it reached a good many. Bro. Howard and his neighbors contributed to their comfort **as far as was** within their power in clothes and provisions.

The next day they were **a little** more composed, as the Indians had not appeared, and **many of** them began to think, with **Bro. Howard,** that the messenger **who, a few** hours **previous, they** considered to be their **best** friend, was **an** unprincipled scalawag. Some of the men went in search **of** him, but could **hear** nothing of him. They gradually left and returned to their respective **homes, and** to their **joy,** found them as they had **left them, and** they never **had** another Indian scare.

Monday morning came, full **of** sunshine **and** joy. The news **that** the Doctor's folks had come, ran all through the neighborhood, and **a** good many of the men came to see if they could do anything to assist us—there were about **a dozen** families within four miles—(Bro. Howard kept the stage office, and Bro. Dillworth the post office.) The Doctor secured **a** carpenter to help him. He had discharged the teamster we had brought from the river; got another wagon and **team,** loaded on our goods and drove to our new home, and it was very necessary that I should go along to cook for **the** men.

We had a lot of shrubbery in boxes, with a little dirt in the bottom, and if I had a moment to spare I wanted to be setting that out in our hedgerow, and put in some garden seed, as it was then the first day of June.

The men soon had the floor down and the stove up, and I had a good warm dinner on the table in the bright sunshine, and they all partook of it cheerfully; then the hammers went tip-tap putting up scantling and boards, while the hired man broke the hedgerow, and by sundown we had our rooms almost enclosed and a temporary roof on the house, sufficient to cover our beds; had our shrubbery set out and quite a garden made. We ate supper, and by nine o'clock were comfortably situated for the night. We hung up some quilts and carpet in the part of the house that was not yet boarded up—they had worked up all the lumber.

I looked and looked all day to see if we had any neighbors, but could see only a little sod hut about two miles distant. Most of the people settled near the timber and water, but when it became dark I could see the glimmer of a lamp light in that sod hut. Oh, how it cheered my heart. We awoke refreshed. The Dr. cheerfully started teams after some lumber and shingles, to Tecumseh, nineteen miles away. Thought they would be back that night.

We took the cotton wood we used for our roof and made a small window; made a door and fixed some shelves to set things on. We left our cupboard at the river with many other things—two heavy loads in all—which we could not bring until we got a roof to cover them. Night came but **no lumber,** which did **not** arrive until ten o'clock the next morning. We spread **some** tarred paper **over our** beds that kept off the **dew.** When the teams came next day they had not a shingle on board, but the promise of some in a few days. They had **a** lot of stock boards and some scantling.

The men went to work and put up the rafters and nailed on the sheathing, and this made us quite comfortable, as it shut out the **sun, and** we began to feel quite at home. The **Doctor had** bought a very fine cow for forty dollars.

The kind neighbors brought **us in** quantities of beautiful lettuce, raddishes, **onions** and new potatoes, and some one came to welcome **us every** day, some from as far as ten **miles.** All seemed **so** pleased to think they **had** a good, old experienced physician in the neighborhood, although they did not expect him **to** ride much. We had been there nearly a **week,** the weather had been very fine, and we had enjoyed ourselves very well, only we feared **getting a** wetting if **it** should rain.

We spent Sunday afternoon **in** writing to our friends, telling of our safe arrival and kind reception; that we had found a number of Illinois friends there, Mr. Corbin, Mr. Filley and Mr. Shaw; that they had all come to **see** us and were pleased to find us so comfortable. After finishing our letters we all retired for the night, as we thought, to have a good night's rest, but about two o'clock there came a severe shower, and the rain poured down through the sheeting onto the beds, and through the carpet **onto** our beds below,

The men began to hustle down the ladder, but oh! there was no refuge there, for the rain poured down through the cracks of the chamber floor in streams as large as one's finger, and before daylight everything was as wet as if they had been taken out of a river. The men stretched some umbrellas over the stove, kindled a fire and I got breakfast. The rain slacked up a little, and by noon they began to think of going after the shingles, but found it so slippery that it would not do to attempt it that day. We stood it as well as we could that day by putting on one wrapper after another; when one would become saturated we would wring it out and hang it on some posts the men had fixed up out doors between showers; the wind blew and they would dry some. The Doctor would hold the umbrella over me and the stove while I cooked the meals, and by nightfall it had cleared away and ceased raining, and I fixed the beds as comfortable as I could by taking every thing we had in trunks and boxes. We went to bed, and were quite comfortable in comparison to the night before.

Morning came and brought us a lovely sunrise. My grandson said, "Grandma, give me a bite of breakfast and I will see if I can't get those shingles here and get a roof over your head before you and grandpa suffer this way again." He was soon off, and by four o'clock arrived with the shingles. Everything else was laid aside, even the two breaking teams were stopped—Bro. Corbin was plowing for us —and he took a hammer and went to work. The Doctor, my grandson and Bro. Corbin all worked with energy, I assure, for there was a cloud in the west, and we feared another rain storm. By night they had the last shingle nailed on the west side of the shanty; I had the beds, quilts, etc., all nicely dried, and we set the beds on the west side of the house so the roof would shelter us a good deal if it should rain. But we were spared a wetting, and by noon they had a splendid roof on, the only frame building there was to be seen from Tecumseh, the County Seat of Johnson county, to Beatrice, the County Seat of Gage county, a distance of about thirty-five miles. It was called the "half-way frame house," by a great many.

Now we had been there ten days, had built our frame house, broke up eight acres of prairie, and had it planted in corn, squashes, pumpkins, melons and cucumbers, and our shrubbery out, garden made, sweet potato plants set, and I assure you it began to look like home. There is not many young people who could have done better than we did. We hired some men to dig and wall up a well close to the shanty door. We bought another quarter section of land lying on Yankee creek that had forty acres of timber on it, some of the best in the county; so we had wood and water.

The Doctor hired some teams to haul stone from Mr. Filley's quarry, five miles distant, calculating to build a stone house—the country abounded with splendid building stone, but none very near us.

In about three weeks after our arrival our best horse took sick and died, but a kind providence opened the way so we were enabled to buy another span, although horses were very scarce and high at that time. So we had three horses to plow with, and succeeded in breaking up forty acres that summer.

We had been to Bro. Howard's to prayer meeting two or three times. They were in hopes of having a preacher appointed to their charge at the next conference. There we learned that there would be a quarterly meeting on the 5th of July at Beatrice. They were to have a celebration on the 4th, on the bank of the Big Blue river in a beautiful grove, and Bro. Leman was to be the orator of the day on the Fourth, and the presiding elder on Sunday.

We did not get out to the celebration, but started early and got to the quarterly meeting in time for the love feast; and how surprised and delighted we were to find such a large congregation so comfortably situated in that beautiful grove, where we could hear the water, not of the Junietta, but the Big Blue river, rippling over the lovely white rocks on its way to the Father of Waters, adding a deep solemnity to the devotion of the hour. We had a love feast indeed, glad to mingle together in Christian devotion on the very ground and in the grove where the yell of the savage Indian was heretofore only heard, and the posts of their wigwams still stood. Bro. Leman preached us a sacred gospel sermon, and the congregation seemed to realize that they were in the presence of the Most High. His theme was, "Salvation by faith on the Son of God," at the close of which the elder took up a collection for the supprort of the gospel. We were much surprised when we heard the report of the steward—twenty dollars—especially as the day before was the Fourth. The elder remarked that there was "more than his allowance, such a thing as seldom occurred; what shall be done with it?" One of the stewards replied, "Put it in your pocket, Elder, to pay your horse keeping, I see you had to put it up at the tavern." The Elder then administered the sacrament to nearly one hundred communicants. I understood there were a number of them members of the Congregational church. A good many the Methodists had come a distance of ten, fifteen and twenty miles. We then received the benediction. We found Bro. Ellwood, the preacher in charge, to be the minister who labored so faithfully in the great revival at Rochelle, Ill., and we had a warm greeting, I assure you, and we were kindly invited to his house, met his dear family with great pleasure; formed a good many new acquaintances; found Bro. Dorsey there, whose acquaintance we made at Brownsville in the land office, but he had since moved to Beatrice. We then and there made the acquaintance of Bro. Dorsey's dear old mother, whose family was among the first settlers of Brownsville; they helped set up the banner of the Lord, and nobly did they sustain every effort that was made to spread the influence of literature, science and religion over that new country. The old gentleman had gone to his reward, and the dear old lady was ready to enter that rest that remains for those who love and serve the Lord, and a short time after, bid adieu to mortality with a bright prospect of an endless life, through Christ, our Redeemer. We stayed all night, made some purchases, and returned home in safety.

We now began to think we were in a country where

the gospel was pretty well established. The Capital was prospering nicely, and other public buildings were going up rapidly, and the city settling with a very intelligent and religious class of people; our county offices were filled with enterprising men, and we hoped to see the time when the thousands of acres of rich prairie that lay around would be settled by an intelligent, religious community.

We began to think seriously of building a more comfortable house for winter. We concluded we would have to give up the idea of building of stone, as there were several streams between our place and the best stone quary, over which there were no bridges. They got stuck several times and lost their stone in the creek, and finally gave it up and concluded to get out some limestone that was on our side of Mud creek to underpin with and build a frame house, for if they got stuck there they could be pulled out by farmers as they went to Brownsville to market their wheat, and they would be glad to take on a light load of lumber and bring it through for us quite reasonable, and we settled our minds to do so.

The boys got out and hauled the stone, while the Doctor and Mr. Corbin laid the underpinning. We found a good carpenter near by; the farmers brought on the lumber; the Doctor, Bro. Corbin and my grandson all worked on the siding and shingling, and by the middle of September we had up a good large frame house indeed, with a brick chimney, ready to occupy, all but the lathing and plastering—the lath, lime and hair were in Brownsville. Bro. Corbin wanted to return to Illinois for his family, so Morris

P. Roe, our grandson, took him to Brownsville, near fifty miles distant, and brought the material for plastering. We had two good large rooms above and below, one below much the largest, so that we could have religious meetings in it.

Some one had to go to Illinois to attend to some business. The Doctor thought I could attend to it as well as he, and I had better go and he stay to see to having the house plastered and made comfortable by the time I returned. I could go very safely with Bro. Corbin. I hoped my son, the young Doctor, and his family, whom we left at Malta, would come back with me. I got ready, and in a few days we were on our way to Brownsville. We crossed the Missouri river on the new steam ferryboat, Mr Rodgers as polite and kind as ever; got an early start, and by four o'clock we were safely landed, Mr. Corbin in Rochelle with his family, and I with my dear children in Malta. I found them quite in the mind to go home with me. The young doctor said he could not think of our living out there away from our children, and he felt it his duty to go home with me, and his wife consented to go. So in a few weeks we had our business all arranged and on our way. The Doctor's wife and children were on the cars with me. We had a pleasant trip, arrived safely, found all well to the joy of all. The Doctor drove through with a span of horses and a buggy; found the roads pretty bad, but got to the Missouri river in about twelve days, but the river was frozen over so the ferryboat could not run, but not sufficiently to bear up a team, and he had to stay there eight or ten days.

I wrote to the Doctor as soon as the children had decided to return home with me, and he was delighted with the idea. Just about this time the scarlet fever broke out at Crab Orchard and up and down Yankee creek. Up to this time the Doctor had not prescribed but a few times away from home, but constantly at our frame house, as it was called, every day, more or less, he was extracting teeth, lancing tumors, etc. They came to him from twenty mile around, as we could not think of his taking those long rides; we felt as though he had done his duty at that in Illinois.

The settlers on the creek bottom were very unhealthy, as they invariably used the creek water, and lived in dugouts or sod houses. The Doctor advised them to get out on high land, and dig wells, and where they did so it was a great improvement to their health. But now this awful disease had broken out and was very severe. We were looking for our son, the young doctor, and wished to hold the practice for him. He consented to go, and met with his usual success; but when the fever first broke out the people were not aware of the danger—and everybody goes to see the sick in a new country—and it spread very rapidly.

The young doctor arrived in safety, about the 28th of December and went right into the practice and relieved his father. We had some neighbors, a Mr. Gale, who bought a section of land of Mr. Newhall's partner, who had two hundred and fifty acres broke on it—had moved in on it while I was in Illinois—and brought two other families, a son and son-in-law. They went in and stopped with the Doctor until they could build them a house **similar to** our summer house, only much large, **and** papered **it** with heavy paper, which made it quite comfortable. They built on the northwest corner of their section, and we built on our northwest corner, that made **the** distance **between our** houses one mile, although our sections cornered—their southeast and our northwest corners joined. But I cannot tell the comfort it **was to** our hearts when we realized **that we had** kind neighbors within a mile of us.

They thought we **must** take Christmas dinner **with** them. Christmas came, but no young doctor arrived. This was a great disappointment to all, but we went, hoping **every moment that he would** come; but he did not arrive until next **morning about** ten o'clock. We were permitted to **welcome him to our** new home, which was warm **and** comfortable and contained plenty to eat, with joy. **We** related to **him** the particulars of the arrival of our kind neighbors, and the pleasant interview **we** had **with** them **the day** before, and the promise we had from them to return the favor on New Years day. This was very gratifying to him. He had **worried a** great deal about our being out there so far from neighbors, with no **one to care** for **us if** we were sick, or **to** bury us if we should die. He could scarcely realize that he **was** at our new home in the west, but it was so.

We had not gotten over our first gush of joy when a nice looking old gentleman rode **up to** the door and inquired if the young doctor had arrived—the whole neighborhood was in anxious expectation of his arrival. The Doctor answered, "Yes, Bro. Andrews, he has just arrived; I hope there is no one sick that you need his services." "Yes," said he, "We have some very sick children at our house, and we want him to go to them as soon as possible; and there are others in the neighborhood who are sick, and I know they will want him. "Well," said the Doctor, "wont you come in and take dinner with us? it is just ready, then I think he will go with you." The old gentleman came in, and Morris P. Roe fed his horse. The young doctor requested that his father go with him until he became a little acquainted with the people. His father consented, and they were off for Mud creek. When they arrived they found the people living in a dugout which was covered with mud and straw, and contained two or three rooms, and three very sick children.

They had not been there but a very short time when a gentleman came in to see if they had the Doctor there; "Yes," was the reply. "I am glad to hear it; I hope now we will not have to go fifteen or twenty miles for a doctor and then not get him." After an introduction, the gentleman asked him to go to his house, which was about half a mile distant, saying there were "two or three very sick children at his house, and in others." As soon as they had prescribed for those they were with, they went to the next house, and so on, until they had visited four or five families, and prescribed for twelve or fifteen patients. This was a pretty good call for the first day. The fact was, they all had good crops of wheat, but had put off their threshing until cold weather, and they had nothing but old tattered shoes, some of the boys having none; they all had to help each other. They had been very much exposed, and as all lived in sod houses or dugouts, were all taken down pretty much alike, the disease being pneumonia, and some were very sick, while others were not so bad. This took them until ten o'clock, and we were glad to see them safe home again.

The next morning they went into the scarlet fever district; some were better, while others were just coming down. All were very thankful to see the new doctor, feeling he would relieve his father. He was very successful in prescribing for his patients. Those on Mud creek lost none but very small children, and this success gave him all he could do, and from day to day his practice increased. Our house was full of patients from a distance; they were chronic cases, caused by living in sod houses and dugouts. The doctors urged them to build on high land; haul their wheat to the river, get lumber and build, if it was but small houses. They did so as fast as they possibly could, and by the next spring the country wore a different aspect, and many who were almost gone with chronic diseases were much improved.

We had a pleasant, open winter, with one or two light falls of snow, but at no time was it an inch deep. We raised an abundance of very fine vegetables, and the fall was crowned with large quantities of grapes, wild fruits, and the finest of wild plums, and we gathered them by the bag full. We had raised a considerable crop of sorghum, and had it manufactured into molasses at a nice mill within two miles of our place. We put up a great deal of the fruit in the sorghum—the nicest I ever saw.

Soon after the young doctor came we bought two hundred pounds of very nice pork at ten cents per pound, and all the wheat we needed at fifty cents a bushel; so we were provided with an abundance for the winter, warm house and plenty of wood and water, and felt very much at home. Our friends met with us on New Years day, as anticipated, and we had a nice, social time.

The spring opened nicely. We had twenty acres of wheat sown and our crop of oats in by the 15th of April. We thought we would set out a nice grove of cottonwood on the west side of our house. The Doctor took help and went to Mud creek and took up several thousand nice cottonwood scions, and he and I set them out. Then we went to Yankee creek and got a number of gooseberry, raspberry and plum bushes, mountain cherries and some nice elm shade trees, and the Doctor and I set them out with our own hands; we also set out a nice strawberry bed. There came along a fruit peddler, of whom we bought fifty apple trees, some Siberian, also cherry and plum trees, and set them out. We then went to Mr. Filley's and bought fifty peach scions. They had brought the seeds with them, and had planted them, and they were then fit to set out, and we had planted quite a number of peach seeds we had taken with us; and we also planted some grape roots which we had brought with us, and I assure you, our place began to look as though somebody lived there, and intended to improve it, and dear husband and I enjoyed it very much. We thought if we should not live to enjoy the benefit of our labor, our children might, and we did it, not only with pleasure, but with delight. The Doctor cultivated it with a sulky plow which he bought for the purpose, kept it perfectly clear of weeds, and it grew nicely indeed.

The young Doctor's wife was a little homesick for a little while, but as she became acquainted with the people and the country, she liked it very well, and we found in Mr. Gales' family, and their children's family, very kind neighbors and pleasant associates. Their children were near the age of the Doctor and wife, and they enjoyed each others' society very much.

We had a preacher on the Crab Orchard charge and could attend preaching there every two weeks. Mr. Elijah Filley and a few others organized a school board and levied a tax on a large district including a good deal of speculators' land, and built a splendid stone school house and furnished it with charts and globes, and started a splendid school. We were invited to have our meetings there. We had held meetings in the large room we had arranged for that purpose in our new house, and at one time we sent fifteen miles for Bro. Ellwood to come and hold a protracted meeting with us. He had came a number of times and preached for us, and we had our room well filled with attentive hearers; we had to send a horse and buggy after him, as he had no carriage of his own. He often walked out to appointments near Beatrice, but this was too far for him to walk.

Mr. Elwood came, and there was a general turnout from Mud creek, Yankee creek, Bear creek and Placer creek, also. Those creeks headed in the bluffs of this large tract of table lands where we had settled, and run off to the Big Blue river, and really it was a beautiful tract of country. The people came out and we had some good preaching, and good resulted. There were some who dated their conviction from that meeting, who ultimately found the pearl of great price, and became useful Christians, but who were very wicked before; and if the meetings had continued, I think there would have been many conversions; but there came a severe storm, for that country, and the people could not venture out with their children at night, and the meetings were closed and deferred to some other time. That time came after awhile, and the meeting was opened at the new stone school house in the Filley district. There were a number of conversions. A class of fifteen or eighteen was formed, the Doctor put in as leader, and that charge attached to the Blue Springs charge. Bro. Ellwood preached there every two weeks, so we could enjoy religious services every Sabbath by going to one appointment one Sabbath and the other the next.

We had a good many pious friends who came to the Doctor's for prescriptions, and that was a great comfort to us. Among them was an old gentleman and wife who had traveled in the Black River Conference for forty years or more. They had borne the burden and heat of the day in that country when it was new. He had been a very useful minister of the gospel for many years; had seen many souls converted and brought to a saving knowledge of the truth as it is in Christ, and when he had grown old, he came to Nebraska and located, got him a homestead, had it nicely improved, and he and his wife were living very comfortably in their old age; but their health was very poor. They came to see the Doctor, and we had a very pleasant visit, and our hearts burned with awe while we talked of the rich provision made for a sin-stricken world in the atonement of a crucified Saviour; and we parted with the blessed hope of meeting in that better world, where we would praise the Lord for redeeming grace and dying love. We had quite a number of such visits from the old veterans of the Cross.

The presiding elder, Bro. Leman, made us several visits, and he always left us strengthened in the good old way—it always strengthened our hearts to see men of his ability, natural and acquired, laboring for the good of the church and precious souls. Bro. Mann came to see us often. He was always fervent in spirit, serving the Lord.

The young doctor had two very interesting children, a daughter about six years old, and a son a little over four years of age. They were a great deal of comfort and company to us. The little boy was always with his grandpa, ready to carry the hammer and nails, or anything he could do for him, and the little girl was with me most of the time when working in the garden dropping seeds, pulling weeds, picking peas or berries, feeling that she was a great help, and she was. When in the house she would be at my side learning to knit or sew, making clothes for dolly, hemming a pocket handkerchief for her pa or grandpa. And thus the spring passed by very pleasantly.

Our crops began to ripen, and it made pretty busy times with everybody, and soon the harvest was gathered. Grandpa had a nice patch of melons of all kinds, and the children as well as the rest enjoyed them very much. The young doctor was busy with his patients and long rides, and his wife was busy helping about the house work, and all preparing for winter. The corn, cabbages, beans and potatoes had all ripened nicely. We had a fine crop of tomatoes, ground cherries and citrons, and there was a great deal of wild fruit, and our sorghum was very nice, so we pickled and preserved a great deal of such things and stowed them away in our cellar.

We killed a nice fat pig, and made ready for our journey to Illinois; it was necessary for us to attend to some business, we wished to make a short visit and hoped to bring some of our children home with us. The weather up to this time had been very pleasant. One of our neighbors, an Illinois acquaintance, was going to Nebraska City with a light load of wheat, and said he would put on a nice spring seat and take us to the Missouri river. The day we started it froze pretty hard. That night we stopped with some Chicago friends who lived on the road about half way to the city. They had been up to our place on a visit and to get medical advice; we had a nice time, and they wished very much that we would stop and see them when we made this trip, and we promised to do so. We got there about dusk, they gave us a hearty welcome and a good night's entertainment, and next morning drove into the city with us. Their name was Squiers, and my husband was their family physician while we lived in Chicago. Sister Squiers and I belonged to the same class, attended female prayer meeting regularly every week, and both belonged to a temperance organization called the Daughters of Rechab, which was **very useful** in that city. Mr. Squiers said he feared we could not cross the river; it was not frozen hard enough yet, but it might be in the morning, **so we** would go on to the city, and if we could not cross we could make a good visit with his brother's family who **lived** near there. **We** started for the city and arrived there about one o'clock, and found our friends well and glad to see us. **The** doctor found **Elder Leman,** who made his home **in the** city, and he **was** waiting anxiously **for** the river to **freeze** so he **could** go **over to a** quarterly meeting, and he informed us he would accompany us on the cars for some distance. It snowed a little and froze very hard. The elder came **and** told us it would **do** to cross on foot. So we bid our friends good-bye, took our satchels and walked to the river. It looked dangerous; I had crossed it in a scow, a sail boat and steamboat, but it never looked so dangerous to **me** before. I advised **my** husband to wait another night, but just **as we** were trying to decide, a teamster with a light load drove onto the **ice.** We watched him closely, fearing every moment we would see him, horses, wagon and grain, all sink through the ice. We could hear the ice crack, but he reached the other side, and cried out, "Safe! come on." The elder started on first. Pa said, **"Ma,** do you think you can venture?" **"Yes,"** said I, "if you will let me hold your arm closely." "Well, let's try it," said he. I thought if one went to **the** bottom to be buried in the mud, I would rather have both **go** together. The elder stepped very cautiously ahead, and frequently would stop and examine the ice, and then remark, "Come on, doctor, all safe." And in about half an hour we were relieved of our anxiety, suspense, and I must acknowledge, trembling fear, for every time I moved my foot on the ice I was afraid it would go right through; it did not look thicker than a heavy pane of glass. But we reached the east shore in safety, and we were truly thankful for the mercy shown by the Divine Hand which had led us through such great danger.

On the east bank we had a very fine view of the city, we could see the Court House, and the majestic old Capital Theological Institute which stood on a beautiful eminence. When we got into the car Elder Leman gave us an introduction to the President of the College who was going to Council Bluffs. We enjoyed the conversation, and found him to be a very social and intelligent Christian gentleman, who was trying to do all the good he could in this new country for the spread of the gospel, education, and social society. We gave him our good wishes, and separated at the Bluffs. I loved to look at them; I gazed to catch the last glimpse, there is so much natural beauty and grandeur about them. Then we took the C. B. & Q. road, passed through Cass county, on to Grinnell. There we took a new road, I think they called it the Iowa Central, intersecting the Northwestern at Marshalltown, passed on to Cedar Rapids, and reached our son's about twelve o'clock. Attended Fairview church on Sabbath. Found two of our grand-children very sick with typhoid fever;

our son just getting over the worst of the same fever. Stayed with them several days, then passed on to Ogle county, Ill., and at night we reached our friends in Rochelle during one of the most severe storms I ever witnessed. It blowed and snowed a perfect tempest, drifted the track so the trains could not run for more than a week; now the first part of February, 1870, and we were so shut up we could not visit our friends as we had anticipated. Gladly would we have visited many, many of our dear old friends, but we look to a blessed reunion in our Father's house where our blessed Savior told us there were many mansions. And we thought, perhaps, we would live to come again and visit when it would be more pleasant weather.

A number whom we met said to the Doctor, "Oh, I am so glad to see you looking so well; you have not failed much since you left us; why, you look good for twenty years yet, and hope we may have many more good visits."

"Yes," said I, "if it was not for that scarey old river, which is always in the way, we might stay and have a good visit now."

I have always regretted that we did not, but just as soon as soon as the track was cleared and it began to thaw, we had to hurry to get over before the ice rotted, making it unsafe for us to cross, for sometimes it takes a month or more for the ice to run out, so we had to hurry.

As I said before, we left Dr. U. C. Roe's about the 15th of February, at two o'clock Saturday afternoon. Arrived at Sterling and waited for train from Rockford to Rock Island until four o'clock. Arrived at Rock Island about sundown during a severe snow and hail storm. We had to change cars and go on the Chicago, Burlington & Quincy road. This was severe on us, for we got quite damp, and did not get dry thoroughly until next morning, at Council Bluffs. It was a very unpleasant night, the storm beating heavily against the cars, and often I thought the wind would surely blow the train into the ditch; but morning light found us all alive and safe at Council Bluffs. We were soon hurried to a good tavern, where a good breakfast, warm room and nice bed was furnished, where we could be alone or go into the parlor as we chose. We hoped to get back over the river some time that night, and spend the Sabbath at Nebraska City. They were holding a protracted meeting there, and we should have enjoyed that very much, but heard that the river was impassable, and made up our minds to stay at the Bluffs until we could pass over. The Doctor went to church, but it was so slippery I did not venture out. About two o'clock a lady came in on a train just from Nebraska City, saying she crossed on foot, and they thought it could be crossed until eight o'clock. There was a train going to the city at four o'clock, so we concluded that we would take that train, hoping to cross in safety and get to the evening meeting. So we went to the depot, found the train just ready to start, and had a very pleasant ride down the valley to the city. When we arrived there they told us it was impossible to cross with the cab but they would take us to the ice in the cab, then conduct us as safely as they could; at the other side we would find the Cincinnati House cab awaiting us, and we were anxious to get to our old tavern because we knew the proprietor would attend the meeting, and we wished to go with them and hear Brother Alexander preach, so we concluded to try it. The young man that offered to guide us over said it was very dangerous, the ice was full of holes, but as they had been walking back and forth most of the day, though they could guide us safely over if we would be very careful. They had seen the ice crumbling off around the holes a good deal. When I got out of the cab and stepped on the ice, my heart fairly leaped, and I shuddered all over, but they moved cautiously on and we followed very carefully, and as we looked on either side we could see great holes, and they looked as though they would break through from one to the other every moment, but we moved very cautiously, and gradually neared the other shore, the men on both shores cheering us. At length we reached shore, and I cried out from the sincerity of my heart, "Praise the Lord; my feet are on Nebraska soil once more."

We found the cab awaiting us, and were safely conveyed to the Cincinnati House, where we received kind welcome. We found our kind old friends at tea. We partook with them, after which they lit a lantern and led the way to church; oh! what a splendid church, what a large congregation, and oh! what a sermon from the lips of dear Bro. Alexander. He was not much larger than a fifteen year old boy, light complexion, smooth-faced, clear, bright eyes, a smooth, strong voice, and every word was clothed with the spirit of the Most High.

They were just closing their meetings. There had been a great many conversions during the meetings, and they were rejoicing in the Lord, but still there were many who had resisted the Lord and the spirit of grace, and were saying to themselves, "Woe is me, the harvest is passed and I am not saved; I may not live to see another revival meeting." There was a great deal of deep feeling there. The church seemed a sacred place on account of the presence of the Lord. Many praying fathers and mothers, who had dedicated their sons and daughters to the Lord in the ordinance of baptism, and watched over them for a good many years, hoping they would yield and be saved by grace, and especially during this meeting, must see the meetings close without their loved ones giving any evidence of pardoned sin, and a fixed purpose to serve the Lord, which occasioned some deep feeling. The meeting closed with a good old-fashioned Methodist hand-shake, and some appropriate singing.

Just as we were going out of the church a great crushing noise was heard. I inquired, "What does that mean?" The reply was, "It is the ice breaking up, and is rushing out through the channel." Oh! how thankful I was to the Lord for our preservation through that hour of peril and danger. Those dear old folks in the Cincinnati House were among some of the very first standard hearers in that now large city. They held their first meetings in their little log house, while the Indians yelled and hooted around them, but that night they worshipped in one of the noblest churches I ever saw.

We had a good night's rest with our old pioneer

friends, and after a good warm breakfast, and prayers in their private parlor, and many, many warm, earnest wishes that we two might be successful in building up our new home, and in holding up the banner of the Lord, we took our seats in the stage, which runs from Nebraska City to Beatrice, our county seat, and started for our home forty miles away. The stage run within a quarter of a mile of our house. On our way we met our grandson, who had come to meet us, and we were thankful for it, because the stage was a miserable old rickety thing. We arrived at our home next day, found all well and they were very glad to see us. And we could say with the poet "there is no place like home," even if it were far away in the west. The doctor seemed much invigorated from his visit to the country where he had spent thirty years of his life. The best part of his manhood had been spent in Illinois in Rock River Valley visiting and relieving the sick, with great acceptability and success. Oh! how cordially would his friends grasp his hand and say to him, "Doctor, we are so pleased to see you stand the wear and tear of frontier life so well in your old age." One gentleman said to him, "Doctor, you look as though you were good for twenty years yet." "Oh, yes," said he, "I have a good deal of physical energy yet, but seventy-one years have made their impression on my system." "I hope you may live to make us a number of pleasant visits yet," said the old gentleman, "it does us a great deal of good to shake the hand that has ministered to the relief of pain so often, and it does gratify our feelings to look upon the noble form that has bent over the sick-bed of ourselves and families so often, to our great relief. Don't you remember when you was called to my dear wife when she was so dangerously sick, and how soon you relieved her? and how sick the children were with scarlet fever, and how you saved them to us, while other doctors were losing almost every patient? And well do I remember how kind and attentive you were to me when I had that severe spell of typhoid fever; I expected to go then, but you stuck to me so faithfully and brought me out, and I have had remarkable health ever since, and have been able to raise my family, when had it not been for your skill, kind attention and care I certainly would have gone and left my family orphans to shuffle through the world alone. You must allow myself and others to express to you our gratitude."

"Ah," said the doctor, "Reuben, you must remember the Lord was in all this, to Him you owe the gratitude. The Lord has led me all my days, and to Him be all the glory if I have ever done any good." This was not the only expression of this character given him while on this visit. Although we were shut in by snow and storm, we met with many of our old friends; the expressions from them were of similar character, and the answer was much the same; every good gift is of the Lord. I have ever been thankful the Lord permitted us to make that visit, although we passed through so many dangers to accomplish it, especially thankful after the results of a few months.

Now it was the latter part of March, 1871, and it was time to look around and see about putting in the crops. We were fortunate in hiring a very good man, and our grandson was there to help us. We had two good teams, and had forty acres of fall breaking done for corn. The Doctor was cheerful, and thought he saw the opening for a fine crop.

The Doctor and I kept our shrubbery clean and put in a fine garden and a nice crop of potatoes, while the boys put in about twenty-five acres of spring wheat, twenty-five of oats, ten of barley and forty of corn. The next thing was to plant the hedge-row all around the section. This was broken on the section when we bought it. They broke it well the year before, and now it was broken again and harrowed finely, then re-harrowed until it was as fine as a bed in a flower garden, then laid off precisely in the middle and the osage seed drilled in. The hired man had arranged with the Doctor that when that was done, he was to take time to go west and find him a homestead about sixty miles distant. He worked very diligently until it was ready to receive the seed—it was necessary to have the furrow that was to receive the seed smooth and straight.

The young Doctor had all he could possibly attend to—his father going out as counsel occasionally. His rides lengthening constantly—way out into Johnson and down into Pawnee, even to County Seat, Pawnee City—often as far as thirty miles. He was from home, and the grandson had gone to plow some on his homestead. "Now," said the Doctor, "I can help the man lay off that furrow; I have wanted to do that, because I can lay it off straighter than either of the boys; but I knew you would all object to my doing it, but I shall take pleasure in it." I insisted on his not doing it, but he said, "Oh! it will do me more good than harm; I would like to handle the plow once more. Harness the horses and we will be off." "Oh! pa," said I, "don't go, it is quite warm, and it might make you sick, or you might be sun struck." "Oh! no," said he, "I think not; I will go out and try it; I feel very well this morning." By this time they were off. He seemed to feel very much like a boy going into a new job. The young Doctor's wife and I watched them until they hitched onto the plow and started off nicely. They left the wagon where they hitched onto the plow; but they had gone only about a mile on the hedge row, when the Doctor said, "Hold on, I am about to fall; I feel very strangely." Mr. Maine ran to him, and he let go the plow handles, and Mr. Maine steadied him a few steps to the grass, where he sat down. The man said, "Doctor, I will go and get the wagon and take you home." "Oh! no," said he, "get a little water and bathe my head and chest; I will get over it in a little while; it is just a dizzy spell." He ran to the creek, it was but a few steps—they had a cup along—got some water, bathed his head, unbuttoned his collar, bathed his chest, and he soon breathed quite easy. He remarked to Mr. Maine, "As soon as I centered my eyes on the beam of the plow I felt sick at my stomach, and grew very dizzy, and should have fallen if you had not caught me; but don't say anything to my folks about it; they will be so alarmed about it; I don't think it is anything serious. Lay off the hedgerow as best you can and let it go; I felt a good deal of pride in having it laid off straight, but let it go. You will not be here again for an hour or more, and if I had my cane I might walk home across the section; it would only be about a mile." Mr. Maine looked around and picked up a stick that had been dropped there. "I can walk with that," said the Doctor, "but you had better come around with the wagon, I may not feel like walking, and then you can take me home in it."

After he had lain there, perhaps an hour, he took his stick and walked home very slowly. I saw him coming, took my staff and went to meet him. He said he thought it was "too warm for him to hold the plow, and Maine thought he could do it himself, and I concluded I would come home." He took the rocking chair and I gave him a draught of good cool water. He rested awhile and then laid down on his lounge, took a pleasant nap, awoke and ate his dinner as usual.

Mr. Maine finished the hedge planting and started started the next day for his homestead. Nothing was learned by the family about this incident until Mr. Maine returned home. Previous to this—the latter part of April, after our return from Illinois—the Doctor was attacked with congestion of the lungs, something he had been subject to from the earliest of our acquaintance, as often as once in two or three years. Two or three time I thought it would be his last, but there would be some means sanctified to his recovery; but this time he was more violently attacked than I ever saw him. He had been quite well and busily engaged making garden and superintending the farming business; ate supper as usual; seemed cheerful; had prayers as usual, and when he arose from his knees he said, "Ma, I am afraid I am going to have a spell of that congestion on my lungs, I feel great pain in them." I asked him if he would take something to relieve the pain. He told me what to get; he took it and went to bed, but not to rest; he was in great agony, and I called the young Doctor. He came immediately, and as soon as he entered the room he said, "Pa, you are very sick." "Yes, indeed I am," said he, "if I don't get relief soon I shall not live until morning." "What shall I do for you?" said the young Doctor. "Give me a lobelia emetic." He did so, and it relieved him some, but he continued very sick for several days, I think about ten days, sometimes better and then worse, so that we despaired of his life for several days. The young Doctor did not leave the room day nor night during that sickness.

The congestion left the lungs and receded to his heart, then he had a dreadful bad spell. It then receded to the pleura. He said he could feel it as plainly as he could feel the hand on the surface. From there it receded to the spine, then the Doctor got control of it and gave relief. He said to me when he began to feel easier, "Well, Ma, I think we have routed that congestion from place to place until we have cleared it out of my system, and I shall never suffer from it again." He was very weak and much reduced in flesh, and it took him some time to convalesce, but he came up nicely, and in about two weeks was able to ride to Beatrice in a very easy buggy.

In a few days he went to Tecumseh, the county seat of Johnson county. He had been selling a piece of land, and went there to make out the papers. It was a pretty long ride for him, and he stayed over night with Mr. Charles Mayberry, the gentleman who went with us to look up our land on our first trip. He returned home next day about noon, feeling much invigorated by his ride and visit.

We had been talking of going to Blue Springs to quarterly meeting, which was about nineteen miles distant. We had been there a number of times and enjoyed it very much. But we all thought it would be too much for the Doctor; but after having stood this ride so well he thought we might go to quarterly meeting; so we concluded to go, as there would be some time for him to rest. Early Saturday morning we started, had a pleasant ride, got there in good time, heard Elder Leman preach a good sermon, stayed all night at Bro. Ellwood's, our former preacher at Bethel church, White Rock Township, near our last home in Illinois. They were glad to see us, as they had not met us for some time.

Sabbath morning we had a good old-fashioned love feast and the Doctor enjoyed it very much. He and many others were so happy they scarcely knew whether they were in the body or not. He exhorted more than was usual on such occasions, pleading with the brethren to live faithful to the cause of the Master, especially the young; said he, "Soon, and perhaps very soon, us old folks who are bearing the burden and heat of the day will drop off of the stage, and go to that better world, and then those responsibilities will fall on you. O how near you ought to live to God by faith and humble, devoted prayer." There was deep feeling; some prayed, some wept, while others shouted

—it was a love feast indeed. Just as the love feast was over, public worship commenced. The Doctor sung a beautiful hymn of a farewell spirit, and as he sang he went around the room and shook hands with every one in it. A lady said to me after his death, "Oh! how his face shone, that blessed Sabbath morning; it did seem to me as if the angels hovered over him. I do think the Lord was preparing him for this great and sudden change. We were so glad he shook hands with us all, and we had hoped the Lord would spare him to us, he was doing so much good."

After the love feast closed, Bro. Leman preached one of his best sermons. It was food to the soul, and strength to the heart and hands to go forward in Christian duty. Then we had such a sweet, solemn season at the sacramental altar. There were forty or fifty communicants. With this ordinance the meeting closed. But oh, what a change in that town plot; four years since we met with some of those people, and worshipped in a small log house, there was but two or three houses of any kind, and a number of emigrant tents, but now there were twenty-five or thirty, neat small buildings, and a good stone church, and everything prosperous. We had a good meeting then in the log house, in which was good done and souls blessed, and Bro. Mann sent on his way rejoicing. In the love feast Sabbath morning a brother told something of his experience—he was a backslider at the time of the meeting in the log house four years previous. He was one of the first settlers at Blue Spring; came to this country on purpose to get a farm; and the new town was laid off right up to the line of his farm, and he was deeply interested in public affairs. There was some difficulty grew up among them, and he was led to say and do some things that injured his standing; there was no meeting to go to; he lost his interest and became quite wicked. But at that meeting the spirit of the Lord reproved him for sin, unrighteousness and a judgment to come, and he never found peace until he found it the blood of the Lamb, that cleanseth from all sin through repentance and faith on Him. Now he was rejoicing in the love of God shed abroad in his heart. We were much cheered when the Elder told us how the Lord was blessing the work all around his district.

We had a good social prayer meeting at Bro. Ellwood's; he was preacher in charge at Blue Springs then, later became presiding elder of Beatrice district, and lived in Beatrice. We closed our meeting by expressing a hope of a reunion, at least in our Father's House, where there is rest for the weary. The Doctor had come up so nicely from that severe spell of sickness, that we hoped he would live for many years of usefulness.

We returned home in safety and found all well, and the young doctor rushed with business. Our quarterly meeting was to come off soon at Crab Orchard. That charge was yet to be supplied by the conference, and we were looking for a new elder and a new preacher. We knew but very little about our new elder. The circuit preacher, Bro. Hull, had come on a few days previous to the quarterly meeting; had got located in a little log house about a mile from the school house, in readiness for the quarterly meeting.

We had built a good school house at Crab Orchard the year previous. Formerly the meetings had been held in Bro. Howard's log house. He was a noble pioneer Methodist class leader, and an early settler there, and kept the stage house for years for the line that run from Brownsville to Beatrice when we went there. Many precious seasons have the Doctor and I seen there in the little log house and in the new school house. They had a good revival all winter the first winter it was built. Now we were going to have a quarterly meeting there. We were all anxious to see the the new Elder and circuit preacher.

Bro. Howard knew there would be a large congregation out, and had built a nice leafy bower in front of the school house. We had heard a good many rumors concerning the new Elder; some said he was a formal, dry eastern man, who had joined our late conference; knew nothing about our western frontier habits, manners or meetings, and our hearts were sad; but oh, how soon this veil of sadness dropped when he came to the door of the school house. His form was noble and majestic; his complexion very clear; his eyes dark blue; hair dark brown; his apparel very neat, and how kind and gracefully he bowed as he entered the door, and with Bro. Hull he took a seat behind the teacher's desk. He arose, read a chapter, sung a hymn, took his text and preached a splendid sermon in the demonstration of the spirit of the Lord, and all were very much pleased with the new elder, Bro. Maxwell. We gave him a hearty welcome. In his sermon he referred to his early travels over that country a number of years previous, when he could only find a small settlement once in twelve, fifteen or twenty miles, only two or three log cabins or dugouts and a few inmates composed the settlement. He was the first missionary who traveled over those vast prairies and up and down the streams. The little settlements were all very near the streams for convenience of water and timber. There were a number of those early settlers there that day from a distance of fifteen and twenty miles to see their boy missionary and hear him preach, thankful that he had been faithful to the great commission, and grown in grace and the knowledge of God. While he had been laboring in other parts of the vineyard of the Lord, this country had multiplied into many large settlements, and the little vines he had planted, and those faithful old members of the small classes he had formed had multiplied by faith and prayer, while other faithful ministers had been sent by our infant conference to labor among them, had grown to be large vines with rich fruits, and that day he could stand under the branches and proclaim a free and full salvation.

I was truly thankful that I was permitted to enjoy this reunion with those faithful frontier soldiers of the cross. Sabbath morning we had a blessed love feast, and at half past ten the school house and the leafy shade were closely packed, and the elder stood under the shaded bower and preached another blessed sermon; had a sacred, solemn time at sacrament; the presence of the Lord overshadowed us. In the afternoon Bro. Hull preached an excellent sermon, and at the close the elder asked the doctor to close by prayer; he did so, and oh! what a near approach he made to the Lord, it seemed as though the very heavens were bending over us; some were shouting, some were wonderfully drawn out in prayer, while the penitents were weeping all through the congregation; the doctor still pouring out his soul to God in prayer, especially for the people of this neighborhood, especially the impenitent and backsliders of this neighborhood. I think I never heard him beseech the Throne of Grace with so much earnestness before. Ah, little did we think at that time, it was the last prayer he would ever make at our little school house, but so it was. It was growing late, and some were a great way from home, so the elder closed by singing the doxology and saying the benediction. The place seemed sacred on account of the presence of the Lord. Some went away singing, some weeping, some saying, "Praise the Lord, and all that is within me praise His holy name."

There was a dear old Sister Blue who lived on the road between our house and the school house, in a little log house. She was a widow, very devoted, always happy, and was tenderly regarded and loved by all the class. We asked her to ride with us, and she thankfully accepted our invitation. The doctor assisted her into the wagon—we all rode in wagons then in that new country, although it looked like an old settled country to the elder in comparison to what it was when he, the Pioneer Missionary, rode through it with his hymn book and Bible in the saddle-bags to tell the story, the good old story of Jesus and His love.—and we had a pleasant time in our ride, talking of the goodness of the Lord, and His supporting grace in the loss of her two husbands and several children. And when we arrived at her little gate, the doctor helped her out of the wagon, and she went slowly up the narrow path that led to her lonely little house; everything was neat and cozy around it, but not one smile to greet her nor one foot step to meet her. As we went on our way toward home, I said, "Oh, dear, pa, how lonely that dear old soul must be living there all alone, shall it ever be that I shall be left to live like her? I am glad the Savior is with her to bless and comfort her, I know he is, she is always so happy." "Ma," said he, "we are both growing old, and it is certain, according to the course of nature, we must both go pretty soon." "Oh, pa," said I, "I wish we could both go at the same time." "So would I like that; we have traveled and labored together for nearly fifty years, the 11th of next November it will be fifty years, almost a half century. But it is most likely one will be taken and the other left. I am almost five years the older and it is likely I will go first, but you will have the blessed Savior to lean on who has been with us in so many troubles, and sanctified them all to our good. He will always be with you and comfort you; I know the children will all be kind and good to you." "Oh, yes, but they can never fill your place. I fear you have some idea that you will go soon, if so, pa, you ought to attend to your business affairs; there is all your property, you ought to make some arrangements about that." "I know, but I made a will and acknowledged it before Squire Webb, and Bro. Pitney witnessed it. Do you know where it is? I think it is among your papers, I saw it not a great while ago." "But that wont do, it was written twenty years or more ago." "It was written when you went to California," said he, "but if you have it it is all right, it was my will then, and it is now; if I should write a dozen wills they would all be just like that." "But," said I "that is destroyed by time." "Oh, no." said he, " it would be good for fifty years, if no other was made, so you can rest easy about that if I should go suddenly."

We then talked about where we would like to be buried. Both expressed a wish to be buried at Light House cemetery, because it was our first home in Eastern Illinois, and another reason was we gave the ground for that use, and another was that there were a good many of our old friends lying there who came soon after we did, and we would like to arise on the morning of the Resurrection with those whom we had loved, and labored with to sustain the cause of our blessed Redeemer; and there were a number of our grand-children buried there, but none of our own dear children. Our dear little Mathew II., lay in the family cemetery at Eddyville, Ky. We then talked of the manner of burying people in their usual habit of dress. I said, " Pa, would you like to be dressed in your wearing apparel?" "No," said he, " I think white is much more appropriate for for the burying apparel." "So do I," was my reply. "There is no harm talking about these matters, although we may live many years yet," said I, " then we know each other's mind on the subject if anything should happen." " Oh, no." said he, " don't feel gloomy about it, I have no terror of death since

Jesus has lain there. I dread not its gloom. I have lived my threescore years and ten and you are pretty close after me, but if the Lord will, we can stay ten years more. His grace will sustain us, but I have one great desire, that the good Lord, whom we have served together almost fifty years, will take us home to rest before we become helpless. That is my greatest desire."

We had often talked on the subject but never with so much feeling. Just then we arrived at our home. It was this idea that suggested to me that one or the other would go soon, and also told me that I had better write to the children about coming to see us on our marriage anniversary, the 11th of November, and tell them we did not want any Golden Wedding, it was themselves we wanted to see, and they must be sure to come. Now there were seven letters to write, and I went at it, and all read to the same purport. In the morning the doctor went to tearing down our little emigrant shanty, and intended to use the lumber in adding on some more rooms. He and Morris P. Roe had just finished the summer kitchen and moved the stove in. "Now, Ma," said the Doctor, cheerfully, "you can get the dinner and not suffer so with the heat." I thanked him kindly and went to work.

Just as my dinner was about ready a team drove up to the door, and it proved to be some of Morris P.'s friends from Downer's Grove, Du Page county, Ill. They were hunting land to buy in Nebraska, and had called to see Morris. We were very much pleased to see them, and made them welcome. After dinner the Doctor told Morris to harness the double team for him and he would hitch onto the sulky plow and plow out the grove, and he could take the riding horse and go with his friends and see if he could not find a farm that would suit them, as he knew of several that were for sale. "I would like it," said the Doctor, "if they would buy near us, and then more of their friends would come, and they would be quite an addition to our neighborhood." "Yes," said Morris, "and they are the right kind of folks." The young men were off pretty quick, and the Doctor hitched onto the riding sulky plow, and soon he had his little grove plowed out nicely and called me to see it. "Now, Ma, don't that look so nice? it has only been out a little more than two years, and I cannot plow it any more with my riding plow." "Then you will have to plow it with a crossing plow," said I. "It does look nice, dont it? you can see the furrows clear through the grove." "Now, Ma," said he, "it is pretty nice to raise anything so beautiful in so short a time. One thing that makes it look so nice is, I trimmed it up the other day, and it is so perfectly clean." "Yes, Pa," said I, "there is not so nice a grove in the county for its age." "You are joking, Ma," said he. And oh! what a pleasant smile played over his features as he said, "Oh, Ma, it would not have been so nice if you had not helped me set it out so carefully." Then we both had a cheerful laugh.

Oh! little did we realize that we were raising a grove that was to wave its beautiful dark green leaves over his grave; but it was so. Soon after this pleasant interview and chat about the grove he said, "Ma, where will I find the boiler; I told the boys I would like to have them kill a nice shoat this evening; they said they would be at home by half past five, or six o'clock at least; that will be time enough." He made the fire, filled the boiler, and I helped him put it on. The boys were there on time, butchered the hog, and the Doctor told them to hang it up and let it cool, and he would cut it up in the morning. We had tea, then prayers and retired for the night.

In the morning the Doctor cut up the meat nicely, salted it, and brought up some nice spareribs from the cellar, saying, "Ma, that will be nice for breakfast." Soon all was ready and we were seated. After asking a blessing he helped us all, as was his usual custom, and then sipped his coffee, and remarked, " Ma, this coffee is splendid; if you should live until you were an hundred years old you would not forget how to make good coffee, and fry nice spareribs." "Quite a compliment, Pa," I replied. "Well, it is so; it seems to me as though I never relished a meal better in all my life.,' "I am very glad if it suits you, Pa," was my reply.

After breakfast the Doctor said to Morris, " You had better go with the young men and see those other farms this moring, and I will take the team and plow out my melon patch." He said, "Grandpa, you had better let me do that; you are tired with cutting up your meat, and had better not go out, for it is going to be very warm to-day; I fear it will be too much for you." "Oh, I guess not; you harness the team and I can do it. Grandma thought what I did yesterday would hurt me, but I think it did me good." "But grandpa," said Morris, "it has been very cool for a number of days, and now this morning it has turned very warm, and this is one of the longest days in the year. I think you had better let it be; I will do it carefully." "I guess it will not hurt me; you harness the horses, I will be careful." He did as requested, and the young men went to see the farms, and were to be back by ten o'clock.

The Doctor went out to hitch the horses to the plow which stood near the back door. (The young doctor had been called away some ten miles in the night, and we did not know when to look for him when he went over there, for he had very often to go all around the neighborhood; so when the young men went away there was no man on the place but Doctor. We felt a good deal of uneasiness about the young doctor going out in the night, as the country was full of horse thieves, and one had escaped from the sheriff a few nights previous with handcuffs on, only a few miles from our place, and we thought there was danger from both parties. There were thirty or forty men and officers out after the thief. It was supposed he had gone to some of his own crew not far away, and we feared he might be shot at by either party in the night; he was to cross Yankee Creek near where they caught the one who had escaped a few nights before, and we were feeling very anxious about him.) When Doctor went out at the back door the young doctor's wife and I begged and entreated him not to go out in the hot sun, but he smiled and said, "Don't be so foolish, it will not hurt me." "Oh, Pa," said I, "it is so warm and you have your flannels on, and I see the clouds have passed away and the sun has come out so very hot." "Oh," said he, "do not be uneasy, I will come in if it is very hot." And as he passed around the corner of the house, I said to Sarah, "I hope he will not stay out long." "I don't think he will," said she. "I don't think I ever saw it so hot." She came and got the pail and drew a pail of water. Just then I went to the door to see how the Doctor was getting along, and as I looked out I saw him turn around the corner with his team. I remarked, "Pa, I am so glad you have come in; I thought you did not realize how very warm it is." While he was hitching his team he remarked, "Just as I fixed my eyes on the beam of the plow I grew dizzy and blind, and fell down by the side of the plow, and I do not know long I laid there." Said I, "Pa, you have not been out but a few minutes." Sarah looked at the clock and said, "Not more than twenty or thirty minutes." I said, "Do come in and let the horses stand until the boys come." "I will," said he, and stepped around to the north door and entered the sitting room. I said, "Do take the rocking chair," placing it between two windows and the door. Just then Sarah brought him a draught of cold water she had drawn. He drank it, remarking, "That is delicious." I said, "Pa, you had better take something." "I will take something out of that bottle that stands on the table," said he. "I took a sup as I came in, and it has started the circulation and perspiration; see how nicely moist I am; will get over it soon; my head feels all right now," shaking his head. I remarked, "Pa, I am afraid it is something more serious than you are willing to admit of." "Oh, I guess not." "Shall I get you a bowl of water and wash you off nicely and get some lighter clothes on?" "You may," said he; "I do not think it will stop the perspiration, if I take a little more of those bitters to keep up the action." I unbuttoned his collar and bathed his breast and shoulders, and combed his hair, after which he said, "I feel all right now." "You will when you get those woolen clothes off; shall I get some clean, dry ones?" "Pretty soon; I guess I will lie down on the lounge and rest a little first." We had a lounge in the room where he rested often. He had but just lain down when two of our neighbors came in, one to get the Doctor to go and see a sick child, one whom the Doctor had been to see a day or two before, when the young doctor was out on one of his long trips. The Doctor welcomed them and chatted with them cheerfully for half an hour. After the gentleman had described the symptoms the Doctor concluded to send some medicine, and the young doctor would go when he returned home. He said to our daughter-in-law, "Sarah, if you will hand me thus and thus out of the medicine safe, I will fix some medicine for Mr. Armstrong." Sarah did with pleasure what he requested. He arose, sat on the lounge and prepared the medicine —I think we may say he died at his post, and I think he was truly called of God to that post—and the gentlemen bid us good-morning and started home.

They had but just started when the young men arrived. They were going thirty or forty miles further to see a sister, and I had prepared them some lunch to eat on the way. They had found a farm that suited pretty well, and if they did not find something better on their trip, they would come back and buy. They were in a hurry, putting their things into the wagon, bidding good-bye, etc. When they came into the room to bid the Doctor good-bye, he raised up and sat on the lounge again, and with a smile said to the young men, "Now, boys, I am so glad there is some hope that you will come back here, and I hope you will, and then the old folks will come. Now, if you do come back, I want you to remember that the latch string is always on the outside." (This is an old-fashioned phrase, to express hospitality, that the frontiersmen frequently used, and he meant all it could express.) "Come right here and stay until you can fix up your home, and such as we have we will give unto thee; I want you to feel as though you were coming to your father's house." They thanked him very kindly, and went out to harness and hitch up their horses.

The Doctor said to me as he laid down, "Ma, if you will get an early dinner, I think Morris had better take the team and take us down to Bro. Howard's," (he was Squire just over the line in Johnson county, where the land the Doctor had been selling lay) "and take Lovell along, and all acknowledge those papers; it has been put off too long now." "You don't think you are able to go, do you?" said I. "Oh, yes; I feel all right, only I am a little tired." "Well," said I, "I want you to put on some cooler clothes." "I will," said he. I remarked, "I wish those boys would stay to dinner; I have done my best to persuade them, but they will not stay; they are hitching on their horses now." I spoke to the young doctor's wife, and told her what he had said, and asked her to sit by him while I went and got dinner. "I will, Ma," said she, "I will run up stairs and get my sewing and stay with him; I don't think he ought to be left alone." She ran up stairs, saying, "I will be back in a moment or two." I turned into the kitchen to attend to my dinner.

Just at that moment Morris had bid the boys goodbye, and stepped onto the door sill. I heard something fall, and Morris cried out, "Grandma! come! come! Grandpa has fallen on the floor and is dying, I do believe." Sarah and I both ran, and just as we got our hands on him he drew one gurgling breath and two short gasps, but the air did not go into the lungs. Morris screamed for the boys—they had not gone more than five rods from the door. They came back, hitched their horses, and were ready to do anything they could to assist us; took a horse and rode across the field to our neighbor's who, we knew, would go after the doctor. The other young man stayed and helped us rub him and put draughts on every artery. We tried to get him to swallow, but never got him to take one drop. I clasped his hands when I first got to him and asked again and again, "My dear husband, are you conscious? if so, if you can't speak, do press my hand!" But no motion, not the least, nor the slightest pulsation. After we got to him all was over.

Pen cannot describe the anguish of that hour; every heart was ready to burst with grief. Just at the moment we gave him up, a gentleman rode up to the door, who stopped in Tecumseh, the county seat of Johnson county, a distant relative by marriage, by name, Calvin Mayberry. He was very much surprised and grieved at the scene which was before him; we had just got the Doctor straightened out on a bedstead and a sheet thrown over him. Calvin had been at our house a few days before, and had found him looking so well and feeling so cheerful over our proposed re-union in November, that it was a very great shock to him as well as to us. The messenger who went for the young doctor had told the sad news at the stage house on the road, Bro. Howard then sent word to the post office, and its occupants to Bro. Hull, the new preacher, and in less than an hour the house was full of warm, sympathizing hearts and helping hands ready to assist in any way they could. Even dear old Sister Blue was there, and oh! how comforting her kind words were, and how kindly she said, "Sister Roe, don't grieve so, Bro. Roe has only got into port a little early, a few more struggles and the Master will say, 'It is enough, come up higher, enter into rest.' Bro. Roe has fought the good fight, kept the faith and entered into rest, and if we are faithful we will be permitted to enter with him into the joy of our Lord." And the consoling words of all those, or many of them, with whom he was so very happy a few days ago at quarterly meeting, were like cordial to our wounded hearts.

Mr. Mayberry told the news all along the road and at at Tecumseh; there were a number of our friends living there. About one o'clock friend Ellis arrived with the young doctor all safe. He had rode about thirty miles in pursuit, and returned in two hours and a half. With all our grief there was a current of thanksgiving and deep-felt gratitude to our Heavenly Father that his life had been spared, running through our minds. He regretted he had not been there, and so did we, but he thought it hardly possible that anything could have prevented the sad stroke. Some thought it might have been caused by sun stroke, but I think it was caused by that old congestion which had lingered in his system for many years, and in that severe spell he had in the spring, it then fastened onto the spine, and now it was carried to the brain, and finally terminated in apoplexy. The first symptoms were on the day he was helping Mr. Maine lay out the hedge row; the second, that morning about half past nine o'clock in the garden; and the last, a few minutes before eleven o'clock, June 21st, 1871.

The young doctor got young Mr. Newhall, or he very kindly offered, to go to Blue Springs for Brother and Sister Ellwood. I wanted Bro. Ellwood to preach the funeral sermon, for Doctor and he had labored together through two revivals in Illinois, and ever since we came together in this new country we had been very intimate friends. Our very kind friend Mr. Ellis, went to Beatrice, fifteen miles, for a coffin, and what else was necessary in that line. There were ten or twelve of our friends who stayed with us all night.

Mr. and Mrs. McCann came to our assistance about the first of any, and I assure you they were very kind and helpful. Mr. McCann superintended the digging of the grave. We made up our minds to have it in the little grove that Doctor thought so much of, and there, right across the furrows that he had plowed 48 hours ago, we laid him to rest until we could bring him to Illinois. Brother and Sister Hull stayed all night with us, and I gave Bro. Hull the text I wished to have the funeral sermon preached from: "Blessed are the dead who die in the Lord from henceforth, yea, saith the Spirit, that they may rest from their labors, and their works do follow them."—Revelations, IX Chap., 13th Verse. And I told him it might be possible that Bro. Ellwood might not come, and he would have to preach. He said he would do it. I chose that Bro. Ellwood should preach because he and the doctor were so intimate.

The day was extremely warm, and a good many of the friends had been there from 10 o'clock because the word in regard to the hour of the services had not been given out very definitely, but it was intended to hold the funeral at 3 o'clock. Some had a great ways to go and were getting restless, and, as Bro. Ellwood did not come, it was thought best to have Bro. Hull preach, and he preached a good sermon. Bro. Ellwood arrived when he was about half through, and made some very appropriate remarks. You would have been astonished to see the congregation that was there; both the large rooms were filled to the last foot, and there were more outside than inside. Oh! what attention and what sympathy could be read in every face; it was evident that one had gone who was revered, honored and loved. Had we few who were permitted to follow him to the very nice grave that was shaded by those beautiful leafy boughs, been at home with our kind friends and relatives in Illinois, we could not have received more kindness and sympathy. My heart glows with gratitude while I write, to Him who doeth all things well, and to my kind friends also, of whom I like to think and talk, for the kind sympathy and attention given me.

A few more storms, a few more beating waves, and we will meet in our Father's house to go out no more. There the inmates never say, "I am sick." No death there, we shall live on and on through endless ages to praise him for full redemption. The service closed. Our kind friends left us with kindest feeling, all but Brother and Sister Ellwood. They remained with us until two o'clock next day. This was a great comfort to us, and when they left we were lonely and sad.

Of all the sorrows that I ever passed through I must say this was the deepest. I have lost father, mother, sisters and brothers, and sweet little angel babe, and thought my grief as deep as any heart could suffer, but it was not like this. No, no; the great deep of my heart was all broken up, and part of my grief was that I could not say "Thy will be done," for many years. I had been able to say "Thy will be done," under losses, disappointments and afflictions, and thought, that having meditated, consulted and prayed on this subject so much, I would be able to submit with Christian resignation if he should be taken and I left. But I was mistaken. I could not bear the idea that we should never unite our prayers at the family altar again; never again go together to the public worship, or social prayer or class meeting; never see him at my sick bed, ready to administer comfort and relief; never enjoy a cheerful meal with him as I enjoyed that morning—oh! little did I think that it was the last. No; never have his strong arm to lean on in the day of trouble. I struggled fervently in prayer to my Heavenly Father for grace to say "Thy will be done." I knew if I could be able to say that with all my heart I could bear it so differently. I still struggled, with that faith that takes no denial, and the victory was mine. All was peace and resignation. How calmly I could say, "Thy will be done. I will trust Thee, though Thou slay me." And with what sweet peace and comfort I consecrated my soul and body anew to Him who doeth all things well; and from that hour I have kept the victory amid all the trials I have passed, and they have not been few. I have never felt as though I would call him back if I could. No, never; nor any other of my Christian friends. But often it seems as though I could say with the poet:

> See the happy spirits waiting,
>   On the banks beyond the stream;
> Sweet responses still repeating,
>   Jesus, Jesus, is the theme.
>
> Hark, they whisper; lo, they call me,
>   "Sister spirit, come away."
> Lo, I come, earth can't detain me,
>   Hail the realms of day.

I often think of how I felt as I stood at the open grave. "Go, dearest Pa," I said in my heart, "and rest from your labors. You can't come to us, but by Divine Grace we can come to you, and we will." Oh! what a blessing that thought, that a Throne of Grace is made accessible and Heaven possible, through faith in the all-atoning blood of the Lamb that has redeemed a sin-stricken world.

A few weeks elapsed and duty prompted me to have the will probated. All was left to me, to do with it as I thought best. And oh! the great responsibility. My heart cried, "Dear Lord, I am not sufficient for this great responsibility. Nothing but Thy grace can sustain me; but I have said 'Thy will be done,' with all my heart, and with Thy grace to sustain me, I will try and do the best I can." There were heavy crops to be gathered and sold to meet liabilities; the farm to be rented; the deed and mortgage before spoken of to be seen to, and a multitude of cares. Amid my sorrow and loneliness it seemed a great deal. Oh! what would I have done if I had not a precious Saviour to lean on? And oh! how near He was to me to comfort and sustain.

Dear Pa's remains were laid so near the house that I could sit at my bed room window and look on the spot. I spent much of my time there in prayer and meditation. Oh! what a comfort to feel my Saviour so near, and the more resigned I felt the happier I was in the anticipation of a blessed reunion with my dear husband and many other loved ones who had gone before. And oh! how often, while walking in that lovely little grove and standing by the board fence that enclosed the grave. I felt that nothing but God's grace could sustain me in this great loss and sorrow. And there I would wrestle, Jacob like, until I could say with my whole heart, "Thy will be done." Then there would be such a sweet, sacred peace shed over my whole being, and I could almost realize the reunion I expected, and the precious promises were applied to my heart, such as these: "Where I am ye shall be also;" "These are they who have come up out of great tribulation, and washed their robes and made them white in the blood of the Lamb."

The young Doctor rented the farm for the next year, and it was arranged for me to stay there. There were plenty of room for them and me when I had the two bedrooms furnished, and the grandson, Morris P. Roe, spoken of before, agreed to stay with me until the crops were gathered. Our hired man came back. He had secured a good claim or homestead. My husband had supplied him with money to defray all expenses, and he began to think of sending for his wife. When he came he was willing to work out the balance of his term to pay for what money he had and get more to send for his wife, and the harvest work went off nicely. We had a fine lot of corn, forty or fifty acres, and as good corn as I ever saw grow in any country. Morris P. stayed until the small grain was all harvested and marketed, and when the corn was ripe for husking, my kind neighbors came and husked out about four hundred bushels and cribbed it, and I hired Mr. Maine to husk the rest in the field.

Our friends in Illinois desired to have a reunion at the home of our oldest daughter, Mrs. Mayberry, and have us all meet together to condole the loss of our dearly beloved father and husband, as we could not be together at the time of his death. Our oldest son, Dr. U. C. Roe, had moved back to Illinois, and located in Franklin Grove, Lee Co., and lives there yet; my second son, Dr. F. M. Roe, resided then and does now, at Downer's Grove; the third son, G. B. Roe, is a farmer and lives at Paynes Point, and has for a long time—more than 29 years; the fourth son, Mathew C. Roe, lived then in Lynn Co., Iowa; the oldest daughter married J. C. Mayberry; and the fifth son, John H. Roe, lived in Louisville, Ky; my youngest daughter, Francis M. Conlen, lived then and does now in DeKalb Co., Ill.; the sixth son, Dr. Malcom C. Roe, lived in Nebraska, Gage Co., with me. Now the object was to get them all together once more that we might sympathize with and comfort each other over our great loss, and each one felt it very deeply.

The 5th of February, 1873, found us all there, and Mr. Mayberry gave us splendid entertainment. It was a gracious season; we sang and prayed, and there was deep feeling while we talked of Doctor's kindness, counsel, prayers and death; there seemed to be but one spirit, and that was sympathy for each other, reunion and love; it seemed as though the Doctor's spirit mingled with us though unseen. We spent several days together, and talked of bringing his remains to Light House right away, but I thought it might be possible the children would move to Nebraska, and then we would want him there; and I could not think of living there without his grave being near me; so it was postponed. We enjoyed our visit together very much, and while we were together it was thought best that I should choose a trustee; as the law allowed me to do.

My noble boy from Kentucky had no family, and

he put out his strong arms for me to lean upon. The rest of my children thought it best, and I chose him, and he has borne the burden of my business, and has been very kind, very, for lo! those nine years, and has been very attentive to my interests. Our business is so blended that what is for his interest is for mine, and what is for my interest is for his; but there is one thing about our business that is a little unpleasant, and that is, we cannot be together as much as we would like to, as my interest is in Illinois, and his is in Kentucky, and his business is such that he cannot visit me oftener than once a year; then he rights up my business and goes again; but we correspond about once a week, and oh, how his loving counsel comforts my poor old heart; I can scarcely wait with the patience I should until the mail comes that brings the kind message; I think it one of the greatest blessings of this life that we can correspond so quickly, surely and nicely with those we love.

Soon after this arrangement was made the young doctor, M. C. Roe, began to think of returning to Nebraska. The rest of the children had returned to their respective homes, and when he and his family went, I wished to go also. But about the time they were ready to start I was taken violently sick with lung fever, and was taken to my oldest son's home, in Franklin, Lee county, Ill., and oh, how kind they all were to me, especially dear Emma, the oldest daughter at home, who went down with the quick consumption, and died in about six short months from that time, much lamented by her parents, brothers and sisters, and many loving friends. She was at my bedside, always ready to smooth my pillow, or give me my medicine, and I shall ever, with loving gratitude, remember how tenderly her soft hand was pressed to my aching head, or how gently she would rub my side when I suffered the most severe pain. And her father was so very kind; he scarcely left the room, unless it was to go to the office for medicine, or for a bit of nice beef to make some beef tea, and they fed it to me by the teaspoonful.

One night, when he was expecting the crisis, a gentleman came to get him to go to see his wife, fifteen miles away, who was very sick, and feared she would die. The Doctor told him he could not possibly leave his mother that night. The man told him if he would go he would give him the best horse on his farm, and he had some very fine ones. But the Doctor said, "No, dear sir; I cannot leave my dear mother; there will be a crisis with her to-night, she will be better by morning, or will not be living. I will prescribe for your wife, and you go home and give the medicine as I direct, and I will try to be at your house as soon as I can drive there in the morning." He sat by me all night and watched my pulse and gave the medicine himself, and about twelve o'clock, he said, "Ma, there is a favorable change in your pulse; I hope by morning there will be a very evident change for the better." I told him I could breathe easier. "That is very evident," said he, "and I hope you will be quite comfortable by morning." And as each one came into my room in the morning, they remarked, "Oh, grandma, you are better." I answered, "Assuredly, I am much easier." By nine o'clock the Doctor thought it safe to leave me, and he **went to his** patient and found her much better.

That day the young doctor called to let me know **he was** going to start for Nebraska. He said, " Dear ma, you are better, but so very weak, that it will be a long time before you will be able to travel to Nebraska, but do not be uneasy about home, I will take care of home and do the best I can," and as he stooped down **to** kiss me, the great **tears** dropped onto my face, and as he left the room I said, " My dear son, take **good** care of your dear father's grave."

I gradually improved, but from the first of that sickness I felt that to live, to me, was Christ, but to die would be gain; I should leave a world of toil and care and pain, and **go to a** world **of** peace and joy, to meet those loved **ones** who had gone before; and above all I should **be with** Christ, my living Head. **The** Doctor asked me several times, " Ma, shall I not send for the other children?" "Oh, no," I said, " I have been with them all so lately, and bid them farewell in view of my journey to Nebraska, and testified to them the power of Divine grace at **all** times and under all circumstances, to comfort **and** sustain them, they will know I am leaning on Jesus, and if so **I** shall enter the portals safely." Death seemed to have no terror, and the grave no gloom; I felt that Jesus had lain there, and I dreaded not its gloom. I realized **so** sweetly those beautiful lines:

> There sweetly **I'll rest**
> Till He bids me arise
> In triumph descending the skies.

I gained nicely with **the** kind care I received from

the good doctor and family, and in four weeks was able to start to my western home. My son who lived in Iowa, Mathew C., accompanied me. We had a very pleasant trip, and arrived safely at our western home about the 20th of April, and found my husbad's grave just as I left it, and that the young doctor and family had arrived in safety and were preparing to move to Beatrice, having conditionally rented the farm to Mr. Maine. I took with me from an Iowa nursery a thousand grafts of fruit, with the intention of cultivating quite a little nursery. I had grapes, currants, gooseberries, raspberries and strawberries. After my son had set out my nursery nicely for me he returned to his home in Iowa. After looking the country over a little he made up his mind that he could not sell his farm in Iowa, and come and live in Nebraska with me. He thought our country very fine and our home nice, but he liked Iowa better, and thought it to his best interest to remain in Iowa. I was in hopes he would make up his mind to come the next spring at least, and with this hope to encourage me I tried to be reconciled to my situation. I rented the farm to Mr. Maine, I was to furnish the seed and team and he to do the harvesting and receive half the profits. He had let a large, destitute family into my largest and best room, in a very severe storm, for a few days, until the storm should abate. They were making their way to their homestead west of us about seventy-five miles. We had had previous to this very mild winters, but this winter was very severe, but there was plenty of work they could get to do. They were two old men and two young men, and they found themselves well housed in a good warm house, with plenty of unhusked corn in the field and plenty of good wood in the grove near by, a nice large stove in the room, and the man I left there hired them to haul his wood and gather the corn on shares, and they never left there until the first of April. There were nine in the family, and they had made dreadful work with my house, tore off the plastering, broke out the glass, burned the floor, and destroyed things in general, and with the loss in old corn and wood and destruction in the house, I suffered over an hundred dollars loss, and no one to pay me in either gratitude or money.

The Doctor moved to Beatrice. His object in doing so was to concentrate his practice; he thought the people would not go so far for him, but they did; went from the settlements all around where he had practiced before, and plead so hard, that he would go. It was very sickly that fall, and his change of residence eventually made his practice harder on him than ever before.

I was left alone with the tenant and his kind wife; she was very kind to me, but her husband was very unkind, cross and crabbed; but I was enabled, through divine grace, to bear it with a good deal of patience, as it was such a comfort to me to be so near my dear husband's grave. I planted roses, mosses and trailing flowers all around it, which amused and interested me some.

I had a nice garden, and worked in my nursery some. The tenant would not help me, because it was not so stated in the lease; would not even so much as plow it for me; and was not willing the team should be driven to church on Sunday; said it must rest; so I had but little means of grace that summer, but had the word of Life and a present Saviour to bless and comfort me. I took the *Christian Advocate* to read, and occasionally my Christian friends visited me, and the Doctor would call every time he came near my place, and that was quite often. Those visits were a great comfort to me; and I could visit my husband's grave as often as I wished, and to watch the rose buds open, the vines twining over and around it, and the flowers shedding their sweet fragrance over it, did my heart good, and brought to my mind the cheering doctrine of the blessed resurrection of the body that lay there crumbling in the dust, and often my mind was led to reflect on that morning when the trumpet shall sound and the grave shall give up its dead, and this mortal shall put on immortality and rise to meet the Saviour in the sky, with ten thousand thousand angels around Him, and we shall see Him as He is, and we shall be like Him, and where He is, we shall be also. I had rather a pleasant time, although there were many lonely hours and days.

I received a letter about the middle of June from my son John, who was in Kentucky, saying he would visit me about the first of July. He had never seen our new home or any part of Nebraska. I thought I would like to have my home look as cheerful as possible. As I had anticipated this visit, my old carpet being quite worn, I had prepared a nice new rag carpet and sent it to the weaver's. Dear old Sister Andrews had arranged with a plasterer to plaster my rooms that had been so much abused. I could not get lime then, but had heard of some at Blue Springs. I hired a team, wagon and boy, took some milling and went to Blue Springs to get some lime, and had the privilege of staying all night with dear Sister Ellwood and family, and a number of my friends called to see me while there. They were much pleased to meet me; but to my great disappointment I found there was no lime; it was all used up; but I learned of some on my way home, not far from where my carpet was. They had sent me word that my carpet would be done that afternoon, and I intended to call and get it. After calling on a few friends in the morning we started, but had to go by a different road from what I had traveled with my husband, and oh! how I felt the need of his strong arm to lean upon then. We traveled a few miles on the road I was acquainted with, then turned off into another road. The boy was rather stupid, and did not understand much about traveling. It was an extremely warm day, very much such a day as that on which my dear husband died, just a year previous. We were on a large prairie, and the already dim road became invisible, so we no longer knew which way to go, and I was very much overcome by the heat. We were then on the bluffs of Mud creek. I told the boy I knew if we went any farther in that direction we would pass the house. We seemed then about a mile from the house. We went down the bluff into the creek bottom, and as soon as we did so the bluffs shut out all air from us, and my clothes being black, besides holding a large black umbrella over us, seemed to attract the rays of the sun to us. I could scarcely get a breath of air and could not see. I told the boy to hurry the horses, as I was afraid I could not live until we could get to the house. He did so, and when we got there the kind friends had to lift me out of the wagon, into the house and onto the bed. They dashed me with cold water, gave me some of Dr. Roe's ready relief, rubbed my extremities with it to divert the action to the surface, and I soon began to breathe with more ease, and could see and hear better. After an hour or two I took a cup of tea and some other refreshments.

About five o'clock we started on our way for the lime. Sister Andrews and family urged me stay all night, but I told them I thought I would rather go, as the man would be at my house to do the plastering, and I had but little time in which to have the plastering and cleaning done and my carpet down, before my son would arrive, and I thought we could get the lime loaded before dark, and there would be a nice bright moon, and I would rather risk riding by the moonlight than go in the morning when the sun shone. They said perhaps it would be better, and one of the young men went with us to help load the lime, and Sister Andrews said he might go all the way home with us, too, but as I knew the way perfectly after I got onto the Beatrice road, I did not think it necessary.

We got the lime loaded, and got onto the Beatrice road just as the moon was rising, and we had only seven miles to go then, and the road was good, but our load was heavy, team poor, **and** we necessarily had to go slow. We did not reach home until about eleven o'clock.

Early **the next** morning the plasterer was there, and prosecuted and finished his job of plastering nicely, and I got my house cleaned, and carpet made and down, and everything in comfortable order by the time my son arrived. But the mason said that if I had not got home that night he would have taken another job, and **I would** have been disappointed. We had **a** good visit. **The Doctor** and family and some other friends came and visited with us, and **I** went with my son and called on them and a lady who **had** lived in Kentucky when he first **went there** and taught **school**; she was a little girl then, and went **to** school to him, but was **now** married **and** had **two** sweet little children, and resided **in Beatrice. When** she heard **he was** coming she left a standing invitation **with the** Doctor for him to call and **see** them and bring his mother. He and the Doctor's family had **a** pleasant visit **with** them. The lady's mother lived with her, and they were delighted to see **their** old friend and teacher; and he was much pleased to find there in that far-off new country an **old** friend and pupil. The greeting was cordial, I assure you, and I cordially invited them to visit us, and they thought they would, but it **was** quite a distance and his stay was short, so they could not avail themselves **of** the pleasure, but **we** visited **often** at the Doctor's.

My son could not stay long on account of business at home, but he rode out several times with the **Doctor when visiting** patients. He liked the new country very much, especially our new home, and he left us with the hope that he would visit us again in the future, but thought it sad to leave me so lonely.

Now all my sons had seen the new country but Giles Bolivar, and he talked of coming soon. F. M. Roe had made a short visit in the spring after we got home.

My tenant did not do much with the farm, and was so unpleasant that I felt as though I could not keep him another year, and began to think of looking for another tenant.

As the fall came on sickness increased, and the Doctor rode day and night, until he was taken very sick himself with billious fever, and his life was despaired of. All the physicians within a great distance came to see him, and all had their doubts about his case, but Doctor Webb, a graduate from the Cincinnati Eclectic College, was his attending physician. He was very attentive and kind, and succeeded in bringing him safely through, and in a few weeks he was at his post again, and while he was recuperating, the second ride he took, he took me home to the farm. —I had been with him during his sickness—and while there he made up his mind to rent the farm and carry it on with hired help, and give up the town practice. as he could not stand both, and while carrying on my farm he could cultivate and improve his own farm of one hundred and sixty acres which his father had given him a deed to before his death. This was very gratifying to my feelings, and in a few weeks he moved his family in with me, as there was no house on his farm yet. The tenant remained until the crops were secured and then left. After his departure we had plenty of room for the winter. It was with some regret that the Doctor and family left Beatrice, it being then quite a large and promising town, and the citizens were very anxious to have them remain.

When my husband and I first visited Beatrice to attend the quarterly meeting spoken of, it was but a little clump of houses mostly log, with a few stone dwellings, and a very small frame school house to worship in; the court house was a very inferior building, although there was a good deal of business done there, the goods being brought there by freighters from the Missouri river. In less than three years we attended the dedication of a beautiful Methodist stone church, with a membership of one hundred. There was also a large brick church about ready to be dedicated by the Presbyterians, a large brick court house of a very attractive appearance, a fine Baptist church in progress, a fifty acre addition to the incorporation and that building up rapidly, a large elegant hotel, and several fine business houses all of stone, and last but not least, a large public school house built of brick, graded, and manned with teachers, two hundred scholars, and it has kept ahead ever since the railroad reached it. No freighters are now to be seen camped on the road side all along from Beatrice to the Missouri river, as was the custom when we first went to that country. I recollect one time when we ate a meal with some freighters on the road. They had stopped quite early, their teams being all tired out, and had a nice fire started and the coffee-pot steaming. They were on their way from Brownsville on the Missouri to Beatrice with a heavy load, and our team was on the way to Brownsville to convey Mr. Corbin and myself to the cars, on our way to Illinois, and then to return with lumber for our new house. The men folks halted to inquire about the situation of the road. We were nearing the Nimebaugh, a large stream, and the river bottoms were generally very muddy. We asked about the road, and the freighter replied, "You will find it bad enough, I assure you. you. Are you going through to town to-night?" "Yes," was the answer. "Well, you had better stop and water and feed your team, and if the old lady would like a cup of coffee I have plenty on the fire. I know you will not find any chance to get a cup of coffee between this and Brownsville, and it will take you until ten o'clock to get there. I have plenty to eat, all but bread." "Well," said Mr. Corbin. "we have plenty of crackers and cheese, and some apples. We thought we would get there by late supper time." "Oh, well;" said the freighter, "let's join and take supper together." The gentlemen said "All right," and just as we were about to eat, there was a gentleman drove up who was also going to Brownsville for lumber. He lived at Blue Springs. He concluded to stop and take his supper with us, which made five in all. He boiled his coffee in a few minutes, and we were soon enjoying ourselves as well as at a tea party, first one and then another telling something that was interesting about our experience in this country. The gentleman turned to me and said, "Grandma, I think I saw you at Blue Springs something over two years ago, when you and your husband were looking for a home in this country. Were you there?" "Yes, sir;" I replied. "Your husband is a doctor?" "Yes, sir;" I replied, again. "You attended a meeting there on a Sabbath?" Again I answered, "Yes, sir." "Well, that was a good meeting, and one I shall always remember. I had enjoyed religion, and did when I came here; but I became all absorbed in business, and anxious to become rich in this world's goods. I neglected prayer, and of course, lost my enjoyment and became very wicked. I could swear like a pirate. That day I thought I would go to meeting, as there were a number of strangers there who were viewing our country, and see who they were and what they were; and while you and your husband were talking about the great importance of the early settlers of this beautiful country living faithfully and setting up our banner for the Lord, and laying the foundation of a religious society in this new country, the spirit of the Lord awakened my soul to see what I had been doing, and I had no peace of mind day or night until I found it in a sense of pardon through the atoning blood of Jesus and the love of God shed abroad in my heart. And now I would not exchange it for all the wealth of this world." I told him I was glad to find him in such a state of feeling, and I hoped he would live faithful and do all the good he could in the world. He asked me where we were located. I told him, and he said he knew where it was. "Now," said he, "I do hope you and the venerable old doctor will come and see us. We have a good class there now, and are talking of building a church." We did go, and found a great change. I think I have spoken of his telling his experience in love feast. The Blue Springs class built the first church in the Blue River Valley in Gage county. I felt as though I had been to a class meeting. The men hitched on their horses and we drove to Brownsville that night, although it was very muddy and took us until eleven o'clock. We left the good old freighter and his son alone, to sleep in their wagon and make their way to Beatrice the next day. We found the cars ready next morning, and pursued our way, reaching our home and friends in Illinois at half-past two o'clock next morning.

FUNERAL SERMON.

Delivered at the Re-interment of Dr. John Roe, by Rev. Thos. R. Satterfield, Pastor of Light House Point M. E. Church, Ogle Co., Ill.

"Blessed are the dead which die in the Lord." Revelations, 14: 13.

Dr. John Roe was buried in Nebraska in June, 1871. Being on the frontier of a new state, he was away from nearly all of his old friends and relatives, his wife and one son only being present to drop a tear. By the affection of his wife (who has made her home in Illinois) and children, his body has been brought to this place for re-interment, and to-day are gathered in this house his children and friends. They have come from Kentucky, from Iowa, from Chicago, from Malta, from Ashton, from Franklin Grove, from Chana, and from Mt. Morris, to be present at this re-interment, and it is thought best to improve this occasion by an appropriate funeral sermon, and I know of no more appropriate words for the occasion than the words selected, "Blessed are the dead which die in the Lord."

Man is unwilling to consider the subject of death. The shroud, the mattock and the grave, he labors to keep out of sight. He would live here always if he could; and since he cannot, he would put away every emblem of death from his sight. Perhaps there is no subject of so much importance so little thought of.

The old Egyptians were wiser than we. We are told that at their feasts there was an extraordinary guest who sat at the head of the table. He ate not; he drank not; he spoke not; he was closely veiled. It was a skeleton they placed there, to warn them that ever in their feasting they should remember there would be an end of life. If we were more frequently reminded of our mortality, and would more frequently think of death, it would lead us to set our affections on things above, and not on things below. The text says: "Blessed are the dead which die in the Lord." It is the fate of all that live to die. Both the just and unjust must die. Death is no respecter of persons. Like flowers bitten by the frosts of autumn, generation after generation are swept away. The peasant dies in his hut nestled among the hills; the man of business ceases from his anxieties and breathes his last amid the busy marts in the city full; the student leaves his books and papers, and his feverish brow is cold in death; the prudent physician, after administering to the relief of others, must leave his pills and powders, his bleeding and blistering, and close his eyes upon his patients and open them to gaze on things invisible to us. All that live must die. The monarch must lay aside his diadem and scepter; the savage must part from his sturdy bow, and both repose in the narrow limits appointed for all living. "Our fathers, where are they?" Let the graves answer. Their voices are silent in death, and methinks I hear Abraham say, "Their bodies are in my bosom." Ten, twenty, fifty, or one hundred years hence, and all of this congregation will lie mouldering in the grave. What says the Apostle? "Death has passed upon all men, for that all have sinned." Yet with our text we can exclaim, "Blessed are the dead which die in the Lord."

Before showing that death by grace is turned into a blessing, let me make a few remarks in regard to death. 1st. Let me begin by inquiring in regard to its origin. Why is it that you and I must die? Whence came these seeds of corruption that are sown in these bodies of ours? The angels die not. They know nothing of old age and gray hairs; of aches and pains; of coughs, colds and consumption. Why, then, must you and I suffer and die? Because we have sinned. Sin, thou art the mother of death! Adam, thou hast digged the grave of thy posterity! Sin slays the race. We die because we have sinned. "By one man sin entered into the world, and death by sin; and so death passes upon all men, for that all have sinned." "The wages of sin is death." Oh! how this should make us hate sin. How we should fly from it as from a deadly serpent. How we should detest it, because the wages of sin is death. Brand from this day forward the word *murderer* upon the brow of sin.

2d. But again, let us mark the certainty of death. Die I must. I may have escaped a thousand diseases, but death hath an arrow in his quiver that will reach me at last. " It is appointed unto man once to die, but after this the judgment." Run! run! Fly! fly! But the fleet pursuer is on your track and will overtake you. Like the fox before the hounds, you may run, but the dogs of death will overtake you. We are all right in the center of that stream that is rushing to eternity. Not by the right side of it; not by the left side of it; but right in the center of it. And whether we wake or sleep, whether we are at home or abroad, we are rushing onward to eternity. There is a black camel upon which death rides, say the Arabs, and that must kneel at every man's door, and they must mount and away. At every man's door hangs that black knocker, and death hath but to lift the latch and enter and banquet on our flesh and blood. Yes; die I must. I must cross that river. While many things may be uncertain, death is certain. There are so many ways to get out of this world—by apoplexy; by slip or fall; by a fractious horse; by a falling wall; by a misplaced switch; by assassination; by a falling bridge. Suddenly the curtain falls, the lights are put out, and man's place knows him no more. In my own house there are a thousand gates to death. From this pulpit where I stand there is a straight path to the grave. From your seats there is an entrance into eternity. Just before every man, woman and child in this congregation I see a mattock, a spade, a coffin, a winding sheet and an open grave. Oh! let us think how uncertain life is. "What is your life?" asks Job. "It is even a vapor that appeareth for a little time and then vanisheth away." Again, the Psalmist says, "As for man, his days are as grass. As a flower of the field, so he flourisheth. For the wind passeth over it, and it is gone; and the place thereof shall know it no more." Sometimes it is compared to a post, a mail; to a weaver's shuttle; to an eagle hastening to its prey.

The withered bough by the highway may crush us. The deceitful brook may overwhelm us. The whizzing bullet may pierce us. The calm sky may grow wrathful and with his hoarse voice and red right arm may summon us with lightning speed into eternity. If we escape from without, some secret enemy may do the deed. The head grows dizzy; the blood rushes with unaccustomed speed; the heart sickens and faints; its beatings are hushed, and as the sword leaps from its scabbard, the soul has leaped from the body.

"Time, like an ever-rolling stream,
  Bears all its sons away;
 They fly, forgotten, as a dream
  Dies at the opening day.

"Dangers stand thick through all the ground,
  To push us to the tomb;
 And fierce diseases wait around,
  To hurry mortals home."

Notice, again, the terrors which surround death. The pains, the groans, the dying strife, which make our souls start back from the tomb. To the best men on earth the mere act of dying is a solemn thing. In death we must leave behind all of earth. We must say farewell to the house we called home; farewell to fireside and little prattlers that have climbed my knees; farewell to her who walked by my side during life, and was the companion of my youth; farewell to all things—estate, gold and silver; farewell earth and time; farewell to all the means of grace. No bell shall call me to the house of God. There is no rectification or correction of mistakes beyond the dead line. If I have neglected Christ, I shall hear of Christ no more.

Oh! picture yourself as dying now. Suppose you have now come to the vast, the shoreless, the illimitable eternity like a star; suppose you are now hovering between two worlds! Open that window, that I may get a little air. Gather the friends together to see him die. Telegraph for the son; call the daughter. The friends gather around the bedside. Farewell to you all, a last farewell. A mother bids me follow her upward to the skies. "I know that my Redeemer liveth, and that he shall stand at the latter day upon the earth; and though after my skin worms destroy this body, yet in my flesh shall I see God, when I shall see for myself, and mine eyes shall behold and not another's." "For me to live is Christ, but to die is gain." I have a firm and abiding trust in Jesus; His grace is sufficient for me, but now the lips refuse to speak; we breathe heavily; they stay us up in bed with pillows; the eye-strings break; my hands are paralyzed by my side; there is a hush now in the room;

the clock alone is heard ticking as the soul floats out into the ether, and the friends baptise the cheek with their tears. And where am I now, a naked, disembodied spirit. The battle is fought; the victory is won; rest warrior, workman, pilgrim, physician, rest; thou art crowned at last. "Blessed are the dead which die in the Lord, for they rest from their labors, and their works do follow them."

II. Death is a blessing to the righteous. The text is true to the very letter. "Blessed are the dead which die in the Lord." "Die in the Lord!" That is a most remarkable expression; but is an expression that corresponds to others in the Word of God. For example, the Apostle sometimes speaks of us "being in the Lord," and sometimes of the "Lord being in us." He says, for instance, "Christ in you, the hope of glory." Then again, he says, "I am crucified with Christ; nevertheless I live, yet not I, but Christ liveth in me." "Abide in me and I in you." "He that abideth in me and I in him, the same bringeth forth much fruit; for without me ye can do nothing." We abide in Him by faith, and He in us by His Holy Spirit.

Now, whether the expression be Christ in us, or we in Christ, the meaning is the same so far as it expresses the union that exists between Christ and His people—between the Saviour and the saved. A union more intimate than marriage, which the laws of the land may separate. A union more intimate than the soul and the body, which the whizzing bullet may sever. The union existing between Christ and his people is one of incorporation rather than co-operation. As the trunk and branches of the tree have sap in common, as my body and limbs have blood in common, so Jesus and His people have all things in common. "All mine is thine," he says. His Father ours; His merit ours; His righteousness ours; His victory ours; His glory ours; His immortality ours. And with angels, dominions, principalities and powers, we shall run the high race of glory, and honor, and immortality, the smile of the Lord being the feast of the soul.

To be in Christ, that is it; to be in Christ, that is the thought that hallows the dying hour. This text has no promises to those who are not in Christ. If in Christ you are saved: out of Christ, you are lost, hopelessly, eternally lost. But to be in Christ is to enjoy all the blessings He shed His blood to purchase for me. What more could we have? what more could we wish for? To be in Christ is to be in His Father's bosom, all sins forgiven, heaven sure at last. With Christ we shall be crowned in glory. Well then may the Apostle say, "Blessed are the dead which die in the Lord." They are blessed. They must be blessed: how can they be otherwise? Die? yes, they must, but death has lost its sting. The Apostle asks, "O death, where is thy sting? O grave where is thy victory?" The sting of death is sin. It is sin that gives death its sting. If you extract the sting from a bee, a wasp, a hornet, or any insect, it is powerless to hurt you, its sting is gone. So, if the sin which gives death its sting be extracted by the blood of Christ, death is powerless to hurt you, for its sting is gone. So that it makes but little difference when, or where, or how they die. The dying is nothing, if only it be in the Lord. Whether we die in bed, surrounded with friends, or die in battle amid the roar of cannon, the bursting of shells or whizzing of bullets and groans of the dying, or are like a martyr swinging in the air, or burn at the stake, or are engulfed in the mighty deep, dying in the Lord they are blesssed.

It has proved a comfort to a sinking child to feel a kind mother's arms around it, to expire with its head resting on her bosom. And when the dying can no longer see it is a consolation to have some loved one near. How often I have heard the dying soldier say, "I could die happy if I could only see my mother before I die; or if I could only see my devoted wife before I die." But oh! is it not far better to be able to say with Stephen, "I see Jesus at the right hand of God;" or, with Paul, "I am now ready to be offered, and the time of my departure is at hand. I have fought the fight, I have finished my course, I have kept the faith. Henceforth there is a crown of righteousness laid up for me, which the Lord, the righteous Judge shall give me at that day; and not to me only, but unto all them also that love His appearing." Or with Senator Foot, of Vermont. He called his companion to his bedside and enfolded her in his arms, asking, "Can this be death! has it come already?" Then looking with eyes of celestial radiance, and lifting up his hands he said, "I see it! I see the gates wide open! beautiful! beautiful!" and he was not, for God took him.

But beyond the tender accents of mother, wife or child's voice; oh! how blessed to hear Jesus whispering. "Fear not, for I am with thee. Be not afraid, for I am thy God." We may be ready to sink back saying, "Ah! Lord, the water is dark; the stream is cold and deep." How blessed then to hear Jesus say, "Go forward; fear not, I have redeemed thee. When thou passeth through the waters I will be with thee, and through the waves, they shall not overflow thee. When thou walkest through the fires thou shalt not be burned; neither shall the flames kindle upon thee, for I am the Lord thy God, the Holy One of Israel, thy Saviour."

Christians, let the world shrink from death, not you. Death is the portal of life to those who die in the Lord. Think of it, therefore, not as death, but as glory. Think of it as going to heaven; as going to your Father. If you will think of it as death, let it be the death of sin; the death of pain; the death of fear; the death of care; the death of death. Regard its pangs and struggles as the battle that goes before victory. Its struggles as the swell of the sea on heaven's happy shore. It is life in Christ, and life through Christ, and life for ever more. How much happier and holier we would be if we could look at death in that light; if we could feel every morning, I may be in heaven before night; and every night, I may be in heaven before morning. "When they rest from their labors, and their works do follow them."

III. But in the third place death is a blessing to the Christian, as introducing him into a place of happiness and reunion with those that have gone before.

To the believer death is gain, without any fraction of loss. Do we leave our friends behind in death?

We shall meet our friends up yonder, who have gone before, having washed their robes and made them white in the blood of the Lamb. There we shall meet a Friend that sticketh closer than a brother.

Do we leave our house and comforts here? We gain a house there not made with hands, eternal in the heavens. Do we lose earth? We gain heaven. Do we lose our life? Oh, no; we gain a better far—for here we die to live, but there we shall live to die no more. He ceases to suffer and begins to be happy. "Comfort ye, comfort ye my people, saith your God." No better way of announcing a good man's death than the old-fashioned way, "He is at rest—he has gone home."

"With Thee there is fullness of joy, and at Thy right hand there are pleasures forever more." "Then shall I be satisfied when I awake with Thy likeness." Society in heaven. We shall not find heaven a solitary place. St. Paul says, "Ye are come unto Mount Zion and unto the city of the living God, the heavenly Jerusalem, and to an innumerable company of angels." Angels are to be our companions in the skies. Nor these alone. People from all worlds will be there, and we shall enjoy their society.

Then shall we meet those loved ones who have gone before. Fathers and mothers, brothers and sisters, husbands and wives, parents and children, shall meet at Jesus' feet to part nevermore. The hope of a re-union with friends on the other shore, lights up the dying chamber with a halo of glory.

"Good-bye papa; good-bye; mamma has come for me to-night. Don't cry papa, we will all meet again in the morning." Such was the language of a dying child as the night shades of death closed around her. Yes; thanks be unto God, we shall all meet again in the morning. How that thrills the heart. Do we re-inter our friend in the dark, damp grave to-day; how it cheers us to feel that we will all meet again in the morning. "And I heard a voice from heaven saying unto me, Blessed are the dead which die in the Lord from henceforth; yea, saith the spirit, that they may rest from their labors; and their works do follow them." Oh! for an angel's tongue that words so beautiful might have all their melodiousness, all their music, and all their force. Man's mind and tongue are far too feeble to express them.

Dr. John Roe was born in the city of Philadelphia, Pennsylvania, August 19th, 1800. Married Elizabeth Ann Lyon at Eddyville, Kentucky, in 1822. Moved to Sangamon county, Illinois, in 1827. From thence to Light House Point in the winter of 1834. He was the first settler at Light House Point. The beautiful farms and fine residences of this region were at that time one vast open prairie. When the settlers began to come in, his double log cabin was opened as a place of worship, and was the first regularly established preaching place for this section of the Rock River Mission. The foundations of this strong and flourishing Church were lain through his zeal and piety. He brought God and the Bible with him when he came, and they have remained ever since. He assisted in building the first M. E. Church and the first school house of this place. For many years he was a devoted and successful class leader, saying to the people, "Follow me, as I follow Christ."

In 1845 he moved to the city of Chicago; in 1849 he moved to Mt. Morris; in the spring of 1850, with four of his sons, he went to California; in 1851 he settled at Paynes Point; in 1854 he moved to the city of Rockford; in 1856 he located at Bethel in Ogle Co., Ill.; in 1865, moved to Malta, DeKalb Co., Ill.; in 1869 he emigrated to Gage County, Neb., at which place he died suddenly of apoplexy, June 21st, 1871, in the seventy-first year of his age. To him sudden death was sudden glory.

For nearly fifty years he had successfully practiced medicine. He died at his post, for about the last act of his long and successful life was to make a prescription for one of his patients, and then was himself forever cured. Cicero said, "There is nothing in which men are so allied to the gods as when they try to give health to other men."

Dr. Rush use to say in his valedictory addresses to the students of the medical college, "Gentlemen, have two pockets: a small pocket and a large pocket; a small pocket to put your fees in, and a large pocket to put your annoyances in." But Dr. Roe was a Christian physician; he had the grace of God to help him to overcome his annoyances. To him the Scripture was literally true, "As thy day so shall thy strength be." When he came to doctor the eye he had communication with Him who said to the blind man, "Receive thy sight," and this fair world burst upon his vision. When he treated the paralytic man, he had faith in that God who said to the paralytic,

"Stretch forth thy hand," and he stretched it forth. When he came to treat a case of hemorrhage, he trusted in Him who cured the issue of blood, saying, "Thy faith hath saved thee." In the name of God he had studied the properties of minerals and vegetables, and had become acquainted with the sources of pain, and knew how to apply remedies and assuagements.

When he came to the bedside of his patients, he had the medicine for the body in one hand and the medicine for the soul in the other hand. And when his patients would die, as sometimes die they must in spite of the skill of the best physician, for the irrevocable decree has gone forth, "Dust thou art and unto dust thou shalt return." But, oh! when the feet of the Christian was touching the dark river of death, he could and did hold up the " Lamp of Life " until it lighted his dark pathway clear across the "dark valley and shadow of death," to that world of light and life above. When morphia and chloroform would not quiet the terror of the dying sinner; when he had terror in his eye and terror in his heart, starting back, saying, " Oh ! Doctor, I cannot die; I am not ready to die;" he could kneel down by his bedside and say, " Oh! God, I have done the best I could to cure this man's body, but I have failed. Now I beseech Thee have mercy upon his poor, suffering soul. Oh! Thou Great Physician of souls, apply the blood of the Lamb and cleanse his guilt away; open heaven to his departing spirit; and as Thou didst save the thief upon the cross, so be pleased to save him."

His skill as a physician, his consistent Christian life, his unselfish devotion to all that was noble, pure and good, greatly endeared him to all who had the good fortune to be acquainted with him. The medical profession of this country do more missionary work without pay than any of the other professions. On a cold night, when the thermometer is twenty degrees degrees below zero, they must leave their comfortable quarters and face the storm. Or on a hot day when the thermometer is one hundred degrees above, the doctor must go in haste. He must always go in haste, and very frequently he must go without hope of fee or reward, except the satisfaction of allaying pain and helping suffering humanity. I heard a man say that Dr. Roe had thousands of dollars on his books of gratuitous services rendered.

He truly loved all Christians, and sympathized with all good men. His heart was indeed as broad as humanity. His benevolent feelings allied him to all the race. Possessed of a strong physical frame; of a broad intellect, and of a truly social nature, he attained a well developed Christian character.

He was a man of prayer. He started every morning with a chapter from the Bible and his family on their knees. He forgot not God when employed in the duties of his profession. The morning prayer came on one side of the day, and the evening prayer on the other, forming an arch under which he walked all the day.

His happiness in this life was to make others happy. He lived, not for himself, but for others. His chief delight seemed to be to minister to the sick, comfort the distressed, and help forward every good work that had for its object the amelioration of the condition of man.

He was the father of nine children, eight of whom live to honor his memory. One is not, for God transplanted it to paradise in its infancy.

His wife, the companion of his youth, the mother of his children, the partner of all his joys and sorrows, still survives him. She is here to-day to shed a tear because of his absence. You weep not because your husband is before the throne, because he has ascended to the general assembly and church of the first born; but you weep because you shall see his face no more until you shall greet him on the glorified battlements of immortality. Blessed be God, I can bring my text to-day and lay it as a balm upon your lonely, bleeding, wounded heart. "And I heard a voice from heaven saying unto me write, 'Blessed are the dead which die in the Lord from henceforth; yea saith the Spirit, that they may rest from their labors; and their works do follow them.'"

A wife and children's affection have brought the husband and father's body from a distant State to repose in this soil. The soil of which he was at one time the sole possessor. He had a clear title to it in fee simple; but in the benevolence of his heart he gave it to the trustees of the Light House M. E. church, both as a place in which to erect a church and as a free burying place for rich and poor.

Here, at the scene of his early labors, he desired that his body should be buried. He desired to rest in close proximity to many of his old class-mates, friends and patients; with the early settlers and pioneers with whom he shared the hardships and trials of a frontier life.

It is only his body that rests here. His immortal spirit is "without fault before the throne," on the other side of the river of death. Some of his old patients, who have been forever cured, came out to meet him and to welcome him to the house of many mansions; and the Old Physician of Heaven, "whose head and hairs are white like wool, as white as snow," came out and said, "Come in, come in; 'I was sick and ye visited me;' inasmuch as ye did it unto one of the least of these, ye did it unto me;' 'Enter thou into the joy of thy Lord.'"

When this church was erected his memory was not forgotten; and while his memory is enshrined in the hearts of a loving people, the affection of his children has placed a memorial window in the east end of this church. Over that window is the emblem of the Holy Bible. That Bible was the guide of his youth and his solace in riper years and his guide to immortality. It revealed that Saviour "Who hath abolished death and brought life and immortality to light through the Gospel." It tells of Him who proclaimed Himself "The resurrection and the life; he that believeth in Me, though he were dead, yet shall he live. And whosoever liveth and believeth in Me shall never die."

"Let me die the death of the righteous, and let my last end be like his."

To his wife and children, let me exhort you to follow him as he followed Christ, and the separation will be short and the re-union glorious.

May God add His blessing, for His Son's sake. Amen.

The following hymn was then sung:

> Why should our tears in sorrow flow,
>   When God has re-called his own,
> And bids them leave a world of woe,
>   For an immortal crown.
>
> Is not e'en death a gain to those
>   Whose life to God were given?
> Gladly to earth their eyes they close,
>   To open them in heaven.
>
> Their toils are past, their work is done,
>   And they are fully blest;
> They fought the fight, the victory won,
>   And entered into rest.
>
> Then let our sorrow cease to flow,
>   God has re-called his own,
> But let our hearts in every woe,
>   Still say—Thy will be done.

DR. JOHN ROE.

FROM THE "OREGON (OGLE CO.) COURIER."

"The announcement that the funeral ceremonies of Dr. John Roe, Sr., would be observed at Light House Point, was sufficient to attract a large concourse of those who had been neighbors and friends of the 'good old doctor' in the days that are passed. It was in the far off winter of 1834 that the then young doctor, poor in purse, but rich in the attributes of true manhood, determined to carve out for himself a fortune in the then almost untrodden west. The mere mention of the struggles and privations of the pioneers of our country, has never failed to fill me with the most lively emotions of veneration and gratitude. We love to look back beyond the fertile fields, the beautiful hedges of willow, maple and orange, the commodious barns, palatial mansions, the countless flocks, and the "flowery orchard trees" of to-day, to the wild, bleak and barren prairies of forty years ago, when

> 'His echoing ax, the settler swung,
> Amid the sun-like solitude.'

"Forty-four years have passed since John Roe 'staked his claim' at Light House, built his log cabin on the wild prairie sod, wheretofore the wild fox had dug his hole unscared. Here this herald of the dawning civilization offered up his fervent prayer amid the primeval solitude. The most utopian fancy can hardly realize the change that has been wrought during the past two score years. Almost on the very spot where Roe's log cabin stood and crumbled by the corrosion of time, stands one of the finest church edifices in Ogle County. And we could not help thinking as we reclined on the cushioned seat, between those walls of marble whiteness and beneath that frescoed ceiling, that these elaborate surroundings were in strange and beautiful contrast with the rugged experience of the early pioneer, whose memory we had there assumed to honor. Methinks that the 'memorial window' erected in his honor, would cost more than the temple in which he worshipped.

> "'Mid whitewashed walls and swinging beam."

"The subject of this hurriedly written article was born in Philadelphia during the first year of the present century. Was married in 1822 to Miss Elizabeth A. Lyon, daughter of Col. Lyon, of Kentucky, and settled at Light House, Ogle county, in 1834, at the close of the Black Hawk war. The fleet-footed antelope passed the cabin more frequently than the slow-paced ox team, and the voiceless solitude gave no token of the iron horse that has since rolled its living tide into the beautiful Rock River Valley, to build up the waste places, and make these "gardens of the desert" blossom as the rose. Methinks that these rugged pioneers must have heard the premonitory "hum of that advancing multitude that since has shape and shadow overflowed." Dr. Roe, finding himself somewhat broken in fortune at the close of the late civil war, removed to Gage county, Nebraska, where he soon acquired a fine estate. Dying during the summer of 1871, he was buried in a beautiful little grove of cottonwood trees which he had himself planted. The affectionate regard of his widow and her sons, has caused his remains to be brought back from a far-distant State to rest among his earlier friends, amid the scenes of his greatest usefulness. He now rests in the ground he himself gave to the community as a free burial ground to rich and poor alike. It was indeed a rich inheritance to possess such a father, and it was pleasant to notice the presence of four sons who had gathered from far-distant States to pay the last tribute of respect to his memory. Elder Satterfield preached a very appropriate discourse from the thoughts suggested in the thirteenth verse of the fourteenth chapter of Revelations: "And I heard a voice from heaven saying unto me, write, Blessed are the dead who die in the Lord, from henceforth; yea, saith the spirit, for they rest from their labors, and their works do follow them." You may search in vain for a higher type of humanity than is found among the large-hearted pioneers. One by one they are passing away to be laid beneath the prairie sod, as we laid the "good old Doctor" on that beautiful Sabbath morning. And the crumbling stone over his grave will bear the inscription:

SACRED TO THE MEMORY OF

JOHN ROE.

DIED JUNE 21, 1871,

Aged 70 years.

The above was published March 7, 1877. Soon after there was erected a beautiful monument on the final resting place of Dr. John Roe, by his devoted family.

Birthday Testimony.

This day, June 11th, 1885, I am eighty years old, being born June 11th, 1805. Was married to Dr. John Roe November 11th, 1821; we enjoyed a happy married life for nearly fifty years, lacking only four months of that time. He departed from this life June 21st, 1871, at the age of seventy-one years. Oh! how we have missed him these fourteen long years as a loving, kind husband, father, counsellor, physician and bosom friend, none but our Heavenly Father knows, but I live with a blessed hope of meeting him in that better world where the inhabitants never are sick or in pain; where there is no night, for the Lamb is the light thereof. Oh, how many of our dear old friends have gone to that beautiful world to praise the Lord through endless day. I hope ere long to be with them, for our blessed Saviour said, "Where I am ye shall be also." Oh! blessed hope given us through the gospel of Christ our Redeemer!

We raised eight children, and the ninth, the oldest

of our family, departed from this life at the age of ten months. He was a lovely child, but he was not for this world, for the Lord took him to Himself. I have often thought the good Lord chastened us, for we almost idolized him. I often think of the chastening of the Lord when I see parents whose hearts are almost broken with grief at the loss of their first born. No one but those who have felt the pang can ever know what it is to those who have or may feel it, and I hope it may be sanctified to their great good, as it was to ours. It led us to lean on the precious promises of the Lord as we never did before. Oh! how sweet were the accents of our Redeemer's lips when he said, "Suffer little children to come unto me, and forbid them not, for such is the kingdom of heaven." By His grace we were enabled to resign all to His will. Bless the Lord who doeth all things well!

The Lord spared us to raise the eight born thereafter. Six were sons and two daughters. The older two and the youngest were each successful, useful physicians, loved and honored by their patrons. One son is a traveling agent in Iowa, and is sowing good seed wherever he goes, and is class-leader and steward of a Methodist church; another an excellent farmer in good circumstances in Ogle County, Ill.; another is a lawyer by profession, but is now General Agent of the Equitable Life Assurance Company, of New York City, for Kentucky and Tennessee, and resides at Louisville, Ky. He has the care of his dear old mother, visits me often, and is very kind and affectionate, and always looks after my health and comfort. Few mothers have six such noble, kind sons.

The daughters are both married and have large families. They are noble, kind-hearted mothers, loved and honored by their families. The eldest is Mrs. Beaulah M. Mayberry, and lives in Cook County near Chicago, her husband is a member of the Board of Trade; the youngest is Mrs. F. M. Contin, who lives in Miland Township, DeKalb Co., Ill.; her husband is a farmer. They have five sons and four daughters, some of them stay with me all the time.

I have in all forty-one grand-children and twenty-six great-grand-children; some have died in the triumph of Christian faith, some in infancy. I have lived a widow fourteen years; was the youngest of fifteen children, and for more than thirty years I have had no father, mother, sister or brother living, but I have been surrounded by my very kind family, and have not felt the loss as much as I would under other circumstances, although few persons ever loved father, mother, brothers and sisters more than I did. But they have all gone, I hope, to that better world where I expect to meet them ere long. Praise the Lord for the hope of heaven and immortality, brought to light through the gospel of a crucified but risen Saviour. Truly I can say with the psalmist, "Goodness and mercy has followed me all the days of my life."

It is sixty years since I started on the way to Zion. Early in life I gave my hand to the Methodist church and my heart to the good Lord, and I have never seen a moment when I was sorry I had commenced the heavenly pilgrimage; but often I have grieved, and do to-day, that I have not lived a more devoted life. I can only say, "Forgive, my Heavenly Father, forgive for the Redeemer's sake." And he said when on earth, "Whatsoever ye ask in my name nothing doubting ye shall receive." When I have erred or stumbled, I have repented, sought and found forgiveness in the name of Jesus, to the comfort of my poor heart. Thus I have traveled on the way rejoicing, most of the time, with the hope of immortality in eternal life.

I have been comforted amidst deep afflictions of body, and hard struggles with our large family. These struggles were especially hard in this new country where we had to go sixty miles for everything we had to eat or wear until we could cultivate the rich land, then it produced abundance, and as the Lord has promised the diligent hand shall have its reward, it was verified truly to us. We grubbed out a large spot in the edge of the Light House grove, and there, in the edge of the grove, we had built a nice little log cabin sixteen feet square. Near our garden my little boys split the trees we had cut to clear the garden spot; they were small and the children could handle them, so they fenced the garden and a nice yard. The yard was beautifully shaded with some of the nicest shade trees, which we had left standing for that purpose, and were so near the house that the limbs lay on the clapboard roof. Hundreds of sweet little birds made their nests there, and at the first gleam of daylight the grove would be echoing with their lovely songs.

In that humble log cabin I spent some of the happiest days of my long life; there I dedicated anew my whole heart, my five little boys, my new home, my husband, and the little all of earthly goods we had there. hailed the missionary with joy. I cannot express the joy I felt when, as our mission had lately been attached to the Galena District, they sent Bro. James McCann to us to preach as a Conference Missionary and form a circuit. We were very glad to welcome him to our little log cabin, and entertain him the best we could, and he was glad to find us, for we had been co-laborers in the Sangamon circuit in former years. Oh! what sweet Christian communion we enjoyed that night in singing and praying and planning for the new circuit. Our little songsters awoke us early next morning to join them in praising the Lord. We had many such treats like this in our little cabin, and after enlarging it by adding another cabin twenty feet long, it became the meeting house. A part of it was used for the school house, and you may say, the hospital, for we often had from six to ten patients in it at a time, to seek the kind advice and treatment of a physician and my care as a nurse. They came as far as ten, twenty, thirty and forty miles. Many came sorely afflicted, but went away rejoicing.

Our cabin accommodated many of the best and noblest humble men that ever graced our conference, such as Brother Brunson, Brother Sumers, Brother Meade, Brother Crews, Brother Luke Hitchcock and family. He has preached many noble sermons in my log cabin. We had a glorious revival commence at the cabin, followed up for three successive years. Many precious souls were converted there; many shouts of new born souls have gone up from those old logs. Some of my dear children were converted there, and many who came from afar off. Precious memories, how it fills my heart with gratitude to meditate on those blessed seasons; but if faithful we will have eternity to tell the good old, old story.

I believe in the Methodist doctrines. I think they will stand the test in eternity. I find them good to live by, and I think they will be good to die by; and would recommend them to all who seek to know the truth. I do not feel like falling out with anybody or person who does not think just as I do. I advise all to be fully persuaded in his or her own mind.

Seek the Lord with all your heart. Read the Scriptures of Divine Truth, prayerfully trusting to know the truth of His Word, for he said, "They testify of Me." I would recommend the Gospel of our blessed Saviour to every creature, and with my latest breath cry, "Behold! behold the Lamb that was slain, but liveth again to intercede for you and for me.

I am now living in my own little cottage, on the C. & I. railroad, seven miles east of Oregon, the county seat of Ogle County, Illinois. I would be happy to see any of those dear old friends, or hear from them or any of their families at any time. It would do me good. I am quite an invalid, and can't go from home, if it takes any effort. Perhaps you can remember, some of my dear readers, that I have at two periods of my life weighed three hundred and fifty pounds. The weight of flesh has broken the ligaments off that surround and keep the joints in their sockets. It is with great pain and difficulty that I can move without the aid of one and sometimes two staffs or **canes.** I have had several severe strokes of palsy, and suffer much from heart disease, so I expect soon to go to our Father's house where there are many mansions—one for you and one for me. May we be so unspeakably happy as to meet there, **to** go out no more forever. Oh! what a happy time it will be when we our friends in Heaven do see, there to spend an eternity in praising the Lord our Redeemer.

> 'Twas Grace that taught my heart to fear,
>   And Grace my fears relieved;
> How precious did that Grace appear,
>   The hour I first believed.
>
> Through many toils and snares
>   I have already come;
> 'Twas Grace that **brought me safe** thus far,
>   And Grace will lead **me home.**

www.ingramcontent.com/pod-product-compliance
Lightning Source LLC
Chambersburg PA
CBHW032055220426
43664CB00008B/1013